Constructing Affirmative Action

Civil Rights and the Struggle for Black Equality
in the Twentieth Century

Series Editors
Steven F. Lawson, Rutgers University
Cynthia Griggs Fleming, University of Tennessee

Constructing
Affirmative Action

The Struggle for
Equal Employment Opportunity

DAVID HAMILTON GOLLAND

THE UNIVERSITY PRESS OF KENTUCKY

Scholarly publisher for the Commonwealth,
serving Bellarmine University, Berea College, Centre College of Kentucky, Eastern
Kentucky University, The Filson Historical Society, Georgetown College, Kentucky
Historical Society, Kentucky State University, Morehead State University, Murray
State University, Northern Kentucky University, Transylvania University, University of
Kentucky, University of Louisville, and Western Kentucky University.
All rights reserved.

Editorial and Sales Offices: The University Press of Kentucky
663 South Limestone Street, Lexington, Kentucky 40508-4008
www.kentuckypress.com

15 14 13 12 11   5 4 3 2 1

Library of Congress Cataloging-in-Publication Data

Golland, David Hamilton.
  Constructing affirmative action : the struggle for equal employment opportunity / David
Hamilton Golland.
      p. cm.
  Includes bibliographical references and index.
  ISBN 978-0-8131-2997-6 (hardcover : alk. paper)
  ISBN 978-0-8131-2998-3 (ebook)
  1. Affirmative action programs—United States. 2. Construction industry—United States.
3. Minority business enterprises—United States. 4. Building trades—United States.
5. Race discrimination—United States. 6. Minorities—Employment—United States.
7. Discrimination in employment—United States. I. Title.
  HF5549.5.A34G65 2011
  331.13'30973—dc22   2010054014

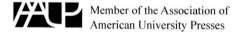

For Lana

Contents

Preface

Richard Nixon wanted to be remembered as a "civil rights president" rather than "Tricky Dick" of the popular imagination. Historians such as Joan Hoff and, more recently, British scholar Kevin Yuill have nearly achieved that goal for him, noting the advances made in equal employment opportunity during the early 1970s.[1] But the reality is that most of these advances were made in the courts, where Lyndon Johnson–era programs and laws were being challenged and upheld.

When pressed to defend Nixon's actual civil rights accomplishments, these modern apologists point to one program: the Philadelphia Plan. They recount how the president, with his Department of Labor deputies George Shultz and Arthur Fletcher, shepherded this first affirmative action program through a heated congressional battle and challenges in the federal courts. But they minimize the *real* history of the Philadelphia Plan, which was developed by Johnson appointees after years of experimental attempts to integrate the skilled building construction trades. Nixon implemented the Philadelphia Plan in order to *appear* to be committed to civil rights, but he abandoned it after the hard-hat revolts less than six months later. In fact, Nixon was not a "civil rights president" at all; by 1971 his black appointees were resigning in disgust, and he even appointed a secretary of labor with a plan to resegregate vocational training.

I wrote *Constructing Affirmative Action* to tell the real story of Richard Nixon and civil rights. But I also wrote it to tell quite another story altogether: the integration of the building construction trades. In the 1950s blacks working in building construction were typically relegated to unskilled or residential work, while the skilled commercial construction work—with its lucrative wages—was done almost exclusively by whites. After years of struggle, the skilled unions had gained control of the hiring process, but their membership—despite increasing calls for reform by their leaders—remained racially segregated. With the postwar increase in federal construction spending, specifically urban renewal programs, the prospect of all-white skilled work crews erecting structures in predominantly black neighborhoods was one of the most obvious—and galling—examples of Jim Crow outside the American South. Civil rights organizations, labor leaders, and the federal government spent two decades working to right this wrong, and their relative successes and failures in integrating the trades are the other story I set out to tell.

This work is due in no small part to the copious assistance I have received over the years. The names are too many to mention, but I shall try. Bob Reynolds, now retired, of the George Meany Archives got me started, with patience and compassion. Jennifer Brathovde, Jeff Flannery, Joseph Jackson, Lia Kerwin, Patrick Kerwin, and Bruce Kirby made the nine-to-five at the Library of Congress Manuscript Reading Room not only tolerable but enjoyable—no small feat. I am grateful to Tab Lewis at the civilian records section of the National Archives in College Park, Maryland; Allen Fisher, Claudia Anderson, Laura Eggert, and Elizabeth McLelland at the Johnson Archives in Austin; and the small but knowledgeable staffs of the Schomburg Center in Harlem, the Urban Archives at Temple University in Philadelphia, and the Historical Society of Pennsylvania. I thank the Johnson Foundation, the Colonial Dames of America, and Thomas W. Smith for the fellowships that kept me on the road, and Harold and Betsi Closter, Cynthia and Jon Simpson, and Tom and Giulia Terbush for the roofs that kept me dry.

   For inspiration along the way, I would like to thank Ervand Abrahamian, Angelo Angelis, Carl Arnold, Anna Balas, Paul Fletcher, Phyllis Fletcher, Tom Kessner, Steve Levine, Vince Macaluso, Lee Malkiel, Peter Miller, Mark Peterson, Jon Powell, Chris Rosa, Brian Schwartz, the late Stephen Stearns, Randy Trumbach, Cynthia Whittaker, and Woody Zenfell. Thanks also to my mother, whose love for history inspired me from an early age to find relevance in the past; Myrna Chase, who was the first to suggest that I become a historian; Michael Holt, my M.A. adviser at the University of Virginia; and Jim Oakes, my M.Phil. adviser at the City University of New York (CUNY) Graduate Center. A large debt is owed to the members of my dissertation seminar, especially Kris Burrell, Matthew Cotter, Carla Dubose, Kate Hallgren, and Alexander Stavropoulos. I am grateful to my informal readers—my colleagues David Aliano and Joseph Sramek, my father Jeffrey Golland, and my wife Svetlana Rogachevskaya; my formal readers—Carol Berkin, Joshua Freeman, and K. C. Johnson at CUNY, and Brian Purnell at Bowdoin College; and my doctoral adviser, Clarence Taylor. I would like to thank the two anonymous readers for the

University Press of Kentucky, as well as Steven F. Lawson, David Cobb, Linda Lotz, and Anne Dean Watkins.

Finally, I must express a very special thanks to Zelda Rose Golland, whose imminent arrival spurred the completion of this work.

Abbreviations

AFL	American Federation of Labor
AFL-CIO	American Federation of Labor–Congress of Industrial Organizations
BART	Bay Area Rapid Transit
BAT	Bureau of Apprenticeship and Training, U.S. Department of Labor
BCTD	Building Construction Trades Department, AFL-CIO
BSCP	Brotherhood of Sleeping-Car Porters
BTD	Building Trades Department, AFL
CCRB	Cleveland Community Relations Board
CEO	chief executive officer
CHR	Commission on Human Relations (Philadelphia)
CIO	Congress of Industrial Organizations
CIU	Congress of Independent Unions
CORE	Congress of Racial Equality
CRC	Civil Rights Commission
DOJ	Department of Justice
DOL	Department of Labor
EEOC	Equal Employment Opportunity Commission
FAA	Federal Aviation Administration
FCCCS	Federal Contract Construction Compliance Subcommittee (Philadelphia)
FEB	Federal Executive Board
FEPC	Fair Employment Practices Committee
FHWA	Federal Highway Administration

GAO	General Accounting Office
GSA	General Services Administration
HEW	Department of Health, Education, and Welfare
HHFA	Housing and Home Finance Agency
HUD	Department of Housing and Urban Development
IBEW	International Brotherhood of Electrical Workers
JAC	Joint Apprenticeship Committee
JOBART	Job Opportunities—Bay Area Rapid Transit
MAP	Manpower Advancement Program, NUL
MCA	Mechanical Contractors' Association
NAACP	National Association for the Advancement of Colored People
NASA	National Aeronautics and Space Administration
NLRB	National Labor Relations Board
NTULC	Negro Trade Union Leadership Council
NUL	National Urban League
OFCC	Office of Federal Contract Compliance
OPP	Operational Plan for Philadelphia
PCEEO	President's Committee on Equal Employment Opportunity
PCEO	President's Council on Equal Opportunity
PCGC	President's Committee on Government Contracts
PCGCC	President's Committee on Government Contract Compliance
RPP	Revised Philadelphia Plan
UAW	United Auto Workers
WPA	Works Progress Administration

Introduction

In April 1969, at a luncheon in Philadelphia sponsored by the Jewish Labor Committee and the Negro Trade Union Leadership Council, AFL-CIO legislative director Andrew J. Biemiller stated that the embattled "labor–liberal–civil rights coalition must be maintained and strengthened because its job isn't done."[1] Biemiller's worry—that a rift was developing in the coalition over the issue of affirmative action—was well founded. The building construction trades' notorious exclusion of most blacks from all but the meanest jobs did not jibe with the umbrella organization's official attitude of equal opportunity. The previous autumn had seen the election of Richard Nixon to the presidency, and whereas President Johnson's secretary of labor, Willard Wirtz, had played an active role in maintaining the rights-labor coalition by promoting programs that aided union leaders in their drive to integrate, Nixon's secretary of labor, George Shultz, had little faith in union efforts to end segregation at construction sites.

Shortly thereafter, President Nixon announced that he fully supported the Philadelphia Plan, an affirmative action program that required federal construction contractors to hire and train minority workers in several of the construction trades in Philadelphia. This decision went against the wishes of the union leadership as well as a large section of the U.S. Congress and especially the General Accounting Office, Congress's taxpayer watchdog. But it had the political purpose of dividing two groups that had coalesced against the administration: civil rights and organized labor.

In the 1950s the building construction trade unions were notoriously segregated throughout the United States, with the vast majority of black members confined to the less skilled "trowel" trades, and the coveted slots in the skilled trades largely passing from white father or uncle to white son or nephew. The federal government was a significant funding source for construction, so the Eisenhower and Kennedy administrations, through Vice Presidents Nixon and Johnson, attempted to force federal contractors to actively seek minority job applicants. The vice presidents pushed the federal bureaucracy to enforce a nondiscrimination clause in federal contracts, and they in turn were pushed by outside actors and events such as

1

civil rights organizations and public protests. At first, the goal was tokenism: breaking the uniformity of whites in the skilled jobs. But civil rights leaders wanted more. With riots breaking out at construction sites, President Johnson (continuing work started by Kennedy) got Congress to pass the Civil Rights Act of 1964, establishing the principle of fair employment.

Whites often viewed the civil rights movement as being committed to "color-blind" objectives in education, employment, and suffrage.[2] The reality was more complicated. Older, established organizations such as the National Association for the Advancement of Colored People and the National Urban League advocated legislation and worked through the courts and with business leaders to achieve equal opportunity; newer organizations such as the Congress of Racial Equality, the Southern Christian Leadership Conference, and the Student Nonviolent Coordinating Committee pursued the same goals through nonviolent direct action, including marches, sit-ins, and boycotts. They seemed focused on obtaining what was often referred to as a "level playing field"—basic citizenship rights for African Americans—and in addition to working to integrate public spaces and achieve voting rights, these organizations attacked job discrimination. They recognized that "color-consciousness" would be needed to overcome discrimination; after all, "color-blindness" would not erase the inequalities that resulted from the history of discrimination. Later, when the nation's urban unemployed erupted into violence, the need to achieve real equality of employment opportunity had never seemed so pressing.

Between 1965, when President Johnson defined affirmative action as a valid federal goal, and 1972, when President Nixon named one of affirmative action's chief antagonists to head the Department of Labor, government officials addressed pervasive employment discrimination in earnest. No longer would it be sufficient merely to eliminate racial discrimination on paper or in rhetoric; no longer would token integration suffice. Employers and union officials would have to actively promote the training, hiring, and retention of nonwhite applicants—and show results to prove it.

Since all Americans were entitled to attend school up to the twelfth grade, the *Brown* decision (that segregation in public schools was inherently unequal) could be heralded as an important advance by all but the most racist southerners. And the Voting Rights Act of 1957 won the support of most northern whites because it confirmed the constitutional right of all adult citizens to participate in the election of their leaders. Blacks in the North had been legally voting for decades; southern black votes did not pose a threat to northern white interests or, for that matter, to the political interests of southern whites living outside the Black Belt.

Equal employment opportunity, by contrast, pertained to the allocation of a limited resource—jobs. By attempting to give members of historically disadvantaged groups a better chance to obtain jobs that had traditionally been limited to whites, affirmative action had the potential to alienate large segments of white society that viewed school desegregation and voting rights from a neutral or even a positive standpoint. By attempting to establish true equality of opportunity, affirmative action meant that some whites—especially the least talented ones—stood to lose the jobs or potential jobs that their skin color had entitled them to in the past. Thus, affirmative action was—and continues to be—controversial.

One function of an introduction is to state up front what the work is *not.* This book is not a history of the civil rights movement; it is a history of a civil rights issue during the period generally referred to by historians as the civil rights era. This is not a book about the American South. During the period under discussion, 1956 to 1973, the civil rights movement in the South was focused on ending de jure (legal) segregation. This work focuses on a civil rights problem arising in the context of a society that had ostensibly left segregation behind—the North and the West. Additionally, although this is a history of affirmative action, it is limited to employment; it is not a book about affirmative action in higher education. This is not a history of deindustrialization, although much of the action occurs in the context of deindustrialization; nor is this a history of the urban crisis, although the long, hot summers of the mid-1960s would influence the decisions made by the key figures under discussion. Finally, this book does not pretend to be a political history of the era, although it touches on matters political and draws conclusions about some aspects of politics.

This book treats the two iterations of the Philadelphia Plan as the collective watershed moment in the origin of affirmative action. Beginning with an examination of the history of inequality in the building construction trades, chapters 1 and 2 cover the period before passage of the Civil Rights Act, when the Eisenhower and Kennedy administrations attempted to compel the federal bureaucracy to enforce nondiscrimination clauses in contracts. The locus of activity then moved from leaders pushing the bureaucracy to the bureaucrats themselves, in some instances acting beyond the intent of elected and appointed leaders. Empowered by the act of Congress and powerful executive orders, the Office of Federal Contract

Compliance spent the bulk of the Johnson administration attempting to implement affirmative action programs tailored to the particular circumstances of individual cities. Chapter 3 details how, through trial and error, federal officials worked in several test cities before developing the Cleveland and Philadelphia Operational Plans in 1967. I examine how these plans worked on the ground and in what areas they did and did not succeed in effecting fair employment.

Chapter 4 shows how the Philadelphia Plan—and, by extension, affirmative action—came under fire from elements in Congress as "reverse racism," ostensibly a violation of the 1964 Civil Rights Act. The Johnson administration, on its way out of office during 1968, did not fight for these programs, but the incoming Nixon administration latched on to a revised version to take on the mantle of civil rights leadership and punish the unions for political opposition. The White House defended the plan against enemies in Congress and in court. In chapter 5 I look at the implementation and prolonged effects of the Philadelphia Plan, its mandatory spin-offs, and its voluntary knockoffs, and I examine how the administration, organized labor, and the civil rights leadership worked to pursue fair employment in the skilled building trades in the 1970s and beyond.

Ultimately, this book makes three arguments. First, Richard Nixon was *not* the "father of affirmative action" or even a "civil rights president" by the standard set by his predecessor in the White House. Nixon and his administration did not contribute anything particularly novel to the cause of equal employment opportunity. Although my treatment of Nixon's presidency does not begin until chapter 4, this argument is developed throughout the book. First, Nixon was an aloof civil rights vice president (chapter 1); second, Nixon's only civil rights initiative, the Philadelphia Plan, was not his own—it was barely changed from the Johnson-era version (chapters 3 and 4); third, he pushed the Philadelphia Plan for his own political purposes rather than to help black people (chapter 4); and fourth, he abandoned the plan five months after Congress acceded to it—as soon as the hard-hat revolts made the plan politically inexpedient (chapter 5). The popular imagination is right: at least when it came to civil rights, Nixon was "Tricky Dick."

Second, the federal bureaucracy, which initially worked *against* the implementation of equal employment opportunity programs through inertia, came to be the most effective player *for* their implementation during the 1960s and 1970s—by thinking "outside the box." Thus, this book also makes the case for an understanding of the federal bureaucracy as an active agent in a representative democracy—especially in chapters 2 and 3. Looking back from 1982, one journalist referred to affirmative action programs as having had "a sort of bureaucratic virgin birth."[3] The popular imagination is wrong: bureaucracy is (or at least it can be) good.

And finally, this book is about affirmative action *as* equal opportunity. Like the Nixon argument, this story is found throughout the book: demonstration of the need for affirmative action (chapter 1), grassroots calls for affirmative action programs (chapter 2), development of these programs (chapters 3 and 4), and implementation of and opposition to these programs (chapter 5). Because some of the original players favored convenient shortcuts, such as quotas rather than the long, hard slog of working toward real equality of opportunity, and because politicians and pundits of the Right have seized on that fault as convenient propaganda, the popular imagination has come to define affirmative action as inherently unequal: less-qualified blacks being employed or promoted rather than better-qualified whites. But that isn't what affirmative action was or is. This book shows that affirmative action—as it was originally intended—is about breaking down barriers to equal opportunity. The popular imagination is wrong: affirmative action in employment is equal employment opportunity.

An employer once told me it's okay to give a less-qualified black a job over a better-qualified white in recognition of the unusual trials he has had to overcome just by being black. Perhaps that's true, if those trials made for a person who was actually more qualified in reality than on paper. There may be a value, in some jobs, to inner-city "street smarts" that a white job applicant may not have, and the reality of the black underclass is that its members must work harder to get to the same place as their white counterparts. But that isn't affirmative action.

Edward Sylvester, President Johnson's federal contract compliance director, put it this way: "affirmative action is anything that you have to do to get results. But this does not necessarily include preferential treatment. The key word here is 'results.'" And President Bill Clinton, in a 1995 speech, said that affirmative action "does not mean—and I don't favor—the unjustified preference of the unqualified over the qualified of any race or gender. It doesn't mean—and I don't favor—numerical quotas. It doesn't mean—and I don't favor—rejection or selection of any employee or student solely on the basis of race or gender without regard to merit."[4]

Affirmative action means carefully identifying areas of inequality, taking a series of positive steps to alleviate that inequality, and following through in the long term. For instance, if the inequality is the result of overt racism, such as a personnel manager who thinks blacks are less capable of completing skilled tasks than whites are, then reassign (or terminate) the manager and hire one who does not share that prejudice. If the inequality is the result of a lack of knowledge of job openings in the Korean American community, then advertise in Korean newspapers and inform community leaders. If the inequality is the result of a dearth of trained Latinos, then create more training opportunities aimed at—but not exclusive to—Latinos.

That is hard work. But that is affirmative action. And in a nation with racial inequality, it is the key to equal employment opportunity.

Chapter 1

Fighting Bureaucratic Inertia, 1956–1960

I am informed that full scale hiring by the electrical contractor on the Southwest Project will begin [in] October. I would like to impress upon you the urgency for taking affirmative action in this matter (the Local 26 impasse) at the earliest possible date.

—Vice President Richard M. Nixon
to the president of the International Brotherhood
of Electrical Workers, September 29, 1958

Thomas Bailey was a skilled brick mason living in Beacon, New York, a sleepy little town in the Hudson Valley between Peekskill and Pough-keepsie. In June 1958, when he applied for membership in the Bricklay-ers, Masons, and Plasterers Local #44, he was told by the union's business agent, Andrew Gallante, that he could become a member of the union only if he was actively working in the trade. Unfortunately for Bailey, when-ever he applied for work—at job sites such as the new Mattawan State Hospital—he was repeatedly told by the construction foremen that he could not be employed without union membership. There was no shortage of jobs in Dutchess County; there were, in fact, "a number of jobs that had been started but where work had been discontinued . . . due to the short-age of skilled craftsmen in the area." Yet Thomas Bailey could not secure steady employment.

Why couldn't Bailey get a job or join the union? Because he hap-pened to be African American. Observers from the National Urban League (NUL) had noted "the absence of Negro craftsmen on the job" at con-struction sites in Dutchess County. Although one local contractor, Mr. Eugene Ninnie, had hired Bailey "from time to time" and found him to be "well qualified," he could never employ Bailey for long: "the Union

. . . had forced stoppages because the Negro masons were on the job" and "had refused [the contractor's] request to admit Negro masons into membership."

As a result of pressure from civil rights organizations, the New York State Commission against Discrimination, and the International Office of the Bricklayers Union, a representative of the union visited Bailey and told him to "consider himself a member." He told Bailey to report to a union job starting the next day, Monday, July 28, 1958. Bailey appeared for work as requested, but he was immediately "subjected to the most vicious kind of pressure" and was "the victim of the worse [sic] kind of intimidation." He strongly considered "throwing in the sponge" but stuck it out, and on Saturday, August 2, he attended his first union meeting, paid his initiation fee and membership dues, "and was promised his membership book within two weeks." An Urban League report saw this as a victory but pointed out that it had "received similar complaints from Negro building craftsmen [suggesting] a pattern of union utilization which is discriminatory against Negro workers in violation of the State Law."[1]

Thomas Bailey's problems were indeed symptomatic of a much larger pattern of racial exclusion in the craft unions, especially (and most visibly) in the building trades. These obstacles were not statutory: by 1958, all unions affiliated with the American Federation of Labor–Congress of Industrial Organizations (AFL-CIO) were officially egalitarian, accepting members without regard to race, creed, or color. Often these obstacles were not the result of racist leadership, either: many union leaders, especially on the CIO side of the federation, personally opposed racial discrimination, and delegates to the annual AFL-CIO conventions consistently affirmed their commitment to the ideal of merit-based employment and union membership. For the most part, although many were far from blameless themselves, labor leaders attributed these problems to entrenched practices and attitudes at the level of the rank and file. This created an inertia that organizations like the NUL found themselves fighting—one worker, one local, and one city at a time.[2]

At the level of public policy, President Dwight Eisenhower and his administration had a solution to these problems: the nondiscrimination clause in government contracts. Since the Great Depression, the federally funded sector of the economy had grown exponentially, aided by wartime (and Cold War) production. For Eisenhower and Vice President Richard Nixon, discrimination was largely a propaganda issue: the Soviets pointed to it as evidence of American degradation when trying to convert newly independent developing nations—especially in Africa—to Marxism. Building on similar attempts by the administrations of Franklin Roosevelt and Harry Truman, Eisenhower issued an executive order prohibiting discrimination in federal contracts and establishing the President's Committee on Government Contracts to enforce it. But like the union leadership, which had difficulty implementing its egalitarian policy among the rank-and-file membership, the Eisenhower administration often found itself largely stymied by the bureaucratic inertia of the federal civil service.

Two other constituencies played a role in this struggle: management (i.e., federal contractors) and the federal legislature. For the most part, management saw equality of opportunity as a matter of business policy rather than a human rights issue. Most businessmen looked forward to the profits that would come when all potential workers were fully utilized, but at the same time, many feared the internal white backlash—usually in the form of strikes—that often followed the initial integration of a firm.[3] Congress, meanwhile, through a southern-dominated Senate and liberal use of the filibuster, did not contribute to the equality effort during the 1950s (notwithstanding the importance of the 1957 Voting Rights Act).

Thus, the reality consisted of a union umbrella organization too weak to enforce its own antidiscrimination ideals, a moderate presidential administration unwilling to take on the federal bureaucracy, and a civil rights leadership fighting token battles. Taken separately, these three groups were unable to effect the changes necessary to achieve real equality of opportunity in employment. Working together, they would make a difference.

This chapter examines the struggles faced by these groups, including an overview of the mainstream civil rights and major labor organizations, and how these actors eventually forced President Eisenhower's committee to take the decisive action required to move federal contractors from outright exclusion to tokenism in minority hiring. It begins with a brief history of the development of inequality in organized labor in general and the building construction trades in particular.

African Americans and Organized Labor, 1860–1955

Racial discrimination in the trade unions, especially in building construction, was built on nearly a century of segregation and exclusion. During the colonial era, many African captives arriving in what would become the United States possessed a variety of skills useful in pursuits other than farming, and the most intrepid and lucky (if such a term is appropriate in a discussion of slavery) were given additional training by their white owners. A generation of scholarship has demonstrated that slaves under the plantation system were skilled in such varied fields as ironwork, salt mining, and building construction. Slaves built Monticello, the stately home of Thomas Jefferson outside Charlottesville, Virginia, and slaves were employed in the construction of southern cities as well as New York City during the revolutionary era. As the nation grew, southern slave artisans' skills were nurtured and protected by slave owners, who earned profits from their slaves' toil and maintained control over any potential competition from nonelite whites. In the antebellum North, freedmen and their descendants engaged in various entrepreneurial pursuits, in at least one case in Philadelphia, parlaying an acquired skill into an extremely profitable sail-making business.[4]

With the coming of emancipation in 1865 and an influx of immigrants, especially in the North, skilled and aspiring whites increasingly sought to marginalize skilled blacks throughout the country through violence as well as other forms of coercion. The methods and results were complicated, but a simplification of the story looks something like this: Emancipation set skilled freedmen out to shift for themselves and removed the planters' incentive to protect their employment. As immigrants continued to flood the country in the late nineteenth century, skilled whites sought to decrease the general availability of skilled labor to maintain wage levels. White immigrants pushed their way into (and in some cases created outright) nascent labor unions, and the unions in turn gained control over the training mechanisms, thereby pushing freedmen and their descendants almost completely out of skilled labor.[5]

Although the leadership of one early union umbrella organization, the Knights of Labor, was racially egalitarian (and, in fact, anti-immigrant), its influence declined after the Haymarket Riot of 1886. The larger Federation of Organized Trades and Labor Unions (which was renamed the American Federation of Labor in 1886 and survives today as the AFL-CIO) rigorously excluded blacks from most unions while maintaining an officially egalitarian policy. Local autonomy was cherished, and the umbrella organization functioned mainly as a national lobbying group. Black workers who did attempt to organize were shunted into lower-paid trades or into segregated "auxiliary" locals as a condition of affiliation; exclusively white unions such as the Boilermakers and Iron Shipbuilders Union were chartered in 1896 after paying lip service to equality by ratifying nondiscriminatory constitutions. Some blacks continued to acquire skills in all industries, but these became an ever-shrinking minority. In building construction, blacks were organized into the less skilled "trowel trades," and those who acquired more specialized skills, even new ones such as electrical work, found virtually all commercial employment closed to them. The earliest umbrella organization for the building trades, the Structural Building Trades Alliance, refused to charter the majority-black Laborers' Union in Washington, D.C., in 1906 (although some liberal carpenters voiced opposition to the decision), and the subsequent Building Trades Department of the AFL continued the practice of exclusion. That said, some construction unions—in particular the bricklayers, plasterers, painters, and especially the unskilled laborers—were egalitarian in their admission policies, and union leaders had a long history of standing up for equal rights on the job. But for the most part, blacks in the construction industry were trained and employed on small residential construction projects, often by other blacks.[6]

After the First World War, large numbers of African Americans came north in search of relief from the overtly Jim Crow practices of the South in a movement called the First Great Migration. Where they didn't encounter covert Jim Crow practices in the North—and overt acts of discrimination—they were welcomed by big business as strikebreakers, especially during the Great Strike of 1919. But when the strikes ended, black workers were routinely dismissed, their usefulness to management exhausted. With the coming of the Great Depression, more and more blacks sought the protection afforded by unions. A new and more militant umbrella organization, the Congress of Industrial Organizations, arose in counterpoint to the AFL and truly welcomed black and integrated unions. The CIO, with its early connections to the Communist Party of the United States and its desire to organize entire factories and job sites, regardless of specialization, quickly assumed the more militant mantle of the old Knights of Labor as well as the Knights' racial egalitarianism.[7]

With the outbreak of a new world war in Europe, the federal government geared up for major production, at first to supply unofficial allies and later, after Pearl Harbor, for national defense. This was a major cause of the Second Great Migration, wherein some 400,000 African Americans left the rural South for cities throughout the nation between 1940 and 1945. Like the rural whites they accompanied, they came in search of jobs in wartime industries or for military service. Unfortunately, jobs in the new trades required for wartime production remained largely closed to blacks. A board member of the National Association for the Advancement of Colored People (NAACP) remembered that "unemployment even among whites had been sufficiently severe so that there were enough of them to fill the new jobs." As the wartime potential for government spending made the New Deal seem small by comparison, the president of the Brotherhood of Sleeping-Car Porters, A. Philip Randolph, saw federally financed employment as a useful lever for change and felt that the eve of war was an opportune moment to demand governmental action. Randolph called for a massive march on Washington to demand jobs, set to take place in the early summer of 1941. President Roosevelt met with the leaders of the movement and, in an attempt to dissuade them from marching, told them that they had "'friends in Washington.' Mr. Randolph is reported to have pounded the table and said it was not friends but jobs they wanted."[8]

The threat of such a massive show of civil disobedience had its effect. On June 25, 1941, the president issued Executive Order No. 8802, prohibiting racial discrimination in defense industries and other federal contract work and establishing the Fair Employment Practices Committee (FEPC), which was empowered to investigate and report on violations of the order. Randolph agreed to cancel the march.[9]

Asa Philip Randolph (1889–1979) was born the son of an African Methodist Episcopal minister in Florida and was educated at the City College of New York, where he initially studied acting but soon gravitated toward politics and economics. Shortly after graduating, Randolph cofounded an employment agency in Harlem and began organizing black workers; he also founded *The Messenger,* a radical Harlem magazine, in 1915. During World War I Randolph became a polished street-corner orator as he assailed the policies of the Wilson administration from atop his soapbox, at one point even being arrested for espionage when he tried to convince black men to avoid military service.[10]

Randolph's wartime and postwar public activities attracted the attention of several employees of the Pullman Company, which provided sleeping-car rail service. The sleeping-car porters were almost exclusively black and had traditionally been hostile to union organizing, given the unions' exclusion of blacks and Pullman's reliability as an employer. But in 1925 employees organized the Brotherhood of Sleeping-Car Porters (BSCP), and the small membership asked Randolph to be their president. Randolph had never been employed as a sleeping-car porter himself, although he had worked as a building porter in college. (He later recalled that he had written on the wall, at one job, "Randolph swept here.") At first the union made little headway, but after ten years it was accepted into affiliation as the first black-majority union in the AFL, and in 1937 Pullman finally signed a collective bargaining agreement with the BSCP. By 1941, with his leadership in the March on Washington Movement, Randolph was clearly the unofficial leader of black labor in the United States, and in 1955 he was elected vice president of the AFL-CIO.[11]

The numbers of African Americans seeking jobs in the nation's cities continued to swell during the postwar period, with nearly 4.5 million migrants leaving the rural South between 1945 and 1970, many with extensive carpentry and masonry experience—useful skills in building construction. Although the FEPC had been helpful in ensuring wartime employment for blacks, it was unsuccessful in breaking down the barriers to black membership in the skilled building trades: the vast majority of blacks at job sites were employed as unskilled laborers. And at the end of the war, the southern-dominated Congress pulled the FEPC's funding. After much advocacy by local civil rights groups, several northern states picked up the slack by establishing their own state versions of the FEPC; by 1959 there were seventeen such agencies nationwide. Since the federal FEPC had been neutered, President Truman tried another tack. In 1946 Truman signed Executive Order No. 9808, establishing the President's Committee on Civil Rights, which issued a report the following year titled "To Secure These Rights." Among the committee's recommendations was legislation "or Executive Order [machinery] to review the expenditures of all government funds, for compliance with the policy of nondiscrimination." With no such legislation forthcoming, on December 3, 1951, Truman signed Executive Order No. 10308, mandating that all federal contracts contain a nondiscrimination clause and establishing the President's Committee on Government Contract Compliance (PCGCC) to enforce the order. The PCGCC consisted of the heads of the main contracting agencies (including the defense procurement agencies and the General Services Administration) and six presidential appointees, in contrast to Roosevelt's four-member FEPC. Funding for the committee's operations came from the represented federal agencies. The first presidential appointees included AFL president George Meany, a representative of the CIO, a newspaper editor from Kansas City, a captain of industry, and a lawyer from Richmond, Virginia. Northern editorial opinion lauded Truman's move. In June 1952, however, after six months of operation, the committee had failed to act against any government contractor and had not even hired an executive director.[12]

Under Eisenhower, the PCGCC became the President's Committee on Government Contracts (PCGC), notably dropping "Compliance" to emphasize, as Labor Department historian Judson MacLaury has observed, "the more voluntaristic approach of the new body" in comparison to the old PCGCC and FEPC. In keeping with the context of fighting for the "hearts and minds" of those in developing nations during the Cold War, Eisenhower named Vice President Richard Nixon as chairman. Although most politicians were anticommunist at the time, Nixon was particularly vociferous in his sentiment.[13] His role in the administration was, like that of so many vice presidents before him, largely ornamental; he had little real power and was used mainly as a sort of ambassador-at-large. As PCGC chairman, he would reprise that role as the administration's unofficial ambassador to the African American community.

Secretary of Labor James P. Mitchell would serve as vice chairman and effectively run the committee, with the Department of Labor providing "office space . . . logistical support, and . . . legal services." Mitchell had a progressive record on racial discrimination; as assistant secretary of the army, he had been responsible for the integration of army bases. MacLaury called him "the most enthusiastic supporter of civil rights of any member of Eisenhower's Cabinet" and "the 'social conscience' of the Eisenhower Administration." But Mitchell too saw civil rights as a tool for winning the Cold War, stating in a 1954 speech that "human equality in America is a weapon against Communism."[14]

Like the PCGCC, the PCGC consisted of representatives from the contracting agencies, as well as representatives from industry and labor. Meany was again named to the committee, along with United Auto Workers' (UAW) president Walter Reuther and retail executive Fred Lazarus. Unlike its predecessor, however, the PCGC quickly named an executive director and got to work.[15]

In April 1955, after meeting with "representatives of organized labor, business and industry, and national private organizations concerned with discrimination," Nixon and the PCGC held a conference at the White House with government officials on the enforcement of the fair employment practices clause in government contracts. According to the vice president, "The purpose of this conference . . . is to acquaint these agencies with the national equal job opportunity program and explore ways in which Federal, state, and local agencies can co-operate." Later that year, based on studies by the Urban League and the committee, Nixon stated that the hiring of blacks was not a problem; rather, the difficulty was getting employers to exercise equal opportunity in promotions. It was largely true that equal employment opportunity in blue-collar hiring had been achieved in government contracts. Many employers had been concerned about violent protests by their white employees should they implement equal employment policies, but according to Nixon, "the fears many companies had about installing a program of nondiscrimination [in hiring], particularly in the South, had not proved justified." The vice president had overlooked three major exceptions, however: the petroleum industry, railroads, and—most notably for our purposes—construction.[16]

Exploring the Boundaries:
Civil Rights Organizations and the PCGC

In 1956 the NUL surveyed the hiring practices of local building trade unions nationwide. Most cities reported difficulty in integrating the skilled trade unions, although in May, thanks to the NAACP's protests and complaints submitted to the PCGC and the AFL-CIO Civil Rights Committee, a black electrician was admitted to the Chicago local of the International Brotherhood of Electrical Workers (IBEW).[17]

The NUL and NAACP were both committed to securing civil rights, but in different ways. Each had been founded in the same era (1909–1910) by a biracial contingent of New Yorkers committed to fighting lynching and ending Jim Crow. The NAACP conducted campaigns to overturn laws dealing primarily with education, voting, and public accommodations, mainly in the South, whereas the NUL worked with industry leaders to integrate offices, factories, and other workplaces, mainly in the North. The NAACP had brought the series of lawsuits that ultimately resulted in the overturning of *Plessy v. Ferguson* by the Supreme Court in 1954, ending legal segregation in public schools. The NUL, in contrast, conducted surveys and advocated on behalf of black workers for employment integration. In short, the NAACP was primarily a civil rights advocacy organization focused on ending southern de jure segregation, and the NUL was primarily a job placement organization aimed at ending northern de facto segregation. In labor matters, the NAACP tended to side with the AFL and the CIO against management, since the organized labor organizations at least paid lip service to the ideals of equal employment opportunity. The NUL, whose contacts with management often led directly to job referrals for constituents, was more ambivalent toward unions.[18]

By the time of the landmark 1954 Supreme Court decision in *Brown v. Board of Education of Topeka, Kansas,* both organizations were run primarily by members of the black middle class, often intellectuals or academics. Their tactics, whether litigious or persuasive, reflected a privileging of bourgeois-style achievement that was irrelevant to many (if not most) African Americans, whose priorities tended to be immediate (wages and buying power) rather than abstract (percentage of skilled blacks with skilled jobs in each community). As a result, their ability to speak as the moral authority for the African American community was gradually being eroded by newer civil rights organizations. Nevertheless, their work to increase employment opportunities (and, especially at the NAACP, fight school segregation) continued to be of immediate importance to many blacks.[19] The NAACP had garnered a reputation as a louder, tougher fighter for civil rights, whereas the NUL appeared more conservative, more willing to compromise. Often the NAACP battled school boards, white citizens' councils, or county voting registrars to force integration, while the NUL quietly went about the tedious process of securing jobs with individual firms or membership in union locals. Nonetheless, both organizations made important contributions to the movement to integrate federally funded construction sites and the unions that supplied the labor.

In August 1957 President Eisenhower signed into law the first civil rights bill passed by Congress in the twentieth century—the Voting Rights Act. He also federalized the Arkansas National Guard to protect nine black youngsters attempting to integrate Little Rock High School. (Among them was Ernest Green, who, by the mid-1960s, was running a training program for black building construction apprentices for the Workers Defense League in New York City.) While the national NAACP concerned itself primarily with passage of the 1957 civil rights bill and issues in the South, the NUL undertook a new study of hiring conditions in the building trades, concluding unreservedly that the skilled trades were excluding blacks at all levels throughout the nation: "In some unions and in some occupations the Negro worker has faced many restrictions not only because of race but also because of the general policies affecting workers in some crafts. The Building Trades Unions seem to have more restrictive practices than others."[20]

Still, throughout 1957 the PCGC plugged onward, addressing about 60 percent of the discrimination complaints that came in. Nixon and Mitchell praised the committee's work as successful, but leaders of the NUL and NAACP called the PCGC largely ineffective. This difference of opinion was a result of the committee's method of handling complaints.

The PCGC—with a staff of twenty-five—functioned mainly as a conduit, without any powers of its own: "contract revocation and other legal sanctions for overt discrimination were solely at the discretion of the contracting agencies and beyond the committee's control." And whereas the PCGC had an interest in equal employment opportunity, the contracting agencies' interest was in contract fulfillment. When it received a complaint, the PCGC first determined which government agency was supervising the contract in question and then forwarded the complaint to that agency, which eventually passed it along to the responsible contracting officer—one of about 5,000. The contracting officer—who had a larger stake in getting the contract completed than in ensuring compliance with the nondiscrimination clause—investigated the complaint and reported back to his supervisor, who passed the information up to the agency head and eventually back to the PCGC. As a result of this laborious process, the disposition of an individual case typically took anywhere from five months to two years.[21] By this standard, Nixon and Mitchell could laud the committee's work as effective, in that it was functioning as an active conduit and clearing its caseload at a steady rate. By the same token, it is easy to understand the frustration felt by the civil rights community. Equal employment opportunity was being stifled by intervening layers of bureaucracy.

Exclusion and segregation were not the only causes of low black attainment levels in areas such as the building trades; the notion that blacks should not enter such fields was endemic in the nation's educational institutions, leading most black youngsters to not even attempt to train as electricians, steamfitters, plumbers, and the like. Unlike whites, most blacks couldn't look to fathers or uncles in skilled jobs as role models, so it fell to high school guidance counselors to encourage them to aspire to their full potential. However, many guidance counselors stereotyped black youths as incapable. Some counselors were simply unaware of the expanding job opportunities now available thanks to equal employment policies. Still more steered promising youths into fields where they felt discrimination would be less of a bar. As a result, the pool of skilled black construction workers and those in training remained small.[22]

In 1958 NAACP labor director Herbert Hill, having conducted a number of studies on discrimination in the building trades, noted that the PCGC had failed to take action against even one government contractor. The committee had received several hundred complaints from individuals and from organizations like the NAACP, citing discrimination in hiring on federally funded jobs as well as discrimination in union membership and official apprenticeship programs run by unions with exclusive hiring privileges with government contractors. Although most of the complaints had been resolved informally (contractors, after being visited by a member of the committee, would agree to hire the complainant or engage in some other satisfactory behavior, such as increasing the number of black trainees), many were still pending due to union recalcitrance or employers' fears of strikes by white workers. Additionally, with new, more militant civil rights organizations being formed as the movement against segregation in the South gained steam, many members of the NAACP felt their organization needed to become more active in response to the accelerating pace of demands for racial equality. Hill concluded that the time for studies had ended, and he resolved to push the PCGC to take concrete action.[23]

Born in 1924 in Brooklyn, New York, Hill graduated from New York University in 1945 and obtained a master's degree at the New School for Social Research under the guidance of noted political theorist Hannah Arendt. A committed member of the Socialist Workers' Party during his college years, the Jewish Hill saw the United States' involvement in fighting fascist anti-Semitism as flawed by the nation's continued relegation of African Americans (and, at that time, Jews) to second-class status. While at the New School, Hill became involved with the NAACP as a volunteer in the organization's local campaign to integrate New York City's recreational facilities. Shortly after graduation he was hired as a full-time organizer, and in 1951 he became director of the NAACP's labor department. Over the years Hill developed a close working relationship with the head of the organization, Roy Wilkins. On issues pertaining to the AFL-CIO and other labor matters, Hill "played the outspoken heavy, while . . . Wilkins maintained a more soft-spoken, congenial public posture, although he protected Mr. Hill from the attacks of labor leaders."[24]

On April 15, 1958, at the request of Wilkins, the PCGC met with Hill. The NAACP labor director took the opportunity to remind committee members that a number of complaints about unequal hiring, promotions, and training had been submitted by the NAACP more than a year earlier and had not been disposed of. These included one complaint against the U.S. Industrial Chemical Company of Ohio and another against American Banner Lines Inc. of New York. Hill pointed out that the committee had yet to revoke a single government contract, and he asked that the PCGC issue a status report on all pending cases more than a year old. The committee agreed and promised a summary by late May. In the interim,

Mitchell asked Hill to send him a comprehensive list of unions with discriminatory practices.[25]

On May 13, 1958, Hill sent Mitchell the list, including national and international labor unions that excluded blacks. In particular, Hill stated that the IBEW, which "has recently admitted Negroes into some hitherto lily-white unions," still excluded blacks "in the North as well as in the South" or placed them in "Jim Crow 'auxiliary' locals." Auxiliary locals, like segregated public schools, were informally (but forcefully) relegated to second-class status. Hill also listed unions that confined blacks to segregated locals, including many in the building trades, and added that the unions controlled hiring as part of "all collective bargaining agreements in the building and construction trades industry." He noted one example in "Terre Haute, Indiana, [where] Negro mechanics have been systematically denied admission into building trades unions and therefore have been denied the right to secure employment in those job classifications where AFL-CIO affiliates hold exclusive bargaining rights." In Cleveland, Ohio, in defiance of an order by the Cleveland Community Relations Board (responsible for executing a local fair employment law), IBEW Local 38 prevented skilled blacks from working on any major construction jobs, including "huge construction projects erected with federal government funds."[26] In short, Hill contended that the unions were using the right to supply labor under collective bargaining agreements to keep blacks off the job, and when a job was federally funded, the government had a responsibility to take action.

That July the PCGC released a newsletter touting its programs and congratulating Major General Cornelius E. Ryan, the executive vice chair, for his hard work. A veteran of both world wars and former commander of the 101st Airborne Division, the retired general now lent his considerable gravitas to the PCGC. General Ryan paid visits to a number of CEOs of important federal contractors, including Alcoa, General Electric, and Bethlehem Steel (but notably *not* U.S. Industrial or American Banner, the contractors Hill had mentioned to the committee; the newsletter gave no explanation for their omission). The newsletter included a column on a new equal job opportunity stamp and touted the distribution of 35,000 "car cards for buses, subways, and trolleys."[27] No actual compliance cases were mentioned.

This focus on "puff pieces" by the public relations arm of the PCGC did not go unnoticed by the NAACP. At its annual convention in Cleveland that month, a resolution reflected a different picture of the committee's activities: "Regretfully we note the lack of vigorous enforcement and broad application of the intent and purpose contained in Presidential Executive Order No. 10479, issued on August 13, 1953, establishing the [PCGC] to enforce the anti-discrimination clause found in all U.S. government contracts. Not a single contract has been cancelled by this committee, although canceling contracts is their only means of enforcement . . . we strongly condemn the lack of meaningful enforcement and the extremely limited application of the intent of the Executive Order by the President's Committee."[28]

The NAACP was not simply trying to excoriate the Eisenhower administration for failing to integrate federal job sites. In fact, the organization—as well as the NUL—viewed the administration as generally friendly to the cause of civil rights. Rather, the NAACP hoped that such a stern, public expression of "regret" would push the administration to act with more vigor to enforce its own policies at the level of the civil service. In short, the NAACP understood that the fault lay with the entrenched federal bureaucracy, but it believed the administration—nominally in charge of the bureaucracy—could have worked harder to tackle bureaucratic inertia.

Later that month Hill asked the PCGC to cancel the federal contracts with U.S. Industrial and American Banner, as well as two southern oil companies, for failure to comply with the nondiscrimination clause. The complaints against these companies included two of the pending cases more than a year old that Hill had cited in his statement to the committee in April. The PCGC never canceled the contracts, and the NAACP convention resolutions of 1959 and 1960 would include similar "regretful" language about the PCGC's "hard work."[29]

The Rift: Herbert Hill, the NAACP, and the AFL-CIO

On December 5, 1955, the AFL-CIO was formed when the older AFL merged with the newer representative organization of mainly unskilled and semiskilled factory workers, the CIO. The merger created one major umbrella labor organization with which national and international unions could affiliate. The umbrella organization would serve mainly as a national lobbying organization for workers' rights and a referee for conflicts between affiliated local unions. The national AFL-CIO had several departments that focused on major industries and other areas of concern, such as the Building Construction Trades Department (BCTD) and the

Civil Rights Department. It also supported local area councils, which dealt with labor issues for individual cities, states, and regions.

One important function of the AFL-CIO during the first decade after the merger was reconciling the differences between unions from its two former parts. With a few major exceptions, the old AFL unions tended to be less tolerant of integration, while the newer CIO unions, which had formed (or split off) during the 1930s, tended to be more accepting of integration—a political calculus that had helped swell their ranks with black as well as white workers.[30]

Most of the building construction trades had been organized under the AFL and consisted of highly skilled, well-trained, and usually better-paid workers. Most blacks working in unionized building construction were members of the less exclusive laborers' or carpenters' unions, requiring less skill and fewer years of training and ultimately leading to jobs with lower pay.[31]

Given the high visibility of public construction projects, the building trades became a focal point for civil rights leaders looking for symbolic as well as substantive victories against discrimination, especially as urban renewal swelled the number of federally funded construction projects. In other words, young blacks were constantly reminded of their second-class status whenever they passed one of the many construction sites in their cities and saw only white faces under hard hats. That needed to change. Under the new umbrella organization's constitution, the AFL-CIO committed itself to equality of opportunity in apprenticeship and training, union membership, and job referrals.[32] Whether it could make good on that promise was another question entirely.

The role of unions in the exclusion of blacks from the skilled construction trades came into sharp relief during the summer of 1956 in Cleveland, Ohio. The Cleveland Community Relations Board (CCRB) submitted a complaint to the PCGC that the IBEW local was not referring any blacks to work on the federally subsidized construction of public schools (indeed, as a "lily-white" local, the union had no African American members to refer). The PCGC appeared "to accept a sort of responsibility" for the matter by agreeing to pressure the contractor to pressure the local to admit blacks (or at least to allow the contractor to hire nonunion or nonlocal blacks) to meet the terms of the nondiscrimination clause. But when the NAACP complained publicly in October of the committee's apparent inactivity, the PCGC's executive director stated that the committee had no jurisdiction over unions because unions didn't sign federal contracts.

This prompted the CCRB to ask the PCGC for clarification, reminding the committee's executive director that "an argument could be advanced that union contracts, particularly the type found in the skilled building trades, are in effect and substance a subcontract admissible as such under the provisions of the presidential executive order."[33] The desired result of this wrangling—the employment of one or more qualified black electricians on the Cleveland school construction project—was never achieved. The electrical work on the new schools—some in neighborhoods without any white residents—was completed exclusively by white electricians.

Yet in other cities there was cause for hope. After the Chicago Ironworkers' Local #1 apprenticeship program twice refused to admit three black youths—Ronald Todd, Michael Coleman, and James Hill—NAACP lawyers filed suit on September 26, 1957. In a banner legal ruling on October 16, Chief Judge William J. Campbell of the U.S. District Court for Northern Illinois, "in what is believed to be the first court order of its kind," ordered the union to admit the three youths to the apprenticeship program "forthwith."[34]

In the fall of 1958, after spending the better part of the year applying pressure to the PCGC, Herbert Hill turned his attention to the AFL-CIO in an attempt to get it to enforce the nondiscrimination aspects of its own constitution. In October he asked the AFL-CIO's Civil Rights Department to "immediately 'initiate a direct frontal attack' against the many affiliated unions which are violating AFL-CIO civil rights policy," including "Local 120 and Local 55 of the Plumbers and Pipefitters Union in Cleveland . . . as well as . . . the Carpenters Union in East St. Louis, Illinois, and elsewhere." He also asked that action be taken against segregated locals. Hill followed up in December, sending affidavits of bias in securing union membership, including one pertaining to the Laborers Union in East St. Louis: a black worker named William Gamble had attempted to use a traveling permit obtained from Local #110 in St. Louis to enter Local #100 in East St. Louis and had been rebuffed. Hill said that blacks were being excluded from building trades unions in both cities, and he included affidavits against IBEW Local #309 in St. Louis, Local #90 of the Plasterers and Cement Masons in St. Louis, and Local #630 of the Plumbers and Pipefitters in East St. Louis. He warned that if these complaints were not positively resolved, the local NAACP branches would be forced to initiate legal action in order to best represent the interests of their members. The next week, NAACP executive secretary Roy Wilkins sent Hill's affidavits to George Meany, president of the AFL-CIO, reminding him that the NAACP had worked with the AFL-CIO diligently on the union leadership's antidiscrimination program and on nonracial matters such as fighting right-to-work laws. He stated forcefully that action must now be taken against discriminatory locals. This correspondence was then leaked to the press.[35]

AFL-CIO president George Meany (1894–1980) was literally born into union leadership as the son of a leader in the New York City Plumbers Union. Meany dropped out of school at age sixteen to become a plumber's helper, and by age twenty-nine he was secretary-treasurer (the second-highest leadership position) of the New York Building Trades Council. By 1934, at age forty, Meany was New York State AFL president, where he became an effective lobbyist during the administration of Governor Herbert H. Lehman. During the summer of 1935 Meany was thrust into the national spotlight for the first time as he battled with the Works Progress Administration (WPA), an arm of President Roosevelt's Depression-era New Deal. The WPA proposed to pay construction workers less than the prevailing union rates. Threatening a strike, Meany honed his skills in two styles for which he would later achieve national renown: he and the WPA administrator "exchanged epithets by day and dinner-table chat by night." By the end of the summer, with the White House becoming concerned about the progress of the talks, the WPA yielded. Not for the last time, Meany had won a major concession from a federal agency.[36]

Meany's successes as head of the New York State AFL led to his election in 1939 as secretary-treasurer of the national AFL, second only to AFL president William Green. Meany, always an anticommunist, used his growing power to keep the federation out of a worldwide umbrella organization that welcomed Soviet labor unions. The other major U.S. labor organization, the CIO, had fewer objections to communist ideology and joined the worldwide umbrella.[37]

In 1947 Congress passed the Taft-Hartley Act, which amended many of the more pro-union statutes of the Wagner Act of 1935, despite growing union influence in Washington. Increasingly, Green's leadership of the AFL was seen as lacking, especially by such outspoken critics as John L. Lewis of the United Mine Workers. Meany, however, supported Green and saw the continuing split between the older AFL unions and the newer CIO unions as the main weakness of organized labor. When Lewis—along with a number of CIO leaders—refused to take a noncommunist loyalty oath, Meany used his own anticommunist history to strengthen Green's administration (and his own dominance of the organization) until Green's death in 1952. At that point, Meany assumed the presidency of the AFL and became committed to arranging a merger with the CIO, a process that would take three years. Although it seemed probable that Meany would lead the new combined organization, based on the relative size of the two organizations and the ascendancy of anticommunist ideology at the time, UAW president Walter Reuther was another strong contender. Nevertheless, at the founding convention of the AFL-CIO in 1955, Meany was unanimously elected the new organization's first president.[38]

The AFL-CIO had come to see the NAACP as an ally, mainly thanks to the latter's opposition to Taft-Hartley. But now, unhappy with its negative portrayal in the press, the federation's Civil Rights Committee met on January 29, 1959, to discuss "how to handle the NAACP." When two committee members suggested trying to push recalcitrant locals to admit blacks or to integrate segregated locals, the chairman rejected such proposals out of hand, apparently feeling that it was more important to pacify Wilkins and marginalize Hill to avoid any additional press leaks on the subject. The two sympathetic committee members advised Hill of the proceedings, who then recommended to Wilkins that the NAACP respond by publicly demanding that the AFL-CIO take concrete action to "prevent exclusion practices . . . eliminate all segregated locals . . . call upon all local affiliates" to refuse "to ratify collective bargaining agreements with separate racial seniority lines," and "establish a functional liaison with all state and municipal fair employment practices commissions."[39]

Shortly thereafter, Wilkins moved to quell rumors (started, according to Hill, by the AFL-CIO Civil Rights Committee in an attempt to marginalize Hill) that he—Wilkins—had disowned his December memo to Meany containing the list of Hill's affidavits. Wilkins confided to A. Philip Randolph that he was dismayed that so many union leaders seemed more concerned with getting past the scandal caused by the press leak than with taking concrete steps to end union discrimination. Wilkins acknowledged the organizational limitations of the AFL-CIO, which had no direct authority over its affiliates, but he believed that strong action by the umbrella organization to cajole and threaten unions that were breaking the law and their own constitutions would be extremely useful in the battle to secure union rights for black workers in all crafts.[40]

With the rift between the AFL-CIO and NAACP leadership now public, Randolph employed his considerable stature among black workers to support the NAACP from within organized labor. In a speech before the Trade Union Leadership Council on February 7, 1959, Randolph pointed to progress in integrating the IBEW in New York and Chicago but stated that this progress had to be more widespread. He also looked with pride to the election of a black plumber as a union local's business agent, even though "Negroes represent less than ten percent of the membership." Randolph praised "the firm action of President George Meany in setting a deadline to compliance with the AFL-CIO anti-discrimination policy by a union guilty of racial discrimination," and he made "reference to a specific complaint by a Negro electrical worker of discrimination . . . by an electrical workers' local union in Cleveland." He stated that "racial discrimination is practiced by building trades unions in practically every community of the country" and reiterated that "since union membership is generally a condition of employment, the refusal to permit Negroes . . . to become members . . . denies qualified Negroes the right to work at their chosen trades."[41]

On March 18, 1959, Wilkins and Hill met with Meany and Randolph to discuss Hill's December memo and possible actions to be taken by the AFL-CIO. Meany assured the NAACP leaders of his "continuing determination to strive for the elimination of discrimination in the . . . trade union movement." Meany and Wilkins agreed that the solutions should be systemwide rather than directed at individual local unions. Hill would wait four months before pressing the matter further, but in July, when the delegates to the 1959 NAACP convention unanimously approved the content of Wilkins's December memo to Meany, Hill asked the director of the AFL-CIO Civil Rights Committee for a progress report.[42] There is no record of a reply.

The alliance between the NAACP and organized labor may have outlived its usefulness, as outside forces seemed set to pull the two organizations apart. The civil rights movement was gaining steam, requiring older organizations like the NAACP to take a more vigorous tack to keep up with the pace of change. Meanwhile, the white union rank and file seemed eager to protect their existing and hard-won advantages, including those based on skin color and family connections.[43]

These developing tensions took a dramatic turn at the annual AFL-CIO convention in San Francisco. On September 24, 1959, A. Philip Randolph, addressing the convention, asked for the suspension of two discriminatory unions in the railroad industry and the rejection of a petition for reinstatement of a third until these unions ended their discriminatory practices. He stated that racial discrimination was just as negative an influence on organized labor as were racketeering and communism, infractions for which unions had been expelled in the recent past.[44]

Meany could have given Randolph a measured and logical reply. After all, there were fundamental differences between racially discriminatory unions and those engaged in racketeering or those sympathetic to communism. Meany may or may not have seen racial discrimination as equally evil to racketeering and communism (he was, after all, an ardent anticommunist and was greatly concerned with the growing public perception that unions were corrupt), but the fact was that racketeering and communism were engaged in by the leaders of only a few unions, whereas racial exclusion was practiced by many unions, largely at the level of the rank-and-file membership. The expulsion of a few corrupt or communist unions had resulted—in almost every case—in the election of new, less corrupt, noncommunist leaders, leading to the union's reinstatement. But to expel the many unions with de facto racial policies would have decimated the AFL-CIO affiliates and probably resulted in little change in their behavior. Better, Meany thought, to keep them in the federation, where they could continue to engage in a dialogue that might eventually have a positive result. What's more, Randolph had been publicly proposing—and Meany and his predecessors had been politically deflecting—similar resolutions as far back as 1935.[45]

Labor leaders like Meany had seen attempts at the compulsion and expulsion of unions lead to bitterness and recrimination, antithetical to the goals of the labor movement. As a result, they had developed a tradition of avoiding formal sanctions in favor of suasion, education, and compromise. Notable in that history was the treatment of the United Brotherhood of Carpenters and Joiners in 1910. To the chagrin of the sheet metal workers' union and the newly formed Building Trades Department (BTD) of the AFL (after 1937, the BCTD), the carpenters resolved to include metal trim work in their own portfolio, and they struck contractors that employed sheet metal workers on such tasks (union or not). The BTD suspended the carpenters' union, but the AFL, under Samuel Gompers, did not. Gompers persuaded the BTD Executive Council to repeal the suspension, and the carpenters rejoined the department in 1913. They continued to do metal trim work and—to the dismay of the plasterers' union—plaster carpentry.[46] So Meany could have calmly drawn from a number of points to deflect Randolph's request yet again.

Instead, exasperated that Randolph hadn't brought these issues before him in the smaller venue of the organization's Executive Council, Meany blurted out, "Who the hell appointed you as the guardian of all the Negro members in America?" The AFL-CIO president was immediately excoriated in the black press, and African American leaders—from the Reverend Dr. Martin Luther King Jr. to the only black U.S. congressman, Adam Clayton Powell Jr.—publicly reaffirmed their confidence in Randolph as the unofficial "dean" of the civil rights movement.[47]

The flap over Meany's unexpected outburst put the NUL in a particular bind, for the organization had recently announced that Meany would be one recipient of its annual Equal Opportunity Day awards. Every year, at the NUL's Equal Opportunity Day dinner, the organization presented one award to a labor leader and another to a business leader for furthering the cause of equal employment opportunity in their respective spheres. Meany's choice as the 1959 labor recipient reflected his hard work, since the 1955 AFL-CIO merger, to promote equal opportunity through union constitutions and proposed federal and state legislation. Most notably, Meany had been at the forefront of organized labor's support of the 1957 Voting Rights Act—the first civil rights law since Reconstruction—which had created a federal Civil Rights Commission with the power to investigate and recommend actions pertaining to unequal treatment under the Fourteenth Amendment to the U.S. Constitution. What's more, and perhaps most critically for the NUL leadership, Meany had already accepted his invitation, and the dinner was scheduled for November 17, 1959. On the one hand, the NUL risked offending a large segment of the black community if it proceeded to give Meany the award; on the other hand, the staid organization could hardly make the social faux pas of withdrawing its formal invitation, thereby personally offending the most powerful man in the labor movement and an advocate for union integration—his outburst notwithstanding. After several meetings among NUL executive director Lester Granger, Randolph, and Meany (and despite the disagreement of two NUL board members, who pointed out that offending Meany would merely equal Meany's treatment of Randolph), the organization decided to give Meany the honor after all. The austere Randolph had hardly been as offended as the black press, and Meany's record as an advocate of civil rights was overwhelmingly positive and outweighed this one intemperate, heat-of-the-moment outburst.[48]

At the dinner, Meany devoted fully half of his speech to the issue of racist locals, explaining that he had not intended to insult Randolph. He noted that the delegates to the AFL-CIO convention had unanimously affirmed that the recalcitrant unions should integrate, but he thought the best way to get them to do so was through pressure from the AFL-CIO leadership, not through a deadline or expulsion, as Randolph would have it. He reiterated that his anger in September had been over the fact that Randolph had brought the black longshoremen's complaints directly to the organization's convention, rather than following the established procedure of having the initial discussion in the AFL-CIO's Executive Council.[49]

Even as ties between the AFL-CIO and the formerly ambivalent NUL were strengthened with Meany's speech at the Equal Opportunity Day dinner, the already strained relationship between organized labor and the once loyal NAACP took another hit. Frustrated that the behavior of racially exclusionist unions had gone unchecked by either the AFL-CIO or the PCGC, Herbert Hill publicly—in a speech in Minneapolis in April 1960—called for the decertification of building construction unions that violated the law by operating what were effectively closed shops prohibiting the employment of blacks. Under the Taft-Hartley Act of 1947, the National Labor Relations Board (NLRB) was responsible for certifying (and decertifying) union locals as bargaining agents for workers in any given plant or job site. One of the main tenets of Taft-Hartley was the end of the so-called closed shop, in which unions could require employers to hire only union members. The NLRB had the power to decertify unions for requiring closed shops, and many construction unions operated such shops through their hiring halls, which were basically union offices to which contractors ceded the responsibilities of staffing. Given the seasonal and temporal nature of construction work, it made more sense for contractors to, in effect, contract out their hiring to the unions rather than to maintain a permanent skilled labor force of their own, and throughout the 1940s and 1950s the NLRB had repeatedly certified segregated and all-white locals operating what were effectively closed shops.[50]

The irony of Hill's call for NLRB decertification was apparent to all who had been watching the rift develop between the NAACP and the AFL-CIO. The NAACP had opposed the closed-shop provisions of the Wagner Act, concerned that "at least twenty-two national unions . . . had formal bars against membership by non-white workers, including . . . the Boilermakers, Machinists, Electrical Workers, Plumbers and Steamfitters, and Sheet Metal Workers." But by 1947, when Congress passed the Taft-Hartley amendments, the NAACP had reversed course, arguing that by weakening unions, Taft-Hartley posed a danger to integration. The NAACP had helped organized labor in its ongoing fight against state right-to-work laws, which prohibited unions from requiring all employees of a particular company to join the union, even when a majority of employees was willing to do so. Still, Hill was careful to point out that the NAACP opposed the use of the closed shop only when it was employed to exclude blacks.[51]

At the annual NAACP convention that June, Randolph supported Hill's request, arguing that the open shop, though generally a noxious antilabor tool, was necessary when unions excluded blacks from employment.[52] But in a presidential election year, when the alliance between the NAACP and the AFL-CIO would have been especially important in advocating for the inclusion of strong civil rights and labor rights planks in the platforms of both major political parties, the rift between the two organizations seemed ominous.

Getting a "Chap on the Payroll": Washington's Southwest Redevelopment Project and IBEW Local #26

The PCGC had the authority to investigate claims of discrimination in federal government contracts. All such contracts included an antidiscrimination clause, and if the PCGC found that a contractor or subcontractor had violated the clause, it could recommend that the contracting federal agency (or the White House, if the agency refused) revoke the contract or even debar a contractor from bidding on future contracts. Where union discrimination fit into this scenario was apparently a tricky question. Were unions that signed collective bargaining agreements with federal contractors in effect subcontractors, and therefore subject to PCGC investigation and penalties? Or were they "third parties" over which the PCGC had no jurisdiction? And if unions were subject to PCGC sanction, what exactly would the penalties be?

In the wake of the 1957 Voting Rights Act, several unions issued resolutions on civil rights. A typical resolution—such as the one adopted by the California Labor Fellowship—stated in part: "Whereas, prejudice . . . cannot be tolerated by freedom-loving Americans; therefore, be it . . . resolved, that we urge our members to act with good will in their hearts and understanding in their minds, to work in their unions, their communities, and in the nation for the elimination of injustice and for a society free of race hate and fear."[53] The membership of the IBEW, in contrast, issued a rather nondescript and frankly blasé resolution on civil rights that year: "Resolved, that the IBEW go on record as being in support of full civil rights for all Americans and be it further resolved, that it be the enduring goal of our brotherhood to assure to all workers their full share in the benefits of union organization without regard to race, creed, color, or national origin."[54] It seemed forced, the absolute least the union would agree to under the pressure it was apparently receiving from the umbrella organization. Weak as this resolution was, it was largely ignored by the membership of IBEW Local #26 of Washington, D.C.

On January 19, 1959, a PCGC newsletter announced that the committee had "called for immediate action by the organized building trades unions to bring success to its two-year efforts to see that Negro craftsmen are not barred from construction work on Washington's Southwest Redevelopment Project, known as Area B." Area B was supervised by the General Services Administration (GSA), the agency responsible for overseeing, among other things, the construction and maintenance of the federal government's physical plant in the nation's capital. Notably, the PCGC was not "ordering" the unions to admit blacks or allow them to work; it was only "[calling] for immediate action." The newsletter included a two-year chronology of the situation, which quoted Vice President Nixon: "I would like to impress upon you the urgency for taking affirmative action in this matter . . . at the earliest possible date." Since the PCGC had formerly claimed no jurisdiction over discrimination by unions, this constituted a sea change in the committee's activities. Despite the relative weakness of the language used by the committee, the NAACP leadership announced that it was extremely pleased.[55]

Still, nine months later, no progress had been made on integrating the job site, while much progress had been made on the construction project itself. In November the contractor, McCloskey & Co. of Philadelphia, offered to bring in black ironworkers from outside the District of Columbia to make up for the fact that the ironworkers' local—which the contractor was obligated to use by a collective bargaining agreement—had only two black members. Still hoping that the project could employ local blacks (and demonstrating the truth of the adage that "the perfect is the enemy of the good"), Nixon "rejected the proposal as evading the issue." AFL-CIO president Meany, seeing the Local #26 situation as garnering particularly bad press for organized labor as a whole, and personally miffed that the local had rebuffed all his attempts to get it to integrate and fulfill its obligations as an AFL-CIO affiliate, "said he would personally recruit [black] electricians for the Washington jobs and see that the union permitted them to work." The matter was particularly embarrassing for Meany because the federation had recently constructed its own headquarters in Washington without employing a single black electrician.[56]

On April 28, 1960, NUL executive director Granger wrote to Nixon, recommending that the PCGC ask the president to debar McCloskey on the grounds that the Washington Urban League had referred five qualified black electricians, but McCloskey had refused to hire them, and the GSA had refused to take action by pulling the contract. Nixon's reply noted that the PCGC had referred the matter to the GSA on April 20. The vice president went on to say, "I can assure you that the investigation now under way by the GSA will result either in the employment of qualified Negro electrical workers on current government building projects in the District of Columbia or appropriate action against the contractors involved for failure to comply with the terms of their contracts with the government." Nixon pointed with pride to the "recent first referrals of Negro rodmen on construction projects in Washington," stating that "this achievement was an excellent example of what can be accomplished when champions of equal job opportunity join hands in fighting racial discrimination." But on May 19, 1960, two GSA panels unanimously concluded that the five black electricians referred by the Washington Urban League were unqualified for the type of electrical work required by the project.[57]

Immediately the NAACP entered the Local #26 fray and claimed that the findings were a direct result of the exclusion of blacks from the local's apprenticeship program. Pointedly, Wilkins demanded by telegram that Meany make good on his threat to bring in nonunion black electricians:

Alleged lack of qualified Negroes is direct result of union discriminatory practices. We note that you previously set October 31, 1956 as an absolute deadline for an end to Negro exclusion on federal construction projects in the nation's capital. This spring you publicly pledged to recruit qualified Negro electricians who were not union members. We believe it is essential that you now carry out your pledge. Further delay in this matter which has already been delayed for too many years will be interpreted by Negro community as additional evidence of the inability of organized labor to eliminate even the most obvious instances of racism within its own ranks.[58]

But Granger saw something even more insidious at work, calling the GSA panel finding a farce. The NUL's executive director was not exactly quick to condemn a federal agency: during World War II, Granger had worked with defense contractors and employees as a special assistant to the secretary of the navy, receiving high praise from President Truman. In short, when Granger criticized the GSA, he was taken seriously. Granger noted that the panelists had merely compared the black workers' written statements of their qualifications with the contractor's list of required skills (which, the NUL claimed, were unnecessarily high) and found the black electricians unqualified without conducting any interviews with them. Granger now called on the GSA to cancel the McCloskey contract, and if the GSA proved unwilling, he recommended that the PCGC ask the White House to do so. For his part, Meany concurred with Granger, calling the GSA panel review a "whitewash." Meany went on to say that the five black electricians were in fact fully qualified (pointing out that one had eighteen years' experience), and he agreed that the contractor should be debarred.[59]

The PCGC concurred with Granger and Meany that something was amiss with the GSA panel's findings, and it requested that the panelists evaluate the white electricians already working on the job site to permit a comparison with the "unqualified" blacks.[60] It remains uncertain exactly who was unqualified—the black workers referred by the Urban League, or the panelists evaluating them on behalf of the GSA. In any event, the referred workers were not hired by the contractor and were not admitted into the union. Meanwhile, work continued, and the Area B project approached completion without employing a single black electrician.

Expressing his own frustration with McCloskey, and in an attempt to break the impasse, the PCGC's executive vice chairman asked Granger to refer qualified black electricians from outside the District of Columbia, owing to "some question of the sufficiency of qualified Negro construction electricians in the District." Since the contractor's previous offer to bring in black ironworkers from Philadelphia had been rebuffed, this request shows that by this point—May 1960—the PCGC had little faith in the contractor's claims of innocence in the matter. Nonetheless, pointing out that Meany had deemed the original five black electricians qualified, Granger refused.[61]

Throughout the summer of 1960, the NUL and AFL-CIO continued to put pressure on the PCGC, and the committee, in turn, pressured the GSA. Finally, in September, with construction nearly complete and the contractor apparently more than willing to finish the job without hiring any black electricians at all, the GSA gave McCloskey an ultimatum: hire a black electrician or lose the contract. It took another month, but on October 20, 1960, after nearly four years of advocacy and negotiations, a black "electrician named James Holland [was] employed by the subcontractor for the

. . . construction project in Washington . . . the chap went on the payroll Wednesday and is expected to report to work today (Thursday)." Thanks to government pressure, McCloskey had been compelled to negotiate with IBEW Local #26. The union did not want McCloskey to lose the contract or bring in nonunion labor, and it knew it couldn't depend on support from the international office or the AFL-CIO in the event of a strike. Holland had been a member of Detroit IBEW Local #58 and, as such, was given a referral card, but he was not granted membership in Local #26.[62]

The struggle for equal employment opportunity in the building construction trades during the 1950s was typified by a largely ambivalent PCGC led by Richard Nixon, who saw the committee's main role as fighting communist propaganda. The committee's work dovetailed with the AFL-CIO's civil rights agenda under the leadership of George Meany, which sought to ruffle the fewest rank-and-file feathers while doing the minimum necessary to appease the national civil rights organizations. Those organizations, the NAACP and NUL, were forced to fight hard—one city, one local, and one job at a time—to achieve only token victories. Finally, at the risk of undermining hard-won personal relationships with powerful leaders in government and labor, and in the midst of major attention-grabbing headlines elsewhere (involving voting rights and school desegregation), the NAACP mounted a vigorous campaign to get the PCGC and AFL-CIO to live up to the ideals of their charters—to actively work to integrate jobs and locals. This pressure forced the PCGC, AFL-CIO, and NUL to work together in the case of Washington's Area B, which forced the GSA to issue a powerful ultimatum to the contractor—the first of its kind. The result, then, was much more than just the token hiring of a "chap . . . on the payroll"; it was the realization that, by working together, organized labor, civil rights organizations, and elected and appointed officials could successfully pressure the heretofore intransigent federal bureaucracy to take real—one might even say affirmative—action. Nonetheless, the bureaucracy was still seen as an obstacle to equality of opportunity, and the notion that the power of the bureaucracy itself could be harnessed to the cause of equality had not yet been considered.

At the start of 1961, civil rights leaders could look back at two decades of progress in voting rights and public accommodation. Yet such progress had largely skipped over employment, especially in the building construction trades. Tellingly, the AFL-CIO leadership still saw employment discrimination as a public image—rather than a human rights—issue, and

Washington still saw civil rights in general as a good job for an otherwise ornamental vice president. In January 1961 Richard Nixon handed over leadership of the contracts committee to Lyndon Baines Johnson. But as a new decade dawned with a young president in the White House, the possibility—and the expectation—of real progress loomed large. Another "ornamental" vice president would ascend to the White House as a result of a national tragedy, bringing leadership in civil rights directly into the Oval Office. And other outside events would serve to change the way Washington—and the nation—saw the role of the federal government in securing equal treatment for all.

Chapter 2

Becoming the Urban Crisis, 1961–1963

It is perhaps unkind to refer to the "Plans for Progress" as a hoax, but it is going to be very difficult to bargain with employers in the future in the event they fail "to progress."

> —Richard C. Wells, Washington Urban League director
> of job development, December 20, 1961

The policeman's blackjack hit Stanford's head—not once, but twice. Another officer struck Daniels, also in the head. The two young men fell to the street, stunned. Both were arrested. Daniels, who had been taking pictures, saw his camera confiscated. As he later recounted:

> I was shooting pictures of the line, when all of a sudden these con-struction workers rushed up and tried to crash through. The police came from everywhere. I never saw so many of them in my life. I saw one of them pull out a blackjack and hit Stanford twice on the head. I was still taking pictures when I felt a blow on the top of my head where some cop had hit me. Then some more officers rushed up and snatched my camera. They claimed I had tried to hit the officers with it. That is ridiculous. Why would I use an expensive camera as a weapon?[1]

The year was 1963, Maxwell C. Stanford and Stanley Daniels were African American, and the police officers were white. But this didn't hap-pen in Birmingham, Alabama. The two had gone to a demonstration at a Philadelphia school construction site at Thirty-first Street and Susque-hanna Avenue to record what the local branch of the NAACP had intended to be a peaceful—if militant—protest against discrimination by local construction unions. The school, like so many other city-funded construction projects, was being built without any skilled black construction workers, thanks to local union control of the hiring process. Whatever blacks were employed at the site were found exclusively in the unskilled "trowel trades"— bricklayers, hod carriers, basic carpenters, and common laborers. Stanford was the twenty-one-year-old son of "one of the nation's top amateur Negro golfers," and Daniels, twenty-two, was a recent graduate of the University of Pennsylvania and a social worker. Like so many of the civil rights workers in the South, Stanford and Daniels were the sons of black America's small middle class.[2]

The protest at the school site was the brainchild of the Philadelphia NAACP's fiery branch president Cecil B. Moore. Earlier that month, Moore had watched as the local branch of the Congress of Racial Equality (CORE) had successfully pushed Philadelphia mayor James Tate to suspend construction on a city office building by staging a sit-in outside the mayor's home and later in his offices at city hall. Moore knew that many in the city's black community saw the NAACP as a conservative, inside-the-system organization with little interest in militant protest, and he worried that with the civil rights movement taking a more militant turn, newer organizations like CORE would attract the scores of unaffiliated youths searching for a way to channel their pent-up frustrations. With construction suspended at the office building site, Moore announced that May 24, 1963, would be the deadline for the board of education, the contractors, and the unions to hire skilled black construction workers at the Thirty-first and Susquehanna site, or he would organize picketing. The city made no move, and the protest began on May 24 as scheduled.[3]

The picketers—at first numbering only a few dozen—intended to march peacefully, but by late afternoon there were hundreds of demonstrators, including several local black celebrities. They had physically blocked all entrances to the site, making it impossible for construction workers and equipment to enter. Large groups of workers attempted to push through, resulting in brief, scattered melees. Then the police took action.[4]

Picketing and violence continued at the Philadelphia school construction site for three days, until the contractors agreed to hire skilled workers without regard to race. Two black electricians, a black plumber, and a black steamfitter were hired to work at the site, with the consent of the Philadelphia AFL-CIO Building Construction Trades Council and the local electricians' and plumbers' unions; the steamfitters' local, however, withdrew from the council in protest. Herbert Hill called the Philadelphia protests "the beginning of a nationwide campaign against discrimination in unions . . . the young Negroes with their magnificent courage will take care of the South. But . . . the time has come for freedom rides in Pennsylvania."[5] Unemployed blacks and their sympathizers would no longer sit idly by; the first long, hot summer had begun.

In its first two years in office, the Kennedy administration proved to be more style than substance on civil rights, despite numerous promises made to black Americans during the campaign.[6] Plans for Progress, the administration's signature equal employment opportunity policy, partnered the government with large corporations; however, it was insufficient for the task of integrating the nation's workforce. The violence in Philadelphia helped push the president, in the summer of 1963, to prioritize a civil rights agenda. The African American community and its white liberal sympathizers would no longer be content with the White House's shunting of responsibility for civil rights to the office of the vice president; equal employment opportunity and other civil rights were now truly national issues that required a national solution with direct presidential involvement, as their proponents made clear in a peaceful march on Washington. But just as President Kennedy began to take seriously his responsibilities toward some of the nation's politically and economically weakest citizens—with major legislation and a vigorous campaign to integrate building construction—he was struck down by an assassin's bullet, throwing into question the future of federal involvement in equal employment opportunity.

Chapter 1 shows how a concerted, unified effort by mainstream civil rights organizations and the national leadership of the AFL-CIO forced the federal government to act against contractors with whites-only hiring policies. In essence, that move was from exclusivity to tokenism. But by the early 1960s, as the beginning of an economic downturn made the racial inequalities seem more striking, tokenism was not enough. This chapter shows how local civil rights leaders and the rank and file took their message to the streets, forcing the Kennedy administration to address equal employment opportunity through powerful legislation and aggressive enforcement of executive orders. It begins with an overview of the building construction trades and the role played in the industry by federal contracts.

The Building Construction Trades and Federal Contracts

Industrial construction in the United States during the 1960s involved twenty-one separate specialties, not all of which were needed on each

project. The vast majority of unionized workers at these jobs were organized into local branches (locals) of nineteen international and national
unions. Eighteen of these unions were affiliated with the AFL-CIO and
its Building Construction Trades Department (BCTD). (The nineteenth,
the International Brotherhood of Teamsters, had been expelled from the
AFL-CIO for racketeering in 1957. The teamsters—truck drivers—were
involved in all phases of building construction, delivering and removing
materials as necessary.) Like the parent AFL-CIO, the BCTD had local
councils throughout the country that coordinated the affairs of the building
trades for their cities and regions. Finally, some local unions around the
country remained unaffiliated with any larger organizations.[7]

The eighteen BCTD-affiliated international and national unions represented the asbestos workers, boilermakers, bricklayers and cement masons,
carpenters, electrical workers, elevator constructors, operating engineers,
laborers, ironworkers, lathers, painters, plasterers, plumbers and pipefitters, roofers, sheet metal workers, marble workers, stone cutters, and gran-
ite cutters. Because different locals had affiliated at different times—some
organizing on their own, and others being organized directly by the parent
international or national union—the names of the actual locals varied. For
example, in many localities the laborers' union was called the hod carriers' union. Some cities had separate locals for plumbers and pipefitters. In
Philadelphia, the steamfitters union was a local of the International Boilermakers Union. Another common local union was the tile setters, which
was affiliated with the roofers.[8]

Building construction work generally includes the construction of
an edifice—the beams, walls, and roof of a building—as well as more
detailed interior work such as plumbing, electricity, and painting. Workers
from different crafts often work together in overlapping schedules, with
cement workers, ironworkers, and operating engineers, for instance, doing
their respective jobs on edifice construction of the higher floors, while
plumbers and electricians work on the middle floors and painters and plasterers work on the lower floors.[9]

Because of the outdoor nature of the initial stages of construction
work, construction projects in northern cities do not usually begin during
the winter but often continue into the colder months as the projects move
into the interior phases. As a result, construction employment is cyclical,
with edifice workers finding more employment during the warmer months
and interior workers finding more employment during the fall and winter.
Construction workers either accept temporary unemployment as a regu-

lar, annual condition or find other work during the off-season. Because workers faced unemployment regularly, the unions tended to focus their activities on limiting the number of available workers in their crafts as a means of ensuring as many employment opportunities for their members as possible.[10]

Many construction contractors and subcontractors for government and other industrial projects had exclusive hiring agreements with their local unions, despite the illegality of such practices under the Taft-Hartley Act. These arrangements were often referred to as "hiring hall agreements," and the union workers available for jobs were called "benched workers," suggesting a picture of unemployed construction workers assembled at their union halls, patiently seated on benches, perhaps reading newspapers. The reality was more complicated (and much more reasonable, from the workers' perspective). Hiring halls existed, but they were usually simply the offices of the local unions, where only the business manager and perhaps a clerical staff member or two spent their days. The benched workers would usually wait at home for referrals, visiting the union hall only to conduct membership-related business or to engage in recreational or fellowship activities. Contractors justified these exclusive agreements because of the advantages they offered: the unions guaranteed that their referred workers were adequately and uniformly trained in the particular craft; workers could be obtained through hiring halls quickly and conveniently, often with only a phone call; and the contractors were often former union journeymen themselves, who knew the locals' practices and many of the individual workers.[11]

To limit the pool of available workers, skilled unions kept membership to the minimum necessary to fulfill these exclusive hiring agreements. To accomplish this, they carefully controlled entry to their crafts by granting journeyman status to the fewest applicants possible. A journeyman is a trained, qualified craftsman, certified by the union to be capable of performing the tasks associated with the trade. To attain journeyman status, the prospective union member usually needed to obtain sponsorship by current members of the local (the number varied) and show evidence of training. Such training might have been obtained in the military, at a vocational school, or through the union's own apprenticeship program. Although such programs were technically governed by Joint Apprenticeship Committees composed of both union members and contractors, youths who met the basic aptitude criteria—usually a high school diploma or equivalent and successful completion of written and oral examinations peculiar to the craft—typically were not accepted into an apprenticeship program unless they could demonstrate that they would be admitted to the union as journeymen upon the completion of training. As a result of this rigorous gatekeeping, plumbers, electricians, and sheet metal workers in particular limited their membership to relatives (especially sons) and friends of existing members. And since nearly all the existing members were white, new members were white as well.[12] (Although loosely based on the apprentice-journeyman-master system of the medieval guilds, no "master craftsmen" existed per se; the contractors and foremen filled such roles.)

Federal government and other large industrial construction projects typically began with a bidding process to hire a general contractor. Prospective general contractors—companies with sufficient staff, resources, and experience in the field—would assess the contracting agency's (or industrial firm's) description of the project, usually as defined by an architect (or team of architects); determine the overall cost of the project and their ability to complete it within the given time frame; add a reasonable profit; and submit a detailed bid. Generally speaking, the lowest-bidding contractor capable of completing the project according to the listed terms would receive the contract.[13]

General contractors would supervise some of the construction activities themselves, including bricklaying and carpentry, but usually they hired, often through a similar bidding process, specialty subcontractors to work on individual aspects of the project. For instance, plumbing contractors would be hired as subcontractors to assemble and install the plumbing, and electrical contractors would be hired as subcontractors to install the electrical wiring, lighting, and outlets. Subcontractors were subject to the same provisions found in the general contract, including the nondiscrimination clause in the case of federal contracts, and they generally had hiring agreements with particular local unions in their field and would request a number of journeymen and apprentices for the job.[14] In sum, building construction functioned as an incredibly detailed and complicated operation.

Depending on the number of federal construction projects being completed in any given city, several general contractors might be under the oversight of individual local representatives of federal contracting agencies, such as the GSA or the Department of Defense. Somehow, these contracting officers were expected to ensure that the provisions of the contracts were enforced, including the nondiscrimination clause. As we have seen, enforcement of this clause was often neglected based on an overriding need to finish a project, and the Truman and Eisenhower administrations had established committees (the PCGCC and PCGC, respectively) in an attempt to strengthen enforcement. In 1961 the Kennedy administration would take another look at the problem. The result was the President's Committee on Equal Employment Opportunity.

The President's Committee on Equal Employment Opportunity

In 1961 the nation saw the advent of a new presidential administration, elected on a platform that included a strong commitment to further the cause of civil rights and equal employment opportunity. President-elect John F. Kennedy assured the leaders of the major civil rights organizations that he was opposed to spending federal dollars on anything that promoted discrimination or segregation, and in fact, he felt he should use federal dollars to wipe out discrimination and segregation where they existed. Meanwhile, the nonwhite (primarily African American) unemployment rate was twice that of whites (in some age groups, three times as high), so Vice President–elect Johnson's staff set to work crafting a stronger federal contract compliance regimen. This became a recommendation for a new presidential executive order dealing with equal employment opportunity in federal contracts and ultimately asked Kennedy to strengthen the power and authority of the existing contract compliance committee—the PCGC.[15]

On March 6, 1961, President Kennedy issued Executive Order No. 10925, combining the PCGC and the President's Committee on Government Employment Policy (which handled complaints of discrimination in federal government employment) into a single new committee, the President's Committee on Equal Employment Opportunity (PCEEO), under the leadership of Vice President Johnson. The differences between the PCEEO's contract compliance functions and those of the old PCGC included a "good-faith" clause, which stated that contractors who demonstrated a good-faith attempt to integrate would be deemed to be in compliance. The order specifically mentioned labor unions and authorized the new PCEEO to attempt to "cause any labor union . . . to cooperate with, and to comply in the implementation of, the purposes of this order" and to hold hearings to that effect. It gave the committee investigatory powers of its own, encouraged it to promote equal opportunity programs in apprenticeship and training, and gave it explicit contract revocation and contractor debarment powers. No longer would the committee have to rely on the actions of the contracting agency or the White House to investigate or censure a contractor. Contractors would now be required to submit progress reports and open their books to the committee, but this requirement could be waived if the committee awarded the contractor a "certificate of merit." As with the old PCGC, the vice president would serve as chairman and the secretary of labor as vice chair, and the membership would consist of the heads of the contracting agencies and a number of citizens appointed by the president.[16]

Vice President Johnson moved quickly to ensure that the new committee appeared to outdo the old PCGC without adding significantly to his own workload. Although Johnson wanted to give the impression that he was actively working to further civil rights (and probably—at least to some extent—honestly wanted to alleviate the plight of African Americans), he also maintained a politician's concern with appearance. He wanted to have a vigorous committee that met often, but he didn't want to actually attend all that many meetings. An assistant recommended that the PCEEO establish subcommittees to meet monthly, allowing the full committee to meet only quarterly. The Nixon committee had met monthly, so the subcommittees would be a device whereby Johnson's committee could meet less frequently yet appear to be doing more work.[17]

Scholars have offered a mixed review of Johnson's record on civil rights as vice president. Doris Kearns mentions the PCEEO only briefly in her teleological chapter on Johnson's vice presidency; for her, the vice presidential years were more of an interregnum in Johnson's rise to power, as if he and his staff were waiting for the assassination of President Kennedy. Hugh Davis Graham depicts the vice president as "oddly free of the racial prejudice that was the hallmark of his native region" and genuinely interested in civil rights, but concerned that he had insufficient authority to manage the PCEEO chairmanship. Dennis C. Dickerson, in his biography of NUL executive director Whitney Young, presents Johnson as more interested than Kennedy in civil rights and frustrated that his subordinate status prevented his pursuit of a more active civil rights agenda. Dickerson glosses over the Plans for Progress program (see later), noting that it cemented Young's relationship with the vice president but failing to see it as most at the NUL saw it—as propaganda. Robert Caro's third volume on Johnson does not cover the vice presidential years (presumably, he will do so in the fourth), but it covers in great detail Johnson's indispensable role in passage of the Voting Rights Act of 1957. His take is that

Johnson pushed the act forward to establish his political bona fides for a national candidacy rather than out of any genuine compassion for black people. Robert Dallek points out that putting Johnson in charge of the PCEEO placed the vice president in a difficult position—subject to flak from northern liberals if the committee wasn't aggressive enough and heat from southern conservatives if it was too aggressive. But Dallek believes that Johnson honestly wanted to improve job opportunities for blacks and credits him with an increase in "federal jobs held by Blacks [of] 17 percent in fiscal 1962 and another 22 percent in fiscal 1963." Finally, Randall Woods depicts Johnson as "committed to the goals of the [committee] but hampered by a president and attorney general [Robert Kennedy served as a member of the PCEEO] who sought a situation where Johnson would receive all of the complaints about the government's role in civil rights (or lack thereof), while the president would take all the credit."[18]

Still, formation of the new PCEEO received qualified praise from the mainstream civil rights community. The NAACP called it "a major step forward to end racial discrimination in this country" and stated that LBJ had "an unparalleled opportunity to set a historic pace in this phase of the march toward fair treatment for all Americans." The Washington, D.C., branch of the NUL lauded the executive order and urged the committee to strive for universal merit employment rather than a token black worker or two.[19]

Kennedy had promised a strong, comprehensive legislative program for civil rights during the campaign, but as president, he needed support from the powerful southern Democratic senators to accomplish the other aspects of his agenda. Choosing Lyndon Johnson as his running mate had been one way of ensuring that support. Kennedy worried that he couldn't be too aggressive on civil rights, and for most of his administration he failed to adequately address the issue. Meanwhile, Republicans such as Senator Everett Dirksen stepped in to fill the breach, pressing some of Eisenhower's old civil rights bills and causing liberal northern Democrats to fear losing their congressional seats in 1962 thanks to Kennedy's inactivity. The liberal Democrats in Congress would press ahead with civil rights legislation, with or without administration approval; meanwhile, the president would, like his predecessor, vest his civil rights agenda in his vice president.[20]

Johnson, knowing full well the political ramifications of vigorous activity, led the PCEEO accordingly, in a two-pronged "attack" on discrimination in employment. First, the committee would concern itself with improvements in apprenticeship opportunities (education being an old paternalistic concern of Johnson's, dating back to his days as a teacher of poor Mexican Americans in Cotulla, Texas). He named AFL-CIO president George Meany—now a member of the PCEEO—chairman of the Subcommittee on Skill Improvement, Training, and Apprenticeship. Second, employment discrimination would be addressed generally by voluntary agreements with big federal contractors, called Plans for Progress, starting with the Lockheed-Marietta plant near Atlanta, Georgia. Otherwise, it was business as usual, and most of the PCGC's staff was retained. By the end of October, a PCEEO newsletter reported that the committee had received 443 complaints of discrimination in contract work. Of these, 322 were under investigation, 50 had been withdrawn or dismissed (for either "no cause" or "no jurisdiction"), and 71 had been "adjusted"—successfully conciliated by staff lawyers for the committee.[21] Like the Nixon committee, Johnson's PCEEO took refuge behind big numbers that ultimately represented few jobs.

Over the course of the summer of 1961, yielding to pressure from the PCEEO to comply (at least on paper) with Executive Order No. 10925, several building trades leaders agreed to include nondiscrimination clauses in their apprenticeship guidelines. On August 8, 1961, Meany's subcommittee commended management and labor organizations for implementing equal opportunity provisions in apprenticeship programs. PCEEO press releases noted that the IBEW and the bricklayers' union, along with their parallel contractor associations, "have adopted strong anti-discrimination provisions in their apprenticeship standards."[22]

On October 6, 1961, the PCEEO executive director called Lockheed's implementation of its plan for progress a success and stated that "after 20 years of failure," the government would now be vigorously enforcing equality of opportunity in government contracts. A press release stated, "within the next month several more of the 50 largest defense contractors are expected to sign Plans for Progress."[23]

Johnson put Georgia lawyer and PCEEO member Robert Troutman Jr. in charge of Plans for Progress. On November 1, Troutman recommended that such plans be signed by the nation's 100 largest employers that were not defense contractors. Troutman was proposing an expansion of Plans for Progress beyond the scope of the PCEEO, that is, beyond federal contract employment.[24] The committee would have no method of enforcing these agreements, but as a public relations ploy, they would do just fine.

By the end of 1961, however, the lid was off the teapot, as the normally reserved Urban League criticized the voluntary nature of Plans for Progress. Stating that the agreements basically explained how contractors were already in compliance—and continued to be in compliance—with the executive order, the Washington Urban League pointed out that "it is entirely possible that a contractor may consider that his 'Plan for Progress,' which was executed in the White House, at least by implication, superseded his responsibilities under" Executive Order No. 10925. Indeed, the last section of the order allowed the committee to grant certificates of merit to some contractors, thereby waiving their reporting requirements, and it was this very loophole that Plans for Progress exploited. "None of the 'Plans for Progress,'" the Urban League's statement continued, "contain compliance procedures or any of the even limited safeguards provided by Executive Order 10925 . . . it is going to be very difficult . . . if not impossible to properly investigate complaints against them while they have a plaque on the wall attesting to their enlightenment."[25]

The Kennedy administration had come to the White House full of high hopes and promise, quickly establishing a stronger enforcement mechanism and the promise to do better than Nixon's PCGC. But after its first year in office, strong questions persisted about the commitment of the PCEEO and its chairman to the cause of equal employment opportunity. Triangulating its political potency among civil rights advocates in the North, powerful anti–civil rights forces from the South, and major corporations, the administration sought to give the impression of working toward civil rights, and at first glance, the PCEEO seemed to be doing that work. In reality, the committee was mainly an empty vessel.[26]

On March 30, 1962, the PCEEO submitted its first annual report to the president, which contained the first real set of numbers since the previous October. At least in comparison with the work of the PCGC, those numbers looked good. With regard to contract employment, the committee received 704 complaints during its first year of operation (compared with 1,042 for the entire seven-and-a-half-year existence of the PCGC), with 215 "carried through to completion. Of these, 139 or 65% resulted in corrective action."[27]

Two weeks later, Herbert Hill addressed the committee on behalf of the NAACP. Although he felt that Executive Order No. 10925 was an improvement over the previous policy, "policy is not practice." Hill told the committee there was still not enough evidence to judge the effectiveness of the PCEEO. He called Plans for Progress just another public relations entity, "part of the same sordid pattern," and he called Robert Troutman a tool of southern senators. However, Hill acknowledged, correctly, that the real responsibility lay not with Troutman but with the president, the vice president, and Secretary of Labor Arthur Goldberg. He called the PCEEO Kennedy's only civil rights initiative and pointed out that the president had not even attempted to get it mandated by legislation.[28]

Although it is easy to disparage Plans for Progress as doing little to actually integrate companies, W. Willard Wirtz, who replaced Goldberg as labor secretary in 1962 after the latter was appointed to the Supreme Court, later cited an "attitudinal change during that period which probably had a significant effect" and helped make passage of the Civil Rights Act of 1964 possible. And the program had at least one notable success: Lukens Steel Company of Coatesville, Pennsylvania. Jennifer Delton reports that before joining Plans for Progress, the company had not "made any effort to ensure equal opportunity," but with the signing of its plan, "'advancing equal employment opportunities' became a top goal of the industrial relations department," resulting in a trebling of the number of nonwhite skilled craftsmen and nearly doubling the number of nonwhite managers over the first three years of the plan. But Lukens was not in the initial group of companies to sign a plan for progress; it signed in 1964, when "joining Plans for Progress may have been a way to put their company in compliance with the impending legislation [the Civil Rights Act of 1964]."[29]

Even as Hill was sharing his concerns about the PCEEO, Meany and Johnson began considering the matter of compliance among the unions. Development of what would ultimately be called Union Programs for Fair Practices began in late 1961, when the PCEEO entered into a discussion with members of the AFL-CIO Executive Council on the subject of creating plans for progress for unions. By April 1962 the AFL-CIO Executive Council and the PCEEO had agreed on a draft and had chosen the new title so as not to confuse labor's "programs" with management's "plans."

Meany's membership on the PCEEO blurred the dividing line between organized labor and the federal government, and the initial drafts of the fair practices programs clearly bore his stamp. Like Plans for Progress, the Union Programs for Fair Practices extended voluntary compliance coverage to constituencies that were already partially covered, but the programs also had the potential to serve as union propaganda, relating the signatories' past compliance efforts and their current antidiscrimination regimens. In brief, the programs committed the union signatories to do what their own constitutions already obligated them to do, in addition to actively recruiting nonwhites for apprenticeship and membership and working with employer groups on Joint Apprenticeship Committees to set up equal opportunity machinery in such programs.[30]

Considering that their constitutions already contained nondiscrimination clauses, that most unions were already instituting (or at least appeared to be instituting) minority outreach programs, and that the fair practices programs were likely to be enforced only as strictly as the plans for progress were (which is to say the union leaders perceived them as little more than window dressing for a rather hollow White House civil rights strategy), it should come as no surprise that 120 union leaders signed the agreements on November 15, 1962. What is surprising is that the leaders of two skilled (and highly discriminatory) building trades unions—the IBEW and the sheet metal workers' union—were not among them. Their refusal to sign such innocuous agreements was an indication of their continuing inability (and, in some cases, unwillingness) to enforce their own statutes at the local level. Ultimately, the union nondiscrimination clauses were a top-down imposition from the AFL-CIO Civil Rights Committee rather than a choice of the largely white, highly insular rank-and-file electricians and sheet metal workers themselves. And their leaders feared that even the act of signing the fair practices programs in the company of other union leaders and the vice president of the United States at the White House might lead to antagonism and discord when they inevitably returned to the company of their own members. Leaders of the IBEW in particular felt they had already gone far enough in 1961 by including strong antidiscrimination language in the apprenticeship clauses of their constitution.[31]

In June 1962 the federal government announced that it would be constructing additional buildings in Washington, as well as overhauling Pennsylvania Avenue. In response to the news, Herbert Hill wrote to Vice President Johnson, reminding him of the problems faced by the Nixon committee in integrating IBEW Local #26 and pointing out that the other skilled construction unions in the district were almost as discriminatory. Hill asked that the U.S. Employment Service—rather than the unions—be used to obtain qualified workers for the jobs, warning of the potential for massive protests otherwise. In response, the PCEEO announced in July that it would undertake a major program of compliance reporting by building contractors in the District of Columbia. By November, the committee had developed special compliance reports for the entire construction industry and announced that the new system would go into effect January 1, 1963 (which was, incidentally, the hundredth anniversary of emancipation).[32] But it would not be Hill's advice that ultimately forced a change in the vice president's attitude toward civil rights and reformed the PCEEO; that would come thanks to renewed flak over Plans for Progress, the committee's showpiece program.

Controversy over Plans for Progress and Troutman's leadership came to a head in late June 1962, when a *New York Times* article described a developing rift between the "forced compliance" method of the PCEEO's executive director, on the one hand, and Troutman's "voluntary compliance" method (Plans for Progress), on the other. The article discussed Troutman's connections with southern industry and politicians and suggested that his work for the PCEEO might have some ulterior fiduciary motive. A subsequent editorial favored the enforcement approach, stating that Troutman's voluntary approach had yielded only 2,000 jobs, and at that rate, it would take thousands of years to end discrimination in government contract employment. The editorial, however, did not provide figures on how many jobs had been created by the enforcement approach. In July the annual NAACP convention passed a resolution calling the "voluntary approach [of Plans for Progress] virtually useless." Finally, in early July, former NUL director Lester Granger joined the anti-Troutman chorus, relating how, a year earlier, he had told Troutman that such "reeducation" of business leaders as advocated by Plans for Progress had been tried since 1947, to no avail, and he thought it was a shame that the PCEEO, which had real power, would waste that power getting businessmen to sign statements that they would continue to ignore. An aide admonished Johnson to take Granger seriously, warning that he was an important voice in moderate black America and pointing out that even if Johnson didn't value Granger's opinion, many blacks did.[33]

On August 20, 1962, vice presidential aide Hobart Taylor became executive vice chairman of the PCEEO, responsible for overseeing Plans for Progress, Union Programs for Fair Practices, and all compliance operations; three days later, Troutman submitted his resignation to President Kennedy.[34] The administration had thus removed a white southerner and replaced him with a black lawyer from Detroit. The question remained, however, whether Taylor represented the new face of a public relations entity or a new direction in the committee's operations.

Hobart Taylor Jr. was the son of a prominent black businessman from Houston, Texas. In 1948 his father had been a delegate to the Democratic National Convention—the first black to hold such a position—and he was a close friend of Lyndon Johnson's. The younger Taylor was educated at

Howard University and the University of Michigan Law School and was a clerk for the chief justice of the Supreme Court of the State of Michigan. In 1949 Taylor became an assistant district attorney in Detroit and corporation counsel for Wayne County, Michigan, and in 1958 he was named a partner in a prestigious Detroit law firm. His brief tenure outside public service ended in 1961 when, on the recommendation of his father, Taylor became a vice presidential aide.[35]

The resolution of the Troutman affair and the appointment of Taylor to run the committee's operations gave Johnson the impetus to overhaul the PCEEO's methodology and, for that matter, his own commitment to equal employment opportunity. Until now, the criticisms of Hill and others had been largely correct: aside from an increase in contract discrimination complaints, the committee was largely a public relations venture, like its predecessor. Week after week, month after month, the PCEEO had churned out press releases touting the numbers—so many complaints resolved, so many companies signed up with Plans for Progress. Considering the enhanced powers of the PCEEO over the PCGC—that is, inherent investigatory and debarment authority—the committee really hadn't accomplished all that much. But by the end of 1962, with Taylor in place and with a newfound attitude that contract compliance was paramount, Johnson resolved to use his political muscle to further the cause of equal employment opportunity.[36]

In 1963 the vice president finally went to work. At a January 17 address to a banquet for Plans for Progress signers, the vice president not only reminded the CEOs that their plans did not relieve them of their obligations under Executive Order No. 10925 but also told them that they were expected to go further, actively recruiting nonwhite trainees for future hiring and engaging in activities to help eradicate prejudice throughout society. Six days later he told an assembly of compliance officers of the federal contracting agencies that ensuring compliance with the equal opportunity clause in federal contracts was the core of their mission. And the PCEEO newsletter that month exhibited a stark contrast to earlier iterations: reports of visits and speeches by committee members and staff were shunted to the back, while the front page consisted of a list of actual achievements for the year, including the debarment of one contractor (the first time this action had been taken for violation of a nondiscrimination clause) and a 71 percent action rate in the disposition of contract compliance complaints.[37]

In February and March Johnson tasked Taylor and the committee staff with getting the electricians and sheet metal workers to sign up for Union

Programs for Fair Practices; meanwhile, Taylor continued with the nitty-gritty work of processing complaints. On May 29, 1963, the vice president commended Taylor and the committee's staff for resolving seventy-five contract compliance cases per month, compared with the old PCGC's record of twenty-three.[38] But as Philadelphia erupted into violence over discrimination in construction employment and other northern cities followed suit, it remained an open question whether the changes instituted at the PCEEO by the vice president would be sufficient to make an impact on employment discrimination.

1963: The First Long, Hot Summer

Philadelphia had been the scene of racial violence before 1963. During the Second World War, white bus, train, and trolley drivers and mechanics had struck the city's rapid transit system after a majority of workers voted to be represented by the Transport Workers Union, an affiliate of the CIO that was more sympathetic to the needs of African American workers than the AFL-affiliated Philadelphia Rapid Transit Employees Union. As the first blacks were promoted out of the shops and placed behind the wheels, some 6,000 white employees walked off the job, shutting down Philadelphia's mass transit system for six days in 1944. According to one report:

> Ugly rumors began to flood the city; hotheads and hoodlums began breaking windows of white shop owners and attacking automobilists in Negro neighborhoods; looting followed. It became unsafe for Negroes to travel in certain areas of the city, and a number of colored travelers were attacked by whites. Three white motorists drove through a Negro neighborhood and without warning or stopping, shot a 13 year old Negro lad—all of the ingredients of a first-class race riot were boiling and brewing in the cauldron of a city of 2,000,000 persons, three hundred thousand of whom were colored, smarting under the insults being heaped upon them by bigoted [Philadelphia Transit Company] strikers and sympathizers.[39]

Thanks to sympathetic media, local and federal government officials, the army, and "the Philadelphia police, which all reports credit for keeping order, rather than creating disorder," tensions were relaxed in Philadelphia. Secretary of War Henry Stimson ordered the arrest of several striking workers and threatened to revoke the draft deferments of the rest, and the strike ended. Philadelphia workers were able to commute to the factories where they continued to participate in America's war effort, and the black drivers remained on the job. Local needs had pressed the federal government into a response. But the sympathy of government and the media rested squarely on wartime production needs. It remained to be seen, as black migrants continued to enter the city in increasing numbers during the 1940s and 1950s, whether Philadelphia could avert worse bloodshed during peacetime.[40]

During the 1950s Philadelphia's growing black community faced a host of challenges. Between 1940 and 1960 Philadelphia's black population more than doubled, from 250,000 to 529,000 (typical of the trend during the Second Great Migration). Many of the new arrivals settled in North Philadelphia, then a middle-class white neighborhood. But as the black population grew, whites fled to the suburbs of Bucks and Montgomery counties or across the Delaware River into New Jersey. As other neighborhoods were "defended" by their white residents—through restrictive title covenants or even violence—North Philadelphia rapidly became the City of Brotherly Love's Harlem.[41]

As the whites left, so too did government and financial interest, and the neighborhood declined. Sewers deteriorated, and garbage trucks skipped over entire blocks. Crime increased, and the white police force began to behave like internal colonialists—keeping at bay a downtrodden culture alien to their own interests and experiences. Residential buildings fell into disrepair. Mostly employed as unskilled workers, domestics, and the like, black workers turned over much of their small incomes to white landlords. Retail businesses, largely owned and operated by whites, took the rest of the money out of the neighborhood.[42]

In February 1963 an article in *Greater Philadelphia Magazine* detailed the problems faced by African American skilled workers in Philadelphia, mostly in the building trades. Unions worked in tandem with the local school board to run their apprenticeship programs. The local office of the Bureau of Apprenticeship and Training, husbanding federal funds, allowed the schools to admit only youngsters who were likely to be employed. Thus the union sponsorship practices, whereby only whites were admitted to membership, served to exclude blacks from federally funded and city-funded apprenticeship programs. Those few blacks who did manage to complete training outside of the formal apprenticeship programs would not be sponsored for journeyman membership in the unions. The article concluded by pointing out that although no Philadelphia locals actually had discriminatory clauses in their constitutions or bylaws, only a few had statutes *against* racism, and even fewer actually had black members.[43]

Working to force the city of Philadelphia to live up to its responsibilities to its black citizens was Cecil B. Moore, president of the NAACP's Philadelphia branch. A native of West Virginia, Moore had served in the U.S. Marine Corps during World War II and attended Temple University Law School in Philadelphia, working as a whiskey salesman to pay his way. During the 1950s Moore joined the Citizens' Committee against Juvenile Delinquency as head of its Law Enforcement Committee, and he later served as that organization's president. In 1959 Moore gained a militant reputation when he organized an electoral challenge to the staid leadership of the NAACP's Philadelphia branch that resulted in the retirement of its president. The subsequent election went against Moore's slate, but his reputation as a troublemaker for the old guard was cemented when he filed a divisive (if ultimately fruitless) appeal of the results with the association's national office. By 1963 Moore's brand of charismatic leadership and militant protest was gaining in popularity. He was elected branch president and immediately declared his intention to move Philadelphia's black community to protest: "I will expect my people to stand up and be counted . . . or have their names listed as an enemy of democracy." With the city's allocation of $31 million for the construction of schools in its black neighborhoods, Moore resolved that the time was right to take action against the discriminatory construction unions.[44]

School construction was not the only area where the city of Philadelphia was paying work crews supplied by all-white unions. Across the street from city hall, the city was constructing the Reyburn Administration Building, and on March 31 the local branch of CORE gave Mayor James Tate a week to take action against racially discriminatory hiring policies at the site, threatening sit-ins and picketing. The city took no action against the contractors or the unions, so on April 14 CORE members picketed the mayor's house. Tate told them, "I've done everything I can" and advised them to "go picket the labor unions, not me." But after three days of watching the picketers outside his family home, Tate—part of a postwar Democratic clique with a moderate outlook on civil rights—made an about-face and "ordered the City Board of Labor Standards to 'face up to the issue.'" The picketing ended, but CORE promised more nonviolent direct action unless Tate took further steps against employment discrimination.[45]

CORE had been founded in 1942 by students at the University of Chicago and James L. Farmer Jr., a Methodist minister who would lead the organization, with interruptions, until 1965. The organization's founding principle was the militant nonviolence pioneered by Mohandas K. Gandhi against British colonial rule in India and later associated most closely with Martin Luther King Jr. Militance was a very different method of pursuing civil rights compared with those employed by the NAACP and NUL, older organizations that preferred negotiation, arbitration, legislation, and moral suasion. Although CORE had participated in organizing the Montgomery bus boycott in 1955, by the time of the Philadelphia picketing, the organization's biggest claim to fame was the Freedom Rides of May 1961. Black and white protesters, carefully selected by CORE organizers, rode Greyhound buses from Washington, D.C., into the Deep South. Blacks rode in the front and whites in the back, and sometimes they sat together— all a direct affront to the segregationist conventions governing bus travel (but perfectly legal under federal interstate transportation laws, thanks to a 1960 Supreme Court decision). The attacks the Freedom Riders suffered at the hands of white mobs in Anniston and Birmingham, Alabama, and their jailing in Jackson, Mississippi, demonstrated the depth of white antipathy to civil rights, as well as the indecisiveness of the Kennedy administration when it came to enforcing federal law to protect some of the nation's most vulnerable citizens.[46]

In 1963 the CORE branch in Philadelphia consisted of seasoned civil rights veterans. Two weeks after the picketing of his home, Mayor Tate was still paying only lip service to the notion that the city should not fund discrimination in employment, so an interracial group of CORE members staged a two-day sit-in at the mayor's city hall office. In response, Tate directed the city's Commission on Human Relations (CHR) to call hearings on discrimination in the building trades. The commission published a notice asking for witnesses to testify if they had been excluded from city-financed construction work, and inviting local civil rights leaders to testify as well.[47] CORE appeared to have won a significant victory.

During the first two weeks of May 1963 the Philadelphia CHR held hearings on discrimination in the building trades. Representatives of the local Urban League testified that Plumbers Local #690, IBEW Local #98, Steamfitters Local #420, and Roofers Locals #30 and #113 practiced discrimination in apprenticeship and journeyman membership and did not refer black workers to job sites through their hiring halls. The Urban League recommended the formation of a joint labor–civil rights–government committee to integrate the unions and suggested that city contracts be pulled from contractors that hired members of unions that did not comply. On May 6 CORE went a step further, recommending that the city take over the hiring process for city-funded construction jobs.[48]

Union officials, for the most part, appeared only after they were served with subpoenas, and most testified that their organizations did not discriminate. An IBEW leader protested that his union was nondiscriminatory, and the head of the steamfitters' local claimed that any shortage of black members was due to the fact that blacks simply didn't apply. But the less disingenuous leader of Roofers Local #113 testified that one-third of his union consisted of blacks classified as unskilled "helpers," and the union had banned the upgrading of such helpers to the next level—"mechanics"— which brought a $2 an hour pay raise. The other roofers' local, #30, had no apprenticeship program at all. A bricklayers' union official "angrily [denied] charges that his local was guilty of discriminatory policies," stating, "out of 1,200 members of the Local about 100 were Negroes, some of whom were stewards." Indeed, the bricklayers' union was more integrated than the others, but it is likely that its statistics included an auxiliary black local or a classification system similar to that of the roofers.[49]

Frustrated with the seeming inactivity of the commission and the ongoing work of all-white skilled crews at the Reyburn building site, the interracial CORE protesters staged another sit-in at Tate's city hall office on May 12, this time demanding that the mayor stop work at the site until the skilled workforce was integrated. Two days later, Tate shut down construction of the municipal building, pending a report from the CHR hearings, citing the possibility that contractors were not fulfilling the equal employment clause of their contracts.[50]

Most construction workers were immediately sent home from the Reyburn site, but Tate's order did not apply to one particular contractor, whose workers remained on the job until the end of the day. At this point the NAACP's Moore entered the fray, telling the press that although he approved of the mayor's decision, the Philadelphia branch of the NAACP would not allow *any* workers to continue work at the site. "If this project isn't shut down by noon tomorrow [May 15] we will throw a picket line around it and we will shut it down."[51]

Moore's threat was not idle. Until recently, scholarship on the civil rights movement (and popular documentaries such as *Eyes on the Prize*) have privileged the activities of CORE during the Freedom Rides, the Southern Christian Leadership Conference in the Montgomery bus boycott, and the lunch-counter sit-ins of the Student Nonviolent Coordinating Committee—not to mention the brutal beatings of black students at

Little Rock High School in 1957 and movement leader John Lewis on the Edmund Pettus Bridge in 1965. This has cemented in the American mind the image of nonviolent black protesters remaining calm in the face of white brutality. But blacks in the North—perhaps because of the greater freedoms and rights they enjoyed—were far less inclined to calmly accept the insults and violence of their oppressors. Whereas participants in King's march from Selma to Montgomery, Alabama, in 1965 sang "We shall overcome," blacks in Philadelphia in 1963 chanted "We! Shall! Over! Come!" Northern civil rights militancy was not necessarily nonviolent, and Moore's fiery rhetoric was the epitome of such militancy. His threat resulted in negotiations, and on May 17 the mayor gave in, and all construction work ceased at the Reyburn site.[52]

White construction workers and contractors did not take the city's action lying down. Angry at being laid off, a group of construction workers marched on city hall, where they encountered Moore and engaged in an angry shouting match. (Some workers claimed they had been out of work for six months prior to getting jobs at the Reyburn site, and they were likely telling the truth. However, they failed to mention the seasonal nature of construction work. Presumably, these workers had a good chance of finding other work now that it was mid-May.) Three subcontractors threatened to sue the city for stopping the work, and the affected unions requested that the city pay their workers while construction was suspended (the request was denied). The unions claimed that they weren't racist, that blacks either didn't apply for union membership and employment or weren't qualified, and that their hiring and membership procedures were fair. One union spokesman called the laid-off workers "innocent victims."[53]

Yet the CHR remained hopeful that its hearings and the Reyburn site shutdown would result in the end of racial segregation in the building trades in Philadelphia. The commission's chairman thought black youths might be encouraged to train immediately to fill the newly available jobs. The Philadelphia NAACP and other local organizations began to actively recruit black men to apply for membership in the skilled building trades.[54]

Following his success at shutting down the Reyburn construction site, Moore resolved that the NAACP would take the lead in fighting racial discrimination in city construction projects. The Philadelphia Board of Education was about to set aside $31 million for schools in black neighborhoods—a positive thing for black education—but the construction would involve skilled union labor, which remained segregated. On May 20 Moore demanded that Mayor Tate either force the unions to end discrimination or shut down the remaining city construction sites. If the terms were not met by May 24, the NAACP would organize picketing at the sites, beginning with the school construction project at Thirty-first Street and Susquehanna Avenue.[55]

Moore's position got a boost on May 22, 1963, when the CHR released its report, which recommended that "City contractors be required to hire a 'reasonable number' of Negroes," who, it said, "have been excluded from employment as plumbers, steamfitters, sheet metalworkers, and roofers." CORE turned the report into concrete demands, asking the city to hire and apprentice enough skilled blacks so that they accounted for 15 percent of all workers on city building sites immediately and 60 percent of all building trades apprentices over the following two years.[56]

In an attempt to avoid picketing at the school construction site, Mayor Tate announced on May 23 that the city, the unions, and a contractors' association had come to an agreement and that work would resume soon at the Reyburn site. But official attempts to mediate with Moore failed, and on the morning of May 24, three days of picketing began at Thirty-first and Susquehanna. As we have seen, the picketing and ensuing violence ended with the hiring of four skilled black construction workers at the school site and an agreement among the NAACP, the Building Construction Trades Council, and the city that more would be hired at other school construction sites around the city by June 12. None of the unions went on strike, although the steamfitters temporarily withdrew from the Building Construction Trades Council in protest.[57]

Moore's success at Thirty-first and Susquehanna was due in no small part to the unmitigated support he received from the national NAACP office. Whereas Roy Wilkins often tried to hold back charismatic leaders in his own city, Moore's fiery rhetoric posed no threat to Wilkins's brand of leadership at the national level. If anything, Moore (like Hill) allowed Wilkins to play the moderate on the national stage when dealing with government officials such as Kennedy and Johnson or organized labor officials such as Meany. For his part, Hill at the NAACP's national office in New York was thrilled by the success of Moore's pickets. In a statement to the *New York Times,* Hill encouraged blacks around the country to follow Philadelphia's lead and picket discriminatory construction sites.[58]

Hill's encouragement didn't take long to bear fruit. During the first week of June, black and white members of several civil rights groups picketed the site of the new Harlem Hospital in New York City to protest local skilled building trades' refusal to admit blacks to membership. After two days, during which the number of pickets and represented groups grew exponentially, the city's acting mayor closed the site and appointed a committee to negotiate a compromise. Shortly thereafter, in Newark, New Jersey, a civil rights organization "presented an ultimatum to Mayor Hugh J. Addonizio saying that it would picket building sites in the city where alleged anti-Negro discrimination existed in the hiring of construction workers. It set a deadline of July 10 for the mayor to set up a Fair Employment Practices Committee." Newark, which had "the largest proportional Negro population of any major population center north of the Mason-Dixon line," was undergoing a massive federally funded urban renewal program that employed scores of white construction workers. Finally, the author of a *New York Times Magazine* piece called the future "bleak" and linked such demonstrations to the increasing jobless rate, which affected nearly three times as many blacks as whites.[59]

The racial unrest in the North took place in the context of major unrest in the South, especially in Birmingham, Alabama, where blacks were protesting their continued exclusion from voter rolls and mistreatment by authorities. Birmingham's police chief T. Eugene "Bull" Connor authorized his officers to use attack dogs and water cannons to quell the protests of schoolchildren.[60] The nation's downtrodden were rising up, and the violence with which white authorities responded—in Birmingham as in Philadelphia—was being televised nightly to a national audience. The cries for equal opportunity could be ignored no longer, and the federal government would have to respond—and fast.

The Federal Response

In May 1963, as Philadelphia's civil rights community erupted against discriminatory construction unions, Vice President Johnson spoke at Gettysburg in anticipation of the centennial of the battle that had turned the tide of the Civil War. Stating that African Americans must no longer be asked for patience, but for perseverance, Johnson said, "The Negro says 'Now.' Others say 'Never.' The voice of responsible Americans—the voice of those who died here and the great man who spoke here—their voices say 'Together.' There is no other way."[61]

Johnson had succeeded in reforming the PCEEO, but as the violence in Philadelphia and other cities demonstrated, the committee's reforms had not yet made much difference at the local level. Its policies had not made much difference in the way workers were hired. A determined federal response to the cries for civil rights throughout the nation would require the leadership of the president.

On June 4 President Kennedy announced that he would amend Executive Order No. 10925, which had established the PCEEO, to specifically include construction contracts, and he ordered Secretary Wirtz to investigate practices in the construction industry as a whole. But this amendment was to be merely a stopgap measure until Congress could pass what the administration called "the Civil Rights Act of 1963." As the president said on June 11, 1963, in a televised address to the nation:

> We preach freedom around the world, and we mean it. And we cherish our freedom here at home. But are we to say . . . that this is the land of the free—except for the Negroes; that we have no second-class citizens—except Negroes; that we have no class or caste system, no ghettoes, no master race—except with respect to Negroes?
>
> The events in Birmingham and elsewhere have so increased the cries for equality that no city or State or legislative body can prudently choose to ignore them. . . .
>
> We face, therefore, a moral crisis as a country and a people. It cannot be met by repressive police action. It cannot be left to increased demonstrations in the streets. It cannot be quieted by token moves or talk. . . .
>
> Next week I shall ask the Congress of the United States to act, to make a commitment it has not fully made in this century to the proposition that race has no place in American life or law.[62]

The president's proposed civil rights legislation addressed federal expenditures in its Title VI and private-sector employment in its Title VII. Title VII's proposed Equal Employment Opportunity Commission (EEOC) would have a stronger mandate than the previous "president's committees" and would be able to act with a confidence unknown to the PCEEO; the White House felt the latter had acted hesitantly out of a fear of reprisals from southern senators (such as funding cuts, which had affected Roosevelt's FEPC).[63] Here at last, more than halfway into his term, was the legislation promised by Kennedy during the 1960 campaign.

For the first time, Labor Secretary Wirtz implemented pre-bid equal employment qualifications. Rather than attempting to police contractors when construction was imminent or after a project was already under way, bidders would be evaluated for their fitness to comply with the equal opportunity clause *before* the contract was signed. "We are saying to the contractors and the unions . . . that these are the standards and if they are your standards you have the bid and, if they are not, we are not going to do business with you." This represented a sea change in the way the federal government conducted business, in that the lowest bidder could now be denied a contract for its perceived inability or unwillingness to employ nonwhites on an equal basis and engage in affirmative programs to help them compete equally. Although Wirtz did not specify what would constitute compliance in terms of minority employment, he expected it to be "more than a token."[64]

Ultimately, however, and contrary to the statements of union leaders like Meany, the major hurdle to equal employment opportunity in construction was union control over hiring, not employer recalcitrance. The Philadelphia demonstrations had ostensibly been to protest contractors' policies, but in the end, compromise had been reached only through union concessions. So the PCEEO was faced with the same question that had earlier plagued the PCGC: were unions that acted as hiring agents de facto subcontractors, or were they third parties?

Unlike the old PCGC, however, the PCEEO had a specific mandate pertaining to unions. Executive Order No. 10925 stated that "the Committee shall . . . cause any labor union . . . to comply with, and to comply in the implementation of, the purposes of this order . . . and . . . may . . . recommend remedial action if, in its judgment, such action is necessary or appropriate." Secretary Wirtz's interpretation of this clause was that the PCEEO had the authority to regulate unions' referral practices with regard to federal construction contracts, with implementation effected through the general contractor's liability for the behavior of subcontractors. That is, Wirtz saw the unions as subcontractors and recommended that the committee threaten to debar any contractor for its unions' noncompliance with the equal opportunity clause.[65]

Armed with the amended executive order and Wirtz's recommendations, the PCEEO's contract compliance regime swung into action. By the end of June more than 400 equal opportunity reports had been collected by the committee out of a total of 1,400 federal construction contracts, with more reports coming in every day.[66]

Field officers for contracting agencies remained on high alert throughout the summer, taking preventive steps to avoid protests by civil rights organizations as well as "payback" strikes by union locals, and reporting to the PCEEO as well as their own agencies. A typical case involved a black Chicago sheet metal worker who quit his nonunion job to take a better-paying job on a union project at a federal contract site. However, the new employer informed the worker that because he was not a member of the union, he would be expected to start at a much lower pay rate and as an apprentice, despite several years of prior experience. The GSA officer supervising the project brought in a PCEEO representative to consult. They met with the employer and representatives of the sheet metal workers' local, and the black worker was restored to his promised rate of pay and granted journeyman status, averting protest demonstrations and possible violence.[67]

By the end of the summer, Wirtz had drafted a comprehensive procedure for implementing the executive orders in apprenticeship programs, the "gatekeepers" of membership in the building trades unions. Ruling out quotas, his procedure asked regional directors to "use all means" to ensure that apprenticeship programs were in compliance and that applicants were recruited and selected based on merit alone. Wirtz devised procedures for pulling federal registration from apprenticeship programs for noncompliance (federal registration allowed students in an apprenticeship program to be employed on federal contracts), as well as the appeals process for such cases. The procedure also defined "merit employment," including the statement that "in some cases what seems to be a fair standard can be discriminatory if it is not essential and serve[s] to eliminate all minority members. . . . For example, the test standards may be set beyond job requirements, and the requirement of relevant work experience, while objective, can reinforce previous discriminatory practices that prevented obtaining this desirable but not essential experience."[68] In short, the "best man for the job" is not necessarily the man with the most credentials. If a high school diploma was not an essential requirement of the job, being a high school graduate would not confer any advantage to an applicant.

The late spring constituted the Kennedy administration's proving ground in the field of civil rights. The previous winter, Johnson had finally found his calling as head of the PCEEO; with the resignation of Troutman, the hiring of Taylor, and the ascension of the dynamic Wirtz, the committee was in a strong position to respond to the crises in Philadelphia and other cities. Now Kennedy himself, who had long shown more style than substance, had finally come out strongly for equal employment opportunity, strengthening his previous executive order and proposing the most comprehensive civil rights law since Reconstruction.

But by midsummer, debate on the president's "Civil Rights Act of 1963" had been postponed by the Senate, and mainstream civil rights leaders were becoming increasingly concerned about the possibility of more violence. To commemorate the centennial of emancipation, A. Philip Randolph resurrected his plan for a "March on Washington for Jobs and Freedom." To channel the energies of the unemployed, frustrated, and angry, the leaders seized on the march as an opportunity to bring together tens of thousands of Americans in a peaceful protest aimed at passage of the civil rights bill.[69]

The August 28, 1963, March on Washington, attended by at least 200,000 people, is probably best remembered for Martin Luther King's now famous "I have a dream" speech, which today serves as an enduring epitaph for the slain leader. But other speakers, most of them lacking King's impressive oratorical skills, decisively made the case for passage of the civil rights bill. Said Roy Wilkins of the NAACP: "We want employment, and the pride and responsibility and self-respect that goes with equal access to jobs. We want a fair employment practices bill as part of the legislative package." Walter Reuther, head of the UAW and a member of the AFL-CIO Executive Council, spoke for organized labor, alluding to the difficulties faced by liberal union leaders in trying to force integration on the rank and file: "It is long past the time for the Congress of the United States to act affirmatively and adequately to secure, guarantee, and make effective the constitutional liberties of every American without regard to race, creed, or color." But the most stirring rhetoric came from the NUL's Whitney Young: "The hour is late. The gap is widening. The rumble of the drums of discontent, resounding throughout this land, are heard in all parts of the world. The missions which we send there, to 'keep the world safe for democracy,' are shallow symbols unless with them goes the living testament that this country practices at home the doctrine which it seeks to promote abroad."[70]

Kentucky-born Whitney M. Young Jr. was already a college graduate with training in electrical engineering from the Massachusetts Institute of Technology when he entered the U.S. Army as a private in a road construction crew during World War II. He was quickly promoted to sergeant as he successfully navigated the resentments of the other men in his all-black regiment and the racial prejudice of the southern white officers assigned to supervise them. After the war Young earned a master's degree in social work at the University of Minnesota and worked at the St. Paul branch of the NUL while he attended school; after graduation in 1947 he was promoted to a leadership position there. As branch president of the Omaha Urban League in 1950, Young became friendly with the national organization's executive director, Lester Granger. For most of the 1950s Young served as dean of social work at Atlanta University, and in 1961 he succeeded Granger as head of the NUL. Young took the organization in a more militant direction in order to keep up with the changing tenor of the civil rights movement, advocating peaceful demonstrations in addition to the organization's traditional backroom negotiations.[71]

Shortly after the march, Young laid out his ideas for equal employment opportunity. "The scales of equal opportunity are now heavily weighted against the Negro and cannot be corrected in today's technological society simply by applying equal weights." To remedy this disparity, he proposed a "Domestic Marshall Plan" aimed at pulling the black community up to the level of the white community by means of federally funded education, employment, housing, and health and welfare initiatives. Young reminded the nation that the black community "is in revolt today, not to change the fabric of our society or to seek a special place in it, but to enter into partnership in that society," because the black man "has given his blood, sweat, and tears to the building of our country; yet, where the labor and initiative of other minority groups have been rewarded by assimilation within the society, the black American has been isolated and rejected."[72]

Had the fate of the civil rights bill been decided by the marchers on the Washington Mall, it surely would have passed by a veto-proof margin. As it was, the weeks of delay in the Senate turned into months as the bill languished in committees in both houses. And looming over the entire proceeding was the threat of a southern filibuster.

On Labor Day, President Kennedy again addressed the nation on the subject of equal employment opportunity:

This year, I believe, will go down as one of the turning points in the history of American labor. Foremost among the rights of labor is the right to equality of opportunity; and these recent months . . . have seen the decisive recognition by the major part of our society that all our citizens are entitled to full membership in the national community. The gains of 1963 will never be reversed. They lay a solid foundation for the progress we must continue to make in the months and years to come. We can take satisfaction that 1963 marks a long step forward toward assuring for all Americans the opportunities for life, liberty, and the pursuit of happiness pledged by our forefathers in the Declaration of Independence.[73]

As seen by his televised speech in early June and his Labor Day address in early September, the president had finally found the political will to defend the rights of the politically weakest Americans.

Unfortunately for the young president, his vision of 1963 as a turning point would indeed prove true, but not in the way he imagined. On Friday, November 22, 1963, an assassin's bullet ended his life as the presidential motorcade drove through Dallas, Texas. The assassination linked Kennedy with Maxwell Stanford and Stanley Daniels—the two young men assaulted by the police in Philadelphia—in a continuum of violence surrounding the civil rights movement that year. The violence was clearly worst in the South, with the brutal murder of Mississippi NAACP leader Medgar Evers and the bombing of the Sixteenth Street Baptist Church in Birmingham, Alabama, which resulted in the deaths of four young girls. But the protests in Philadelphia seemed to be the harbinger of things to come.

When Lyndon Baines Johnson ascended to the White House, he became the first southern president since Reconstruction, and the prospects for passage of the civil rights bill seemed bleak. Despite his activity on the PCEEO and his work as a senator on the Voting Rights Act of 1957, Johnson's maiden speech as a senator had been an earnest defense of segregation, and he enjoyed the respect and friendship of some of the most unreconstructed southerners in Congress. The president, however, acted swiftly to dispel any notion that he was unwilling to further the cause for which his predecessor had fought. Proving that his "conversion" of the previous year had been in earnest, Johnson built on his accomplishments as vice president and gave Secretary Wirtz and Hobart Taylor of the PCEEO the full support of the White House, and he called on Congress to pass the civil rights bill as a memorial to the slain President Kennedy.[74]

Johnson quickly earned the tentative support of Whitney Young, who said that a reconstructed southerner as president might be more effective than a northern liberal in furthering the cause of civil rights. Young went so far as to predict that the assassination would ultimately be helpful to the civil rights bill, in that it made many in the nation wary of the right wing. (Despite the fact that the accused gunman was likely left wing, the 1963 violence against blacks was clearly right wing.) But Young warned that if the civil rights bill wasn't passed soon, the responsible civil rights leaders would lose ground to those he called the "irresponsible leadership"—people who advocated rioting and other forms of violent protest.[75]

In the event, both occurred. In the early summer of 1964, more than a year after the violence in Philadelphia and Birmingham, Congress passed Kennedy's Civil Rights Act. The new law's strongest provisions were Title VI, which established that no federal dollars could be spent on projects that involved racial discrimination, and Title VII, which made discrimination in private employment for reason of "race, color, religion, sex, or national origin" illegal and established the EEOC to enforce the provision.[76]

But as the summer of 1964 wore on, race riots on a scale unseen since World War II broke out in seven American cities. On the night of Friday, August 28, Philadelphia police were in the process of arresting a woman when youths attacked the officers, and the riot spread like a wildfire. Cecil Moore and other community leaders did their best to stop the violence, but the riot wasn't brought under control until the next evening, when Mayor Tate ordered all off-duty police officers into action. Just as the reinvigorated PCEEO, a televised presidential address on civil rights, and a strengthened executive order had been insufficient to prevent violence in the summer of 1963, strong civil rights legislation failed to prevent urban rioting in the summer of 1964. And with the national unemployment rate among black youths still nearly twice that of whites, passage of the landmark Civil Rights Act was not enough, by itself, to prevent another long, hot summer.[77]

Chapter 3

Grasping at Solutions, 1964–1967

It is no mere coincidence to say that there are fewer than 300 licensed [black] journeyman electricians in the entire country.
—Otis E. Finley, NUL associate director, November 4, 1961

In 1962 James Ballard, a "twenty-two-year-old Negro Air Force veteran," applied for an apprenticeship at the office of Sheet Metal Workers Local #28 in New York City. He was dutifully asked to complete an apprenticeship application form. Then he was shown a stack of papers and told "he would just have to wait his turn." This was irregular; the sheet metal workers had never followed a first-come, first-served policy but typically ranked applicants based on less objective criteria. Ballard was also advised that in order to qualify, he would have to pass a "General Aptitude Test Battery conducted by the New York State Department of Labor." Such tests had rarely been used before; clearly Ballard was being put through a more rigorous application regimen than usual to discourage him from entering the program. Even though Ballard passed the test with flying colors (and received the highest recommendation possible from the Labor Department for "jobs in sheet metal at the trainee or apprentice level"), Local #28 did not allow him to enter the next apprenticeship class, and the Joint Apprenticeship Committee concurred. Who was admitted? Only white youths, of whom "more than 90 per cent . . . were sons or nephews of members of Local 28." Ballard faced the same injustice experienced by Thomas Bailey (see chapter 1) and countless other African Americans who had attempted to break the racial glass ceiling separating the better-paying skilled construction trades from the less-skilled trowel trades.[1]

In his congressional testimony advocating fair employment practices legislation, NUL associate director Otis Finley listed the employment problems faced by blacks and pointed in particular to the discriminatory practices of the building trades unions. "One has only to observe the virtual absence of skilled Negro workers on building projects in every major city," he noted, "to realize that some forces are operative to prevent their employment in the building and construction trades." Finley went on to say that "there are fewer than 300 licensed [black] journeyman electricians [and] fewer than 300 licensed [black] journeyman plumbers in the entire country. . . . Since apprentices often are brothers, sons, and relatives of union members, this places further limitations upon Negroes because of the few represented in some unions. Such discrimination," Finley said, constitutes "a serious threat to our free society."[2]

Discrimination in apprenticeships in the building trades was one of the most visible ways blacks continued to be excluded from the benefits of a booming economy during the 1960s. Apprenticeships in the skilled building trades were especially prized, as they often produced future foremen, contractors, and union leaders. And as the federal government increased domestic spending on urban renewal, model cities, and the rest of President Johnson's numerous antipoverty programs, the lack of skilled blacks working at construction sites in the nation's cities represented an affront to all the James Ballards—to every young black man who had been turned away from a job because of the color of his skin or, just as insidiously, because of the dearth of quality educational opportunities available in the inner city. As long, hot summer followed long, hot summer, the young black unemployed collectively constituted a tinderbox that exploded with worsening violence. Besieged on the "Negro problem" from both sides of the political spectrum, the Johnson administration looked to the PCEEO and the Department of Labor (DOL) for solutions. What they developed was a local-based approach that would differ from city to city and succeed or fail based on local conditions and the relative skills and talents of the federal officers—midlevel bureaucrats—in charge of implementing each program. These federal officials were motivated by a belief in the inherent importance of racial equality, the ethos known as Great Society liberalism. But the failure to conciliate—to push the unions and contractors to change on their own—would lead to more dramatic actions.

Chapter 1 shows how mainstream civil rights organizations and labor leaders forced the federal government to push its contractors from racial exclusivity to tokenism. Chapter 2 shows how local civil rights leaders and rank-and-file supporters took to the streets to demand change, forcing the Kennedy administration to demand equal employment legislation.

This chapter shows how the federal officials tasked with implementing the new legislation, operating in a climate where riot followed riot, developed a series of programs tailored to individual cities. The result was use of the manning table—long a staple of contractor bid paperwork—to demonstrate compliance. Although the manning table quickly led to accusations of quota enforcement—arguably illegal under the Civil Rights Act of 1964—it also led to the watershed moment in the origin of affirmative action: the Philadelphia Plan. The chapter begins with an overview of the apprenticeship process in the building construction trades.

Apprenticeship in the Building Trades

Although apprenticeship was not the only method of learning a skilled trade, it was the single most popular way for a young man to attain journeyman membership in the unions. It was also the best way for the unions to limit the number of skilled craftsmen and thus maintain their high wages and avoid the levels of unemployment many old-timers remembered from the Great Depression.[3]

Most skilled apprenticeship programs in the building trades were administered by a Joint Apprentice Committee (JAC), which consisted of union members and contractors. Apprenticeships could last anywhere from one to four years, but they tended to average about three years; apprentices attended evening classes for one or two years—usually conducted by the JAC at a local public school—and each apprentice worked in the craft alongside six to ten journeymen. Apprenticeship programs certified by the DOL's Bureau of Apprenticeship and Training (BAT) were eligible for federal funds, the use of public facilities for classes, and paid on-the-job training on federally funded construction contracts. Contractors paid the wages of apprentices, which started at around half the journeyman scale and increased each year to nearly full scale.[4]

Prospective apprentices came from one of several backgrounds. The most common route was through nepotism for the lucky sons and nephews of skilled construction workers. Once a youth turned seventeen or eighteen, his father or uncle would suggest apprenticeship when the union was accepting applications. The older relative would sometimes take the youth down to the union hall for the first time and introduce him around, virtually ensuring that as long as he had basic mechanical aptitude, an apprenticeship slot would be his. Unions tended to justify their use of nepotism by claiming that youngsters raised by (or near) men already engaged in these often dangerous trades were already steeped in the tradition of job safety, part of what Thomas Sugrue calls "a masculine identity reinforced by close relationships with fellow workers both in and outside the workplace." And according to New York City building trades leader Peter Brennan (who later served as secretary of labor), "when we got a man that came out of a family where he was trained by his father, and his grandfather, we were sure that we were getting a good mechanic."[5]

The second most common way for youths to find out about apprenticeships was in school or through a community organization. Unions or employer organizations would send representatives to "career day" at the junior high schools and high schools, drumming up interest in the craft among the children and forging relationships with guidance counselors and other school administrators so that when the union was accepting applications for apprenticeships, the counselors could be called on to refer a few prospects. Religious, fraternal, and community organizations, such as the Roman Catholic Church, the Benevolent and Protective Order of Elks, and the Urban League, also ran vocational or other youth programs that had links with unions and employer organizations and would refer youths for apprenticeships. Prospective apprentices with school and community referrals had the advantage of being from a "known source" to the union, such as a guidance counselor or trusted local priest, but they usually lacked the advantage of having a relative already involved in the trade.[6]

Finally, some young men found out about apprenticeship openings through advertisements in local newspapers. Youths who applied based on such advertisements were comparatively the least advantaged, ultimately being strangers to the union members. The BAT required that JACs post such advertisements as a prerequisite for certification, but a JAC could try to limit and prescreen the youths who found out about apprenticeships by carefully selecting the publications in which to advertise.[7]

Prospective building trades apprentices had to submit applications and then take a written examination administered by the JAC; those who passed were eligible for an oral interview with a member of the JAC. Each prospective apprentice was then assigned a score, relative to the other applicants, based on the written exam, the oral interview, and other criteria such as educational, military, or criminal background and prior work in construction or some other trade. Different JACs and different trades assigned different weights to each of the selection criteria, ultimately offering apprenticeships to the top scorers.[8] For these lucky few, apprenticeship meant eventual entry into a lucrative trade, membership in a powerful union, and steady—if seasonal—work. But in the short term it usually meant immediate employment at apprentice wages, which, even at half-scale, constituted a fine living for a working-class eighteen-year-old.

There were three primary methods whereby blacks were excluded from apprenticeships. First, the JAC could fail to advertise the upcoming apprenticeship class in black communities, placing the recruiting advertisement in newspapers that black youths were unlikely to read (such as trade publications) or forgoing such advertisements altogether and relying on word of mouth to recruit sufficient white applicants, while risking BAT decertification.[9]

Second, the committee could set admission standards unreasonably high, adding qualifications that were irrelevant to the job. For instance, if a number of white applicants held high school diplomas while most or all of the black applicants did not, the JAC could change the weighting of admission criteria so that having a high school diploma scored a significant number of additional points, even if it was immaterial to an applicant's fitness for apprenticeship in the particular craft. In fact, most skilled trades required a high school diploma, but that requirement was regularly waived for white applicants. Applicants with arrest records could be disqualified, even if they had never been convicted of any crime—a step that would tend to disqualify more black applicants than white owing to discriminatory policing in the inner cities.[10]

Third, the JAC could place undue weight on the oral interview, which tended to be subjective (and thereby promoted the inclinations of the interviewer—racist, nepotistic, or otherwise), and less weight on the more objective written examination. Even some otherwise liberal interviewers might favor white applicants, feeling obligated to ensure that any black applicant who passed was subjected to a more rigorous vetting process—following the dictum that "the first black has to be the best black."[11]

When all else failed, the JAC or union could simply cancel the apprenticeship class (or never accept applications in the first place). This posed the danger that retirees would not be promptly replaced on the "bench," but this situation could be offset, at least for current union members in the short term, by higher wages or fewer seasonal layoffs. If a union required new members but was unwilling to hold an apprenticeship class out of fear of integration, it could always admit whites—with or without military or vocational school experience—directly to journeyman status and provide the necessary training and supervision on the job. Such tactics could not be maintained over the long term, but they were used as a stopgap measure in the hope that outside pressure to integrate would eventually abate.[12]

On June 5, 1963, Secretary of Labor W. Willard Wirtz proposed a plan "to assure that significant opportunities are provided to qualified minority group applicants . . . [and that] such opportunities are provided . . . by taking whatever steps are necessary . . . to offset the effect of previous practices [of] discriminatory patterns of employment." The DOL proposed to analyze union-provided lists of candidates for BAT-registered apprenticeship programs, and where it found a disparity between opportunities for blacks and whites, it would order the union to admit more black applicants to the program under the threat of deregistration. The proposal immediately garnered furious opposition from contractors and union leaders, and the final regulation—issued on December 18—scrapped DOL analysis of the lists and replaced it with a single standard: programs in which the numbers of black apprentices did not roughly correspond to the local black population would have to demonstrate that their selection system was fair and objective. One local got the message and implemented a comprehensive equal opportunity plan for apprenticeships. New York City's IBEW Local #3, under the leadership of Harry Van Arsdale Jr. and in conjunction with willing contractors, took in a record 1,020 new apprentices in 1963, including 300 nonwhites. The result? By 1966 nonwhites constituted 15 percent of the local's apprentice rolls. The New York sheet metal workers, in contrast, engaged in an all-out struggle against integration, fighting Wirtz's order (unsuccessfully) in court for years.[13]

Like American involvement in the war in Vietnam, integrating the building trades—through apprenticeship opportunities or otherwise—was going to be a long, hard slog that constantly threatened to descend into quagmire. And the government official directly responsible for implementing the provisions of the president's executive order and Wirtz's regulation—the General Westmoreland of the battle to integrate the building trades, one might call him—was Vincent Macaluso.

Implementing the Executive Order: The Area Coordinator Program

In June 1963 President Kennedy responded to the outbreak of racial violence in Birmingham and elsewhere by proposing comprehensive civil rights legislation—what would become the Civil Rights Act of 1964—as well as by amending Executive Order No. 10925. Congress spent a year hemming and hawing over the proposed legislation, with southern senators threatening a filibuster. Meanwhile, the PCEEO spent the same year developing new compliance machinery for the construction industry. After Kennedy's death, President Johnson recommitted the White House to passing the legislation, and Secretary Wirtz took over as de facto PCEEO chairman in the absence of a sitting vice president. On June 8, 1964, a cloture motion—to overcome a southern filibuster—was filed in the Senate to consider what would shortly become known as the Civil Rights Act of 1964. That same day, the *New York Times* published an article about PCEEO's creation of a task force to study problems of equality in employment in the construction industry. After a year, concrete action had finally been taken on both fronts.[14]

The PCEEO divided its new construction industry task force into teams of three to four people each and sent them to cities representing ten regions around the country. The *New York Times* reported that "with major emphasis on New York, Chicago, Cleveland, Philadelphia, and San Francisco, the teams will visit contractors' associations, building trades unions and major individual contractors . . . they will check construction sites and where it is evident that discrimination is occurring, will seek to have it corrected." Although the legislation—which would end discrimination in all employment, not just federal contracts—had yet to be signed, these PCEEO teams would also be investigating the nongovernment work of federal contractors. A federal contract could be revoked (and a contractor debarred from future contracts) if the contractor was using unfair hiring practices on private job sites, even if the contractor's federal work was technically in compliance.[15]

Vincent Macaluso, who had recently been appointed special assistant to Hobart Taylor, the PCEEO's executive vice chairman, was named to coordinate the project. The following week, Macaluso's teams fanned out across the nation. The NUL indicated that it was "impressed" with the plan and recommended several black construction contractors around the country for Macaluso to include in his investigation.[16]

Vincent G. Macaluso was born in 1922. His father was a civil engineer, so Vincent grew up wherever his father could find work building tunnels, including Waterville, Canada; Antwerp, Belgium; and Tuxedo, New York, where he learned to ski. During World War II Macaluso interrupted his studies at Yale University to serve with the U.S. Army's Tenth Mountain Division—the skiing soldiers—and he saw action in northern Italy during the winter of 1944–1945. After the war he completed college, attended law school, married, and in 1951 took his first civilian job with the federal government—as a staff lawyer with the National Labor Relations Board (NLRB). He served at the NLRB through 1954, at which point he entered the private sector as a labor lawyer. At the start of the Kennedy administration, Macaluso was working as a staff lawyer for ARMA Corporation, a defense contractor, and when that company joined Plans for Progress in 1962, it was Macaluso who drafted the firm's plan.[17]

In September 1963, through a family connection, Macaluso was hired by the White House to serve as executive secretary of the President's Committee on Labor-Management Relations, where he became acquainted with Taylor and Wirtz. Two months later, Taylor recruited Macaluso to work as a staff lawyer for the PCEEO. Macaluso spent the winter and early spring of 1964 investigating discrimination at a defense plant in Huntsville, Alabama, and in June he was put in charge of the PCEEO's new construction industry task force.[18]

The task force teams spent the summer and fall of 1964 assessing compliance conditions in their assigned cities and meeting with union representatives, contractor associations, individual contractors, local officers of contracting agencies, and civil rights groups. In December Macaluso reported to Taylor on the teams' findings. Although conditions varied in individual cities, the report stated that opportunities for nonwhites were generally poor, mainly owing to the use of union hiring halls and the racist attitudes of local union business agents. This was the case despite the apparent willingness of many contractors to hire without discrimination and get the "best man for the job."[19]

Meanwhile, the DOL continued to implement its plan for equal opportunity in apprenticeship programs. Secretary Wirtz issued new guidelines that became effective May 1, 1964. BAT-certified apprenticeship programs would be required to exercise equal opportunity in the selection of apprentices. In addition, the BAT began placing apprentices with contractors independently of the JACs, and on July 6 the DOL announced the graduation of three black construction apprentices in Washington—an architectural draftsman and two carpenters—who were promptly awarded "certificates of journeyman status" by the BAT. (These men were not, however, accepted into union membership at that time.)[20]

The DOL's work in ensuring equal opportunity in apprenticeship programs became more important as rioting broke out in several cities, transforming the season of the 1964 Civil Rights Act into the long, hot summer of 1964. By the end of August, seven northern cities had seen outbreaks of violence. Professionals at the BAT and elsewhere in the DOL linked the black unemployment rate—and the idleness and poverty it indicated—with the propensity to violence in the inner city. Black unemployment was still double that of whites, and it was increasing among working-age teenagers faster than among their elders. The DOL's work now took on special urgency. To inform nonwhite youths about available opportunities, the BAT opened apprenticeship information centers in Washington, Boston, Chicago, Cincinnati, Detroit, Newark, Baltimore, and Cleveland, resulting in apprenticeship placements with four skilled building trades: the plumbers, steamfitters, electricians, and carpenters.[21]

In the fall of 1964 the DOL partnered with the NUL to establish several on-the-job training programs aimed at inner-city youth, again bypassing the JACs. The NUL submitted a proposal, and Wirtz agreed that the league's local branches would administer the programs under contract with the DOL. The NUL moved quickly to establish on-the-job training programs in four cities, including Cleveland, where "350 long-term unemployed workers would have the opportunity to learn a skill." (The others were Evansville, Indiana; Pittsburgh, Pennsylvania; and Harlem in New York City.) Finally, using funds procured under the Economic Opportunity Act, the DOL set up the Neighborhood Youth Corps program to pay "modest wages for part-time jobs" to help alleviate the continuing problem of unemployment among inner-city youth.[22]

In tandem with the efforts of the DOL and NUL, the PCEEO established a locally based program in contract construction known as the area coordinator program. During the spring of 1965, the committee appointed twenty area coordinators in selected cities to work, under Macaluso's direction, with unions, contractors, and local representatives of federal contracting agencies to implement the provisions of the equal employment clause in contracts as well as those contained in Title VII of the 1964 Civil Rights Act. As Taylor put it:

> The coordinators will be responsible . . . for making sure that all federal agencies act as one in regard to equal employment opportunity . . . each coordinator will conduct discussions and negotiations with contractors, subcontractors, apprenticeship committees, unions, building trades councils, builders' associations, community groups and other interested parties to assure that equal employment opportunity is provided in all employment practices and policies and all relevant training and apprenticeship programs.

> The coordinator also will . . . encourage private organizations,
> unions, schools and other sources to identify minority personnel
> who are qualified and seek apprentice or journeyman positions.[23]

For the most part, these area coordinators were already federal employees who were familiar with their assigned locales and with jobs related to construction. The area coordinator for St. Louis, for instance, Woody Zenfell, was the Interior Department's on-site engineer for construction of the Gateway Memorial Arch. Although most of the area coordinators were white, which gave them something in common with union leaders, Charles Doneghy in Cleveland was black, which purportedly gave him common ground with black community organizers. Most of the financing for the program—meaning the salaries of the area coordinators themselves—would be supplied "by the agencies involved in the largest dollar volume of construction" in the area.[24]

On April 21, 1965, Macaluso sent his first memo to the area coordinators, setting out guidelines for their work. He would expect weekly reports detailing their activities, including the names of people at meetings they attended, the significance of each reported event, appraisals of each contractor's compliance situation, and projected activities for the following two weeks. He asked that they maintain up-to-date lists of union apprenticeship rolls, hold "kick-off meetings" with pertinent members of their communities, and submit recommendations for how the area coordinator program should function in the future.[25]

Never before had a federal agency engaged in such a hands-on, detail-oriented program to ensure compliance with the nondiscrimination clause in federal contracts. The PCEEO was clearly taking construction industry compliance seriously. But unlike the higher-profile Plans for Progress, the area coordinator program would hold no fancy dinners or signing ceremonies at the White House, and it received little press attention. This was not a public relations ploy to make it appear that the administration cared about civil rights; here, at last, was real evidence that the Johnson administration was serious about living up to its own rhetoric on equal employment opportunity and enforcing the applicable law.

Taking a Stand: Lyndon B. Johnson and Civil Rights

The president had already set a high bar with his own rhetoric. In the wake of police violence against civil rights demonstrators in Selma, Alabama,

Johnson addressed Congress on March 15, 1965, pushing for new voting rights legislation and using the language of the movement to do so:

> What happened in Selma is part of a far larger movement which reaches into every section and state of America. It is the effort of American Negroes to secure for themselves the full blessing of American life.
>
> Their cause must be our cause too. It is not just Negroes, but it is all of us, who must overcome the crippling legacy of bigotry and injustice.
>
> *And we shall overcome.*[26]

For the president of the United States to recite such a phrase was similar in impact to Abraham Lincoln's meeting with Sojourner Truth and Frederick Douglass in the White House. Whitney Young immediately commended Johnson for what the NUL leader called the "most powerful statement ever made by a President of the United States."[27]

Johnson had traveled a long road to that congressional address. For much of his vice presidency, the PCEEO had received little more attention from his office than its predecessor committee had received from Nixon. Johnson had organized photo opportunities for showpiece programs such as Plans for Progress and Union Programs for Fair Practices, which basically confirmed promises already made by companies and unions not to discriminate. But during his final year as vice president, he had hired Taylor to run the PCEEO and had begun to take his responsibilities toward black citizens seriously. And in his first year as president, largely in response to the March on Washington, Young's call for a "Domestic Marshall Plan," and Martin Luther King's call for a "G.I. Bill for Negroes," Johnson had defined civil rights—especially in employment—as one of the most important policy areas of his administration.[28]

The Civil Rights Act of 1964—passed mainly through Johnson's legerdemain and clout with his former colleagues in the Senate—devoted nearly half its text to "Title VII—Equal Employment Opportunity." That title rendered illegal any act of discrimination in employment or union membership on the basis of "race, color, religion, sex, or national origin." As we have seen, however, passage of the act failed to prevent the large-scale rioting seen that summer, although it did harden the support of the mainstream civil rights leaders for the president's reelection campaign. Roy Wilkins, Martin Luther King Jr., Whitney Young, and A. Philip Randolph issued a manifesto on July 29 (James Farmer of CORE and John Lewis of the Student Nonviolent Coordinating Committee agreed in principle but did not sign) decrying the riots and declaring a moratorium on marches and protests until after the election.[29] With the support of civil rights leaders and most of the nation, Johnson handily won the election. Now he could take concrete steps to enforce his civil rights vision and live up to his own rhetoric.

Early in 1965 Johnson moved to overhaul the government's civil rights and equal employment machinery and give it his own presidential stamp. Two major factors influenced his thinking. One was the new vice president, Hubert H. Humphrey, who as a senator had played a leading role in passage of the Civil Rights Act of 1964. He expected to play a leading role in civil rights in his new position as well, just as Johnson had before the Kennedy assassination. The other factor was the new legislation itself. Title VII of the Civil Rights Act of 1964 went into effect on July 2, 1965.

President Kennedy's vision of equal employment opportunity lived on in the PCEEO, which oversaw semi-independent programs such as Plans for Progress and Union Programs for Fair Practices and handled complaints of discrimination in federal government and federal contract employment, and in the new Equal Employment Opportunity Commission (EEOC), which would receive and conciliate complaints of employment discrimination in the private sector, which was now illegal under Title VII (the EEOC had no enforcement power of its own and would have to coordinate with the Department of Justice to bring suits against violators). In short, the PCEEO was now responsible for enforcing Title VI, while the EEOC focused on and enforced—in coordination with the Justice Department—Title VII. In addition, there was the Civil Rights Commission (formed to enforce the Voting Rights Act of 1957) and the contract compliance and equal opportunity offices of the other federal agencies.[30]

On assuming the vice presidency, Humphrey sought to impose his own vision on this federal civil rights machinery. The several agencies, committees, and commissions now constituted an increasingly large arm of the government, and Humphrey believed it would operate best with unified oversight through his own coordination. To that end, he proposed forming a new body, the President's Council on Equal Opportunity (PCEO), which he would chair. To avoid adding substantively to the growing civil rights bureaucracy, the PCEO would have minimal staff and would not actually perform any functions except oversight of other agencies. Busy pushing his new voting rights legislation and a comprehensive domestic agenda—

not to mention fighting the escalating war in Vietnam—Johnson acqui-
esced to the wishes of his new vice president and created, by executive
order, the PCEO as the supreme oversight body on civil rights.[31]

On June 4, 1965, in a commencement address at Howard University,
the president defined affirmative action as the key to equal opportunity:

> You do not take a person who, for years, has been hobbled by
> chains and liberate him, bring him up to the starting line of a race
> and then say "You are free to compete with all the others," and
> still justly believe that you have been completely fair.
>
> Thus it is not enough just to open the gates of opportunity. All
> of our citizens must have the ability to walk through those gates.
>
> This is the next and more profound stage of the battle for civil
> rights. We seek not just freedom but opportunity—not just legal
> equality but human ability—not just equality as a right and a the-
> ory, but equality as a fact and as a result. . . .
>
> To this end equal opportunity is essential, but not enough.
> Men and women of all races are born with the same range of abili-
> ties. But ability is not just the product of birth. Ability is stretched
> or stunted by the family you live with, and the neighborhood you
> live in, by the school you go to and the poverty or the richness of
> your surroundings. It is the product of a hundred unseen forces
> playing upon the infant, the child, and the man.[32]

The president announced that the following year he would host a White
House conference titled "To Fulfill These Rights"—consciously recalling
President Truman's 1947 conference "To Secure These Rights"—at which
public policy and civil rights professionals would discuss possible solutions to the nation's continuing racial inequality.

Five days after the president's commencement speech at Howard, an
NUL press release stated that tensions in the nation's cities were cooler
overall than during the previous summer. The report warned, however,
that if tokenism continued, especially in the building trades, riots might
erupt again.[33]

Then came Watts.

On August 11, 1965, fierce rioting broke out on the streets of the Watts
section of Los Angeles, California. When two white police officers questioned black Marquette Frye on suspicion of drunk driving, Mrs. Frye
came out to scold her twenty-one-year-old son. A crowd appeared, and

one of the officers became involved in a "scuffle" with some of the people on the street. The officers called for assistance, and the scene erupted into a full-fledged melee. The neighborhood quieted the following day as local ministers and gang leaders attempted to negotiate with the chief of police, hoping that a street fair might channel the energies of the neighborhood's young, unemployed blacks into more peaceful pursuits. But a permit for the fair was not granted, and on the evening of August 12, policemen—and any other whites who ventured into the neighborhood—were attacked with clubs, bats, and Molotov cocktails. Over the next six nights, businesses were looted, and attacks against members of the police force continued. Not until August 19 was the police chief able to declare the situation under control.[34]

In the aftermath of the Watts riot, police chiefs around the country considered plans to quell future disturbances, and conservative commentators excoriated the president for not sending in the National Guard at the first sign of violence. But in the opinion of some black leaders, including A. Philip Randolph, jobs were the antidote to further incidents, and it was their advice the president took. Johnson understood that he could not prevent riots in the immediate future any more than he could push back the tide of nearby Chesapeake Bay, but he thought that the energetic application of sound and just public policies could lessen the likelihood of violence in the long run.[35]

This feeling was soon borne out by the conclusions of a California commission, which blamed the Watts riot on the lack of jobs and proper education in the inner city. The commission's report stated that tokenism would not solve a problem faced by 350,000 unemployed African Americans. The solution lay in the systematic, long-term education and training of all Americans on an equal basis.[36]

As a first step, the president moved to reconsolidate the civil rights machinery of the federal government. Although ostensibly requested by Humphrey, the resultant changes in fact reflected Johnson's wishes rather than those of his vice presidential "civil rights czar." Executive Order No. 11246, issued September 24, 1965, abolished Humphrey's PCEO as well as the older PCEEO. Plans for Progress and Union Programs for Fair Practices, already semi-independent entities run largely by their corporate and union signers, were moved to the DOL. Because the new EEOC could only conciliate complaints under Title VII and had no real power, whereas the PCEEO could revoke contracts and debar contractors, contract compliance—including Macaluso's area coordinator program—was moved to the DOL as well. There, these programs would continue to enjoy executive powers in the new Office of Federal Contract Compliance (OFCC) under the leadership of Edward C. Sylvester.[37]

Since the EEOC had no enforcement authority—lacking the power to issue cease-and-desist orders or even bring lawsuits as an independent agency—the most promising area of Johnson's civil rights agenda remained federal contract compliance, which was now covered by actual legislation—Title VI—in addition to the successive executive orders. Within the OFCC, the billions of dollars spent annually on federal construction and the rampant discrimination practiced by the building trades in their apprenticeship programs gave Macaluso's area coordinators program the real ability to make a difference. If the Johnson administration could integrate one of the most visible areas of employment discrimination, perhaps future rioting could be averted. But, like turning back the Chesapeake tides, integrating skilled building construction would be no easy task.

Area Coordinators in Action: Three Cities

In 1989 Hugh Davis Graham linked the development of the Philadelphia Plan with three earlier, similar plans: the St. Louis Plan, the San Francisco Plan, and the Cleveland Plan. He described the development of these plans as an "experimental process of trial and error" leading inexorably to the Philadelphia Plan. This formulation has been echoed by scholars ever since.[38] In fact, the development of these plans was much more complicated, and hardly linear. But the Philadelphia Plan was developed with these earlier experiences in mind, and it is for that reason that we now turn to the experiences of the OFCC area coordinators in St. Louis, Cleveland, and San Francisco.

With the establishment of the OFCC within the DOL in October 1965 and the dissolution of the PCEEO, Vincent Macaluso's construction area coordinators program was transferred from the oversight of White House aide Hobart Taylor to that of OFCC director Edward C. Sylvester. Macaluso's new boss, like his old one, was from Detroit. But unlike Taylor, Sylvester was a native of that city and had attended Wayne State University, where he studied engineering. During World War II Sylvester attained the rank of first lieutenant, serving in the Pacific theater as well as Europe. For most of the 1950s he worked as a civil and structural engineer in Detroit, and by 1958 Sylvester was president of a timber company in Liberia. He returned to the United States in 1960 to join the national staff of Democratic presidential candidate Stuart Symington and ultimately went to work for the Kennedy administration in 1962, serving in Wirtz's DOL as deputy administrator at the Bureau of International Labor Affairs. As a young black administrator, he impressed the secretary, and when Johnson issued Executive Order No. 11246, Wirtz tapped Sylvester to head the new OFCC.[39]

With forty-one employees and a $700,000 annual budget, Sylvester's OFCC was but a small cog in a great machine, but it was a critical cog, in that it bore responsibility for ensuring compliance with the nondiscrimination clause in contracts totaling approximately $35 billion. The area coordinator program dovetailed nicely with the overall methodology of the OFCC, which differed greatly from that of the EEOC. The EEOC, a quasi-independent body whose members served at the pleasure of the president, received major press coverage, handled complaints by individuals and groups, and focused on patterns of discrimination—which it then forwarded to the Department of Justice for litigation. The OFCC, in contrast, was a bureaucratic agency in a large federal department; it received little press but was proactive: instead of acting on complaints, the OFCC initiated programs to seek out and eliminate discrimination in government contracts. And whereas the EEOC, created by statute for private-sector complaints under Title VII, had only the rather blunt weapon of conciliation at its disposal, the OFCC, created by executive order under Title VI, had the president's imprimatur for an arsenal that included the power to revoke contracts, withhold funds, and debar contractors from bidding on contracts in the future. At the old PCEEO, Macaluso had been Taylor's "special assistant." Now at the OFCC, Macaluso's position was assistant director for construction.[40]

With threatened protests at job sites in Cleveland (a new state office building with no skilled black construction workers) and San Francisco (a new transit system hiring white union members from out of town rather than skilled local blacks) and boycotts by white unions in St. Louis over the hiring of nonunion black construction workers to build the visitors' center for the Memorial Arch, Sylvester moved quickly to develop what he called the "1966 Federal Contract Construction Program." Based on Macaluso's reports on the activities and experiences of the area coordinators, and in consultation with the heads of contracting agencies engaged in construction, Sylvester's 1966 program consisted mainly of the requirement that all contractors submit "written Affirmative Action Programs" to the contracting agencies and the OFCC. These affirmative action programs might contain a variety of options, but Sylvester's program strongly suggested that they include minority outreach for apprenticeship opportunities (which could involve establishing relationships with high school guidance counselors in black and Hispanic communities or funding programs to send speakers to junior high school classes to interest students in construction), the hiring of a specific number of black apprentices (and the maximum possible number of apprentices overall, to make room for them), a vigorous recruitment search for black journeymen both inside and outside the unions, the establishment of centralized hiring procedures and a pledge that such procedures would be based on the principle of nondiscrimination, the training of foremen in nondiscriminatory practices, and the promise to enforce the same program among subcontractors.[41]

Although the construction area coordinator program involved fifteen coordinators assigned to twenty-two cities, the experiences of three area coordinators in particular most influenced Sylvester's thinking in the development and evolution of the 1966 program.[42] These were Woodrow W. Zenfell, area coordinator for Kansas City and St. Louis, Missouri; Charles Doneghy, area coordinator for Cleveland and Columbus, Ohio; and Robert Magnusson, area coordinator for San Francisco, California. Their accumulated experience helped Macaluso and Sylvester understand how best to approach the thorny problem of integrating the unions and the job sites.

St. Louis: Woody Zenfell

In 1960 World War II veteran and Vicksburg, Mississippi, native Woodrow W. Zenfell was working as an engineer on the Blue Ridge Parkway in Tennessee. An employee of the National Park Service, he was asked to become the chief structural engineer for the Gateway National Expansion Memorial, known colloquially as the St. Louis Arch. Zenfell immediately relocated to St. Louis, where he served "as liaison between the builders and the National Park Service" and found himself "in the thick of just about every decision made." During his five years working on the arch, Zenfell acquired a wealth of local experience and technical knowledge and was even exposed to the issue of equal employment opportunity when two black men scaled the arch to protest the lack of minorities employed in its construction. Woody talked the men down, reportedly using his "Southern charm and a soft, Mississippi drawl." Clearly, he was the right man for the job of OFCC area coordinator for construction, and his appointment went into effect on April 30, 1965.[43]

Zenfell had his work cut out for him. In 1965 St. Louis had "173 federally-involved construction projects ($50,000 or more) having a total valuation of $500,000,000." None of the skilled trades had a single black youth enrolled as an apprentice, and four of the skilled trade unions—the pipefitters, plumbers, electrical workers, and ironworkers—had no black journeymen either. Zenfell spent the summer and much of the fall of 1965 trying in vain to get the ironworkers to lower their apprenticeship standards, which he felt were too high.[44]

Certainly the most visible of the federal construction projects in St. Louis was the one at which Zenfell had recently been employed. Intended as a grand entranceway to the American West, the arch had been completed earlier in the year, as had the edifice of the visitors' center. In the fall of 1965 the general contractor opened the bidding process for a plumbing subcontractor to work on the visitors' center interior. Granting a subcontract proved difficult, however, as several plumbing companies withdrew their bids when they became aware that the OFCC would be scrutinizing the project for compliance. The contractors had exclusive hiring hall contracts with the local plumbers' union, which required that only union plumbers be employed on any given project. The plumbers' union had no black members and not a single black apprentice out of a class of 100 youths. In neighboring East St. Louis, the plumbers' apprenticeship program was so discriminatory that the BAT decertified the program. Zenfell engaged in meetings with interested parties, and the award ultimately went to Elijah Smith Plumbing, a black-owned business from East St. Louis. The owner was active in the local NAACP and a member of the St. Louis Commission on Human Relations. He employed plumbers from an integrated (but mostly black) plumbers' union affiliated not with the AFL-CIO but with the Congress of Independent Unions (CIU), a local umbrella organization.[45]

The decision to award the plumbing subcontract to Smith was greeted with disdain by the St. Louis Area Building Trades Council of the AFL-CIO, which unanimously voted on December 27, 1965, to walk off all construction jobs related to the arch as long as non–AFL-CIO plumbers were employed by Smith on the project. The walkout, which occurred on January 7, 1966, effectively shut down the project, for there were no electricians to string temporary lights so the CIU-affiliated plumbers could work.[46]

With a black subcontractor and black plumbers, for once the threat of contract revocation—the OFCC's most important weapon—was contraindicated. Sylvester would need to try a different tactic. He asked his men on the ground, including Macaluso and Zenfell, to prepare all their documentation involving the situation with the plumbing subcontract. This paperwork was then turned over to U.S. Attorney General Nicholas Katzenbach, with the request that he file the first "pattern or practice" lawsuit under Title VII of the 1964 Civil Rights Act. At the same time, the case was submitted to the NLRB for investigation of the walkout as an illegal "secondary boycott." In 1949, at the urging of the NLRB, the U.S. Supreme Court had declared it illegal under the Taft-Hartley Labor Relations Act of 1947 for one union to strike an employer simply because another union was doing so. In essence, the OFCC was asking the NLRB to determine whether the AFL-CIO electricians' walkout in protest of the employment of the CIU plumbers (or, put more succinctly, the nonemployment of AFL-CIO plumbers) constituted an illegal "sympathy strike."[47]

The OFCC team had chosen its soldiers carefully. Katzenbach was no stranger to the cause of civil rights: as assistant attorney general under Robert Kennedy, he had been the federal officer at the famous "schoolhouse door" showdown with Alabama governor George Wallace over integration of the state university. And Macaluso knew how to pull the levers at the NLRB, having worked there as a staff lawyer. The Justice Department and the NLRB pursued the matter in a combined case in St. Louis federal district court, where on February 8, 1966, the judge found that the walkout by the Building Trades Council constituted an illegal secondary boycott and issued a temporary injunction, ordering the electricians back to work on the visitors' center.[48]

The fallout from the district court decision in St. Louis was quick and positive. Unable to strike against nonunion contractors, and fearing the loss of their lucrative hiring contracts, the St. Louis building trades unions embarked on a campaign to integrate their membership and apprenticeship rolls. IBEW Local #1 signed a working agreement with a local black electrical contractor, officially making his projects "union" projects and opening the door for his mostly black employees to apply for and obtain journeyman membership in the union. Said the contractor, "I guess the Arch fight is bringing about a change all around." By early March 1966, Zenfell was pushing the sheet metal workers to decrease their journeyman-to-apprentice ratio, thereby paving the way for a large apprenticeship class; by the end of the month, he had succeeded in getting the St.

Louis lathers to admit the first two black apprentices in the union's history. But the group that took the matter most seriously was the previously all-white pipefitters' union, which created a six-month "crash" program that allowed ten skilled black pipefitters to go straight to journeyman membership in the union.[49] The "lily-white" St. Louis building trades, threatened by Zenfell's activities, had thrown down the gauntlet. The OFCC had taken it up and—aided by a sympathetic court decision—won a decisive victory.

Cleveland: Charles Doneghy

In April 1966 the U.S. Civil Rights Commission (CRC) held hearings in Cleveland on the state of civil rights in the city and its environs. The CRC had been established by the Voting Rights Act of 1957 mainly to investigate disenfranchisement in the South, but in 1964 President Johnson delegated the commission to investigate and report on all civil rights issues by holding public hearings in cities throughout the nation.[50]

If the EEOC had little power, the CRC had even less. The OFCC could revoke contracts and debar contractors, and the EEOC could conciliate with offenders and recommend cases for prosecution by the attorney general, but the CRC could only hold hearings and write reports. The public announcement of the Cleveland hearings stated that they would be "part of an in-depth study of civil rights problems in areas of education, employment, housing, health and welfare, and police-community relations."[51]

Because Cleveland had seen protests at construction sites in 1963, the CRC devoted one full day of the weeklong hearings to discrimination in the building trades. One witness, a black plumbing contractor, "had tried from 1933 to 1963 before he got any of his Negro workers into Local 55 of the Plumbers Union," according to a newspaper account. After three decades, he had succeeded in obtaining union membership for only two of his black employees, who together constituted more than half the black union plumbers—there being only three in all of Cleveland.[52]

A staff researcher for the commission testified that only 2.4 percent of whites in the building trades were unemployed, whereas the figure for blacks was 8.9 percent, almost four times as high. He went on to say that five skilled construction unions in Cleveland—the IBEW, the sheet metal workers, the ironworkers, the plumbers, and the pipefitters—had a total of 7,786 journeyman members, of whom only 53 were black, and only 8 of those were currently employed in the building trades. Thus, employed blacks constituted slightly more than one-tenth of 1 percent of the membership of these unions. These same unions also had a total of 367 apprentices, of whom only 1 was black. Of the five trades singled out at the CRC hearings, only the IBEW lacked an apprenticeship class.[53]

In the face of such overwhelming evidence of discrimination, construction area coordinator Charles Doneghy resolved to integrate one of the most discriminatory trades in the city: the electrical workers. He targeted the biggest government contractors first, with the intention of pushing the union to admit blacks afterward. One such contractor was Lake Erie Electric, which held a contract with the National Aeronautics and Space Administration (NASA) for a seven-month, $78,000 project. The company had an exclusive hiring agreement with IBEW Local #38, which had no black members. Threatening debarment, Doneghy pressed Lake Erie to sign a pre-award affirmative action agreement that contained the following four provisions:

☐ Contractor understands that "affirmative action" under the EEO [equal employment opportunity] clause in his contract in this situation means that his firm will actively recruit minority group employees for work in the trades where they are not now independently represented.

☐ Contractor understands that mere reliance upon union referral does not satisfy the EEO clause in his contract.

☐ Contractor understands that his "affirmative action" under the EEO clause in his contract requires that he actively seek minority group candidates for apprenticeship classes through local public school administrators and teachers and local civic and church leaders, and through newspaper advertisements and all other media which effectively reach the minority groups.

☐ Contractor understands that the EEO clause in his contract means that he will instruct his subcontractors to take the same kind of "affirmative action" that he is taking, where it is appropriate, and that the compliance of the subcontractors is his continuing responsibility.

Lake Erie checked each of the four boxes, indicating acceptance of all the provisions. According to what Doneghy told Macaluso, the contractor's attitude was, "if it were necessary to integrate his work force" to avoid contract cancellation, "that is what he would have to do."[54] Then Doneghy began working with the company to devise the details of an affirmative action plan that would comply with the provisions of the pre-award agreement.

With the pre-award agreement in place, Doneghy turned his attention to IBEW Local #38, so that Lake Erie and other electrical contractors could draw from qualified black electrical workers to meet their affirmative action obligations. Local #38 had no black members and did not even have an apprenticeship class. Threatening BAT decertification of its JAC and the possibility that jobs would dry up without federal dollars, Doneghy was able to convince the union to call a new apprenticeship class and even announce publicly that it was seeking black applicants. The Cleveland Urban League immediately referred thirty-one graduates of its Manpower Advancement Program (MAP), a local pre-apprenticeship training program.[55]

Then came Hough, the worst riot in Cleveland's history. On July 18, 1966, after a white bartender refused to serve a glass of water to a black patron, the Hough neighborhood erupted into violence. For seven days the area between Superior and Euclid avenues, stretching west for one and a half miles from Rockefeller Park, was akin to a war zone. The governor deployed the Ohio National Guard in an attempt to quell the disturbance, which resulted in four deaths and at least thirty injuries. Two hundred thirty-five residents were arrested (but none was charged with any crime). Three of the four fatalities were black, including one woman who was apparently killed by a spray of police gunfire while leaning out her second-floor window, and a man who was killed by a white mob while waiting in a car near his job in a predominantly Italian American neighborhood. Due to a delay in mobilizing the National Guard from an air base in Kentucky, the violence ended only when heavy rains came on July 24. The need for more employment opportunities for Cleveland's black youth had never seemed more urgent.[56]

A week after the riots ended, newspapers reported that thirty of the NUL-MAP applicants for IBEW apprenticeship had passed the written exam. But Doneghy's hopes were dashed in September 1966 when all thirty-one NUL-MAP applicants were rejected by the IBEW following a series of oral interviews with union leaders. As had happened so often in the past, the interviewers had ensured that the black applicants did not advance into the union's apprenticeship program. "They asked question [sic] that didn't seem to tie in with electricity," reported one applicant. Said another, "I believe that the written and oral test that I took were not scored upon fairly because I believe I passed the oral as well as written."[57] Yet another wrote carefully:

I, Kenneth D. Roberts, a student of Manpower Advancement Program, took on July 9, 1966 a Written Examination For an electrical apprentiship [*sic*], given by the Electrical Workers Union Local 38. And also received a notice to take an oral exam which was given at the Elec Workers Union Local 38, in which I also took. And on a later date I received a notice stating that I did not qualify. But I, with a considerable reasonable doubt, I believe that I successfully qualified on both examinations, and declaring that a discriminatory act was produced by the Electrical Workers Union Local 38, against me because of race or color.[58]

Clearly, the writing skills of these applicants were not perfect (but good electricians need not be good writers). Nevertheless, their written statements conveyed the earnestness of their belief that they were qualified and had been fraudulently kept from apprenticeship opportunities due to racism.

These and other statements were collected by the NUL, sworn and notarized, and forwarded to the EEOC in Washington. Although the EEOC could not impose official sanctions or even sue the unions in court, these complaints would ultimately become part of a 1969 Department of Justice lawsuit, *U.S. v. IBEW Local 38*, wherein the district court held that the union was not required to seek minority members; in other words, the black applicants lost the case. (This decision was rendered moot later the same year by the Fifth Circuit Court of Appeals in *Local 53, International Association of Heat and Frost Insulators and Asbestos Workers v. Vogler*, which ordered the union to refer black and white members on a one-to-one ratio until blacks were no longer underrepresented on local job sites.)[59]

Although Doneghy succeeded in getting contractors such as Lake Erie Electric to agree to integrate, he suffered a setback in the battle to increase black apprenticeship in the IBEW. Part of the reason may have been his own color: unlike white southerner Woody Zenfell, Doneghy could not easily move among the lily-white leadership of the local unions. But Doneghy was also trying to get the unions to effect change from within, whereas Zenfell had the advantage of a Justice Department lawsuit with a favorable outcome.

Meanwhile, Macaluso and Sylvester were working on a comprehensive program for Cleveland that would address apprenticeship, journeyman membership, and actual contract hiring, but first they would try out a version in San Francisco.

San Francisco: Bob Magnusson

In 1966 San Franciscans were constructing new post office buildings, several hospitals, an atomic energy laboratory, and a handful of housing projects, all fully or partially financed by agencies of the federal government. But the largest project under construction at the time was the new Bay Area Rapid Transit System (BART).[60]

BART was financed in part by the federal government's Department of Transportation and in part by a public bond issued by the three affected counties—San Francisco, Alameda, and Contra Costa. The system had four major legs, terminating in the northeast at Concord, in the north at Richmond, in the southeast at Fremont, and in the west at West Portal in San Francisco County and Daly City in San Mateo County. There were major hubs in Oakland and central San Francisco, and the most labor-intensive (and expensive) component of the project was the trans-bay tube, connecting the two. The projected cost was $350 million, which would pay more than 8,000 workers to dig ditches and tunnels, lay tracks, build trestles and viaducts, and construct stations.[61]

The problem was that public funds (from both the bond issue and the federal government) were being used to finance projects on BART that employed all-white union labor. The head of the local NAACP wrote to Secretary Wirtz, stating that although he had "been extremely critical of BART for its minority hiring practices," he was beginning to see that "a greater share of the blame rests with the subcontractors who are doing most of the construction work and who have to use union members." These unions, he noted, "have very poor records of hiring minority workers and unless drastic action is initiated, their ranks will remain for the most part 'lily' white." If the current conditions persisted, he warned, "the bitterness of unemployed Negro workers will grow and we can anticipate possibly disastrous confrontations between Negroes and white persons before the construction has been completed."[62]

The number of skilled construction workers needed for BART was so large that at various stages of construction, the three participating counties lacked sufficient union journeymen in particular crafts to fully staff the project. To meet their projected needs, contractors sought additional workers from unions in surrounding counties, despite the fact that there were trained black nonunion journeymen in San Francisco, Alameda, and Contra Costa. Advocates of local black construction workers resolved to fight this practice, forming an organization called Job Opportunities–BART

(JOBART). JOBART's main goal was to lobby—with local elected officials, BART officials, federal officials, and even the construction unions—
for the implementation of a single principle: hiring for BART should
exhaust the lists of qualified construction workers in the three counties
paying for the bond—union and nonunion alike—before turning to unions
in neighboring counties.[63]

The building trades had fought a similar battle before, and won. In
1935, President Roosevelt's Public Works Administration had proposed
hiring local workers for projects in Dover, New Hampshire, and Gainesville, Georgia, where union members were unavailable. When the lathers'
union protested at the DOL, the result was the liberalization of local hiring
rules, allowing union members residing elsewhere to work on the projects
rather than hiring nonunion men. But that battle had been over wage rates:
the Dover- and Gainesville-based workers had been willing to work below
the prevailing union wage.[64] There was no evidence that skilled black San
Franciscan construction workers were willing to accept anything less than
union wages.

Soon after his appointment as San Francisco's area coordinator for
construction, Department of Housing and Urban Development (HUD)
officer Robert C. Magnusson held separate meetings with Macaluso and
Sylvester in the spring and early summer of 1966. BART was clearly the
most important project on Magnusson's desk, but very little of its funding came from the federal government, and California's fair employment
practices law did not have a strong enforcement regime. Sylvester's 1966
Federal Contract Construction Program was now in effect, and it required
that all federal contractors attend pre-award meetings with the contracting
agency and the area coordinator to discuss affirmative action activities.
Magnusson thought that equal opportunity could be achieved throughout
the BART construction project by requiring federal contractors to meet
Sylvester's standards (and those of Executive Order No. 11246) on all their
contracts, including those not funded by the federal government. So Magnusson went to work drafting a standard affirmative action plan that would
be offered to contractors willing to "play ball." Sylvester, Macaluso, and
Magnusson were gambling that the contractors would not simply throw up
their hands at union recalcitrance and forgo their federal contracts. With
Bay Area construction already coming under fire from local grassroots
organizations such as JOBART, the OFCC officers hoped the contractors
would agree that integration was inevitable and decide not to fight it. As
in Cleveland, the OFCC was relying on conciliation to effect change from

within, but there was no Justice Department lawsuit in the works to force compliance, as there had been in St. Louis.[65]

Nevertheless, they won the bet. On October 1, 1966, the General and Specialty Contractors' Association of Berkeley, California, resolved to favor local residents for employment on BART and other publicly financed contracts. Three weeks later the general manager of BART said, "There are no particular problems for [BART] in participating in a specific, forceful, affirmative action program as long as it is not placed in a competitive disadvantage in obtaining bids."[66]

With BART management and Bay Area construction contractors willing to entertain affirmative action plans, Magnusson, Macaluso, and Sylvester began working on a comprehensive program to tailor the nationwide 1966 Federal Contract Construction Program to the specific needs of the San Francisco area. In particular, the program would consider the fact that despite the size of the BART project and others, union unemployment in the construction industry was higher in 1966 than it had been in the previous thirty years, with Alameda County alone registering a 30 percent unemployment rate (this was possible despite BART employment owing to the different stages of construction, which employed many workers in the individual crafts, but only for short periods). Meanwhile, the overall unemployment rate in San Francisco's black and Hispanic neighborhoods was skyrocketing to nearly 50 percent (if those who had given up the job search were counted). Magnusson understood that the San Francisco unions would fight tooth and nail against any proposed growth in their journeyman membership. Despite the promise of work on BART, the fear among skilled white construction workers was that new black union members would be competing with existing white journeymen for scarce jobs once the BART project was complete. A more feasible route for San Francisco lay in apprenticeship, where the contractors' willingness to implement affirmative action plans could be exploited to hire and train the maximum number of black youths. If the union-controlled JACs didn't approve, they could be decertified. On December 22, 1966, Sylvester sent a preliminary order to the heads of contracting agencies with projects in the San Francisco area, advising them of BART's willingness to cooperate in affirmative action and setting forth the basic conditions that would, after several drafts, become the Operational Plan for San Francisco Bay Area Contract Construction Program—the San Francisco Plan.[67]

As expected, the plan's nine provisions focused on integrating apprenticeship and emphasized cooperation with unions.[68] The program expected each contractor to do the following:

1. Cooperate with the unions with which it has agreements in the development of programs to assure qualified members of minority groups of equal opportunity in employment in the construction trades.
2. Actively participate individually or through an association in Joint Apprenticeship Committees to achieve equality of opportunity for minority group applicants to participate in the apprenticeship programs.
3. Actively seek to sponsor members of minority groups for pre-apprenticeship training.
4. Assist youths with minority group identification to enter each apprenticeship program.
5. Improve opportunities for the upgrading of members of the construction force.
6. Seek minority group referrals or applicants for journeymen positions.
7. Make certain that all recruiting activities are carried out on a non-discriminatory basis.
8. Make known to all of its subcontractors, employees and all sources of referral of its equal employment opportunity policy.
9. Encourage minority group subcontractors, and subcontractors with minority group representation among their employees to bid for subcontracting work.[69]

Sylvester formally issued the order on February 6, 1967. Unfortunately for skilled and aspiring black San Francisco construction workers, the OFCC quickly deemed the plan a failure. The emphasis on cooperation—which was clearly all Magnusson could expect, given the overall employment situation—allowed contractors to get away with little more than lip service and tokenism.

At HUD, the largest federal contracting agency in the Bay Area, senior officials marginalized the San Francisco Plan as well as Magnusson himself. Still on the HUD payroll, Magnusson was relegated to a shared eight-by ten-foot office without access to a secretary; for several weeks, until Sylvester was able to prevail on Magnusson's supervisor, the San Francisco area coordinator was reduced to submitting handwritten reports and making frequent visits to the HUD mailroom. The San Francisco Plan was met with virtual contempt from the contractors, unions, and government officials responsible for its implementation, and they saw Magnusson and the OFCC as an impediment to lucrative contracts. Thus, by early July, the San Francisco Plan had failed to produce any tangible results.[70]

The experiences of the area coordinators in these three cities during 1966 proved to Macaluso and Sylvester that the differences outweighed the similarities when it came to crafting a comprehensive integration program for the building trades. In St. Louis, sufficient trained blacks could be moved directly into journeyman status due to the unions' fear of court injunctions. In Cleveland and San Francisco, integration in apprenticeship seemed to be key, but the different experiences of Doneghy and Magnusson with their local JACs showed that these cities required different approaches as well. Unlike in St. Louis, no federal lawsuit accompanied the work in Cleveland and San Francisco. The inability of Doneghy and the NUL to place trained pre-apprenticeship graduates with the IBEW, and the outright hostility faced by Magnusson at HUD, led to growing frustration at the OFCC. Stronger measures were required.[71]

The Cleveland Plan

As a nationwide policy, Edward Sylvester's 1966 Federal Contract Construction Program faced daunting odds and achieved questionable success. In 1967 the EEOC reported that black representation in the skilled building trades remained incredibly tiny: 0.2 percent of the plumbers, 0.4 percent of the elevator constructors, 0.6 percent of the electrical workers, 1.6 percent of the carpenters, 1.7 percent of the ironworkers, 3.7 percent of the painters, and 4.0 percent of the operating engineers. If the national problem was to be tackled through local solutions, those solutions would have to be more intense.[72]

Whereas the San Francisco Plan focused on apprenticeship and conciliation and was confronted with high unemployment both inside and outside the construction unions, despite the $350 million BART project, the drafting of an operational plan for Cleveland posed different problems altogether. In January 1967, which was normally the industry's slow season, union unemployment in the construction trades was extremely low and dropping. This trend continued as the winter deepened, and by mid-February, Doneghy reported that "the bench is bare," a circumstance that

Macaluso immediately likened—in a reverse metaphor, given the season—to "snowballs in July."[73]

Unlike in San Francisco, where much of the work involved a single major project, Cleveland was rife with smaller but still substantial construction projects. In addition to Lake Erie Electric's NASA project, Western Reserve University was constructing new campus buildings; the University of Akron was constructing a Cleveland campus; and there were senior citizens' homes, a hospital, and several housing complexes on their way up—all relying, in whole or in part, on federal funds.[74]

Several grassroots organizations were operating to train black youths for apprenticeships in Cleveland. As we have seen, the NUL had MAP, which had successfully trained youths for the written IBEW apprenticeship exam the previous summer. Fresh from his success training youths for construction apprenticeships in Brooklyn, New York, Ernest Green (of the Little Rock Nine) brought his Workers' Defense League–sponsored program to Cleveland in early 1967. And the Reverend Leon Sullivan of Philadelphia opened a Cleveland branch of his Opportunities Industrialization Center in April of that same year. These programs put the lie to union and contractor claims that no qualified black youths were available for apprenticeships.[75]

Based on the overall unemployment rate, Doneghy's experience with the local IBEW, and the presence of minority-oriented training programs, Sylvester and Macaluso resolved that Cleveland was an opportune place to launch a more aggressive plan, and the Cleveland Plan was just that. Building on the affirmative action plan forged with Lake Erie Electric, it called for the now usual pre-award conferences between contractors and federal contracting agencies, and it expected all bidders to meet DOL criteria for equal opportunity certification and to submit an affirmative action plan. Unlike the San Francisco Plan, it was confrontational rather than conciliatory: contractors were expected to hire journeymen from nonunion sources if the unions could not provide sufficient nonwhite employees, and apprenticeship programs without black apprentices would be decertified.[76]

In the midst of implementation of the Cleveland Plan, a major court case pushed the OFCC to take even more direct action. On May 17, 1967, Judge Joseph P. Kinneary of the federal district court in Columbus ruled in *Ethridge v. Rhodes* that construction of a $12.8 million medical science building at Ohio State University be stopped until the trade unions working on the project, or the general contractor and his subcontractors, integrated. The suit had been brought on behalf of black construction workers denied employment at the site because they weren't union members. The court found that Governor James A. Rhodes had waived federal equal employment regulations (beyond his authority as a governor) and even his own executive order to sign the construction contracts. Basing his opinion on the equal protection clause of the Fourteenth Amendment, Judge Kinneary ruled that the state had primary responsibility for ensuring equal employment opportunity at construction sites and could not do business with firms that worked with unions with a history of racial discrimination. The governor's office did not appeal the decision.[77]

The next day, spurred to action by the court ruling, Macaluso ordered that $48 million in federal funds for a variety of Cleveland projects be withheld until each contractor could demonstrate that it had an integrated workforce; he announced that the OFCC would make a decision on an additional $60 million within three or four weeks. For the first time, all federal construction expenditures in an entire city were halted for noncompliance with the nondiscrimination clause.[78]

The stoppage of funds by Macaluso represented a major step forward. During the 1950s, when the antidiscrimination clause was first added to federal contracts, the contractor's signature was deemed sufficient to release funds. In 1960 token compliance became necessary to continue to receive funds (as when McCloskey & Co. put "a chap . . . on the payroll"). With Sylvester's Federal Contract Construction Program, successful bidders were expected to at least pay lip service to the ideals of equal opportunity by attending a pre-award meeting and submitting a plan for affirmative action, but little follow-up was required, and few such plans were fully implemented; in any event, the money always continued to flow. Now the OFCC was taking compliance a step further. The default position of federal expenditures was reversed: instead of having to make promises to *keep* the money flowing, contractors would have to demonstrate compliance to *start* the money flowing. And until they did, the federal government would not spend a dime on construction in the seven-county Cleveland area.

Predictably, the skilled craft unions opposed Macaluso's decision. They had achieved their goal of full employment, which would be lost if they were forced to accept new black members or share jobs with non-union men. Full employment meant not only that all union members were employed—and that they could depend on significant overtime pay—but also that the unions could successfully demand that contractors accelerate wage increases. If additional workers were allowed onto the job sites, union or not, their swelled numbers might slow down pay increases. And the boom times were almost certainly temporary; few expected the bench to remain bare for long. If there was a time to take advantage of low membership, this was it. The plumbers, for instance, were not starting a new apprenticeship class and would not replace members who retired. Rather than comply with the Cleveland Plan, the plumbers sought work on nonfederal jobs until the federal money started flowing again (which they and others predicted would happen eventually, whether the job sites were integrated or not). The union began referring newly available members to the nonfederal construction projects of Republic Steel of Cleveland. But even Republic Steel was not immune to the Cleveland Plan; it had some contracts with the GSA, and Sylvester wrote to the agency, hoping to plug this potential loophole.[79]

Federally assisted institutions had mixed reactions to the Cleveland Plan. For instance, Western Reserve University, whose federal construction funds came from the Department of Health, Education, and Welfare (HEW), welcomed the opportunity to force integration on contractors and unions alike. Federation Towers, a housing project for union retirees being built by the local AFL-CIO with funds from HUD, challenged the decision, claiming that it changed "the rules of the game" after contracts had already been signed. And one hospital with a HEW-funded construction contract complained to Ohio senator Frank Lausche in the hope that his office could convince the OFCC to restore funding (the senator was placated after Sylvester explained that the contractor for the project had failed to submit an acceptable affirmative action plan).[80]

Most contractors welcomed the decision. One saw it as an opportunity to "get his house in order." Some also saw it as an opportunity to weaken the stranglehold the unions had on hiring.[81] But there was still the question of demonstrating results: how could a contractor effectively prove to Macaluso that its workforce was integrated when the funds weren't flowing and the work wasn't being done?

The solution was to add a column to the manning table. The manning table was essentially a list of employees in each craft for a given project (or each subcontractor's portion of a project), and it was a long-established practice in contract construction reporting. Fred Kerr of the Gillmore-Olsen Company, general contractor on the NASA project that had hired Lake Erie Electric, proposed adding the total number of nonwhites in each craft (table 3.1). NASA immediately agreed, Macaluso and Sylvester concurred, and the project funds were released to Gillmore-Olsen. Other contractors—both to demonstrate compliance and to ensure that they

Table 3.1. Kerr's Original Manning Table, June 1, 1967

Crafts	Total Required	Total Minority	Approximate Months on the Job
Operating Engineers	5	2	5
Plumbers	4	1	4
Ironworkers	6	1	5
Electricians	7	2	12
Sheet metal workers	2	1	3
Steamfitters	4	1	4

Source: Fred M. Kerr to Sherwood Holman, June 1, 1967, Records of the Department of Labor, Papers of the OFCC, Collection of the OFCC Assistant Director for Construction, box 8, "Cleveland Correspondence" folder, National Archives and Records Administration, College Park, MD.

didn't lose bids to contractors providing the new affirmative action manning tables—quickly followed suit. By June 27 federal funds were again flowing to four of the thirteen Cleveland-area contractors, and two more had meetings with their respective agencies scheduled for the next week, at which they would present new affirmative action plans and amended manning tables.[82]

The use of manning tables to demonstrate compliance with the equal opportunity clause in federal contracts would later be decried as a quota system by politicians, union leaders, and journalists. These critics generally lacked an understanding of how common such forms had been prior to their use for this purpose, and they failed to recognize that this new use had initially been proposed by the industry, not by government officials. The government merely agreed to accept it (and would later require it) as evidence of compliance for each construction project. It was not a list of quotas for future contracts.

One might reasonably ask, as Terry Anderson has done, why contractors were being required to prove compliance at all. After all, "since a citizen is innocent until proven guilty in America," the burden of proof should fall on the government; that is, the OFCC should have to prove that a contractor was failing to comply with the nondiscrimination clause in order to justify contract revocation or debarment from future contracts—the two main weapons in the OFCC arsenal. But in fact, no such burden of proof exists outside of criminal law in the United States; in civil law, the plaintiff and the defendant have an equal obligation to prove their cases, and when it comes to federal contracts, the potential contractor has an obligation to demonstrate an ability to comply with the terms of the contract. As Graham puts it, "a presumed state of *innocence* in criminal . . . law . . . was not the same thing as a state of *compliance* in contract law."[83]

In any event, manning tables soon had the force of common law. When Cuyahoga Community College rejected a low bidder for failing to add the nonwhite column to its manning table, the contractor sued. In *Weiner v. Cuyahoga Community College,* the Ohio Supreme Court declared that the use of manning tables to demonstrate nondiscrimination was consistent with the Civil Rights Act of 1964, and the U.S. Supreme Court refused to hear the contractor's appeal.[84]

Kerr's manning table concept represented an entirely new paradigm for affirmative action. Prior to its introduction, affirmative action meant taking concrete, race-conscious steps to help blacks and Hispanics compete on an equal footing with whites—or, to paraphrase President Johnson's Howard University address, to allow them to compete under the same conditions from the same starting line. Affirmative action, frankly, was difficult to accomplish. It took work. It meant funding scholarships and training programs, creating new jobs, and engaging in follow-up and oversight to monitor each program's progress. For JACs, it meant advertising apprenticeship opportunities in black newspapers, forging and maintaining social relationships with black community leaders, and actually visiting black neighborhoods. For unions, it meant seeking trained black craftsmen to admit as journeymen, thus enlarging the local and risking a fuller bench and slower pay increases. And for construction firms—as seen in the affirmative action agreement with Lake Erie Electric—it meant breaking exclusive hiring agreements with lily-white unions at the risk of having an inadequate supply of trained workers or, worse, a strike.

The manning table—for all its convenience in terms of reporting (which federal officials such as Macaluso and Doneghy certainly appreciated)—represented the easy way out. On the one hand, the contractor could simply break its promise, fulfill its other obligations under the contract, collect its money, and later claim there were no trained blacks to meet the projection—or that the union had failed to provide them. On the other hand, if the contractor hired the promised number of black craftsmen, that ended the contractor's—and the OFCC's—larger responsibility for long-term improvements. The contractor was not required to post advertisements or forge long-lasting relationships in the black community, let alone provide training opportunities to prevent the next generation from slipping back into segregation. In short, the manning table—which led to goals and ranges, then to quotas, and ultimately to hiring decisions that could arguably be called "reverse racism"—subverted President Johnson's vision that affirmative action was necessary to equal employment opportunity. The manning table rendered a laudable moral goal with the potential to reshape American race relations into a simple matter of hiring the minimum necessary to keep "big brother" happy so the federal funds kept flowing.

Following on the heels of Macaluso's order withholding funds for Cleveland, the NAACP, at Herbert Hill's behest, notified local branches nationwide of the *Ethridge v. Rhodes* decision and asked them to investigate employment conditions at local construction sites. Executive director Roy Wilkins telegrammed forty-two state governors, asking them not to approve any construction contracts involving state funds until the building trades or contractors in their states integrated; he sent a similar telegram to Labor Secretary Wirtz, asking that all federal construction funds be stopped.[85] A turning point, Hill and Wilkins felt, had clearly been reached. Unions and contractors had failed to adequately integrate the skilled trades after OFCC conciliation; only tougher measures—the withholding of funds or the debarment of contractors—would result in serious changes in the racial makeup of the workforce.

For his part, Wirtz wasn't sure that nationwide action ought to be directed at the building trades. Although the secretary was aware that discrimination existed in the skilled building trades in a number of localities, and although he certainly supported the activities of Sylvester and Macaluso in fighting it, he knew that neither federal construction nor the unions—many of which, he believed, were not engaging in discrimination—would be served by a blanket withholding of funds. The building trades included some of the most visible examples of discrimination, but they also included majority-black unions, such as the laborers. Furthermore, those few blacks who had succeeded in breaking the color line in the skilled unions would be penalized just at their moment of triumph. They didn't deserve, as Wirtz put it, "finger-pointing."[86]

He may have had a point. The secretary had commissioned a report from University of Texas professors F. Ray Marshall (later President Carter's labor secretary) and Vernon M. Briggs entitled *Negro Participation in Apprenticeship Programs,* which stated: "It is our conclusion that pre-apprenticeship programs . . . are effective means of . . . providing opportunities to these youngsters and supplying qualified applicants to apprentice programs. . . . Racial discrimination . . . has declined in recent years and . . . measures to recruit, train, and counsel qualified applicants currently are much more important."[87]

Another future labor secretary, George Shultz, agreed. As dean of the University of Chicago's Graduate Business School, Shultz argued that there were other ways to obtain construction employment besides apprenticeship. In the construction trades, he noted, apprenticeships—which included formal schooling—were as apt to produce future foremen, contractors, and union leaders as they were rank-and-file union members. One apprenticeship program, that of the New York City electricians (IBEW Local #3), required apprentices to attend college and earn an associate's degree (with tuition paid by the union). As seen with the direct admission of black journeymen plumbers in St. Louis, other routes to integration were available.[88]

The road ahead, as far as Wirtz and Sylvester were concerned, did not involve blanket sanctions of the entire industry. Instead, they preferred to continue the city-by-city approach, with individual plans tailored to different localities. However, the conciliatory San Francisco Plan, in a high-unemployment area, had had little impact, as was now arguably the case with the local plan for St. Louis, where little progress had been made after the initial moves toward integration following the arch walkout. In Cleveland, the confrontational style in a low-unemployment area had worked only when a district court decision prompted Macaluso to pull the plug on federal funds.

Cleveland area coordinator Charles Doneghy was incredibly busy during the summer of 1967, meeting with unions, contracting parties, and federal contracting agencies; attending pre-award conferences; and reviewing manning tables and affirmative action plans from anxious contractors. The OFCC detailed an intern to Cleveland, and the Nashville area coordinator temporarily moved to Cleveland to help out as well. But Doneghy found time in July to present his experience with the Cleveland Plan and the success of the manning tables to a group of federal officials preparing a comprehensive affirmative action program for construction in Philadelphia.[89]

The development of federal civil rights policies demonstrated that the federal bureaucracy, when managed effectively, can improve the lives of citizens in areas other than the common defense—a position liberals had been taking since the Great Depression.[90] When elected leaders—in this case, President Johnson—can identify and give voice to the needs of society—

in this case, the rising demands for true equality of opportunity—they can influence appointed officials and bureaucratic civil servants alike in the service and development of these policies. And when the bureaucracy is effectively motivated (as was the case in St. Louis), or when conditions are ripe (as was the case in Cleveland), it can foster positive change. When conditions are poor and bureaucrats are uninterested (as was the case in San Francisco), the system breaks down, and government fails.

Lyndon Johnson, the Kennedy administration's civil rights czar, ascended to the presidency at the peak of the civil rights movement. By 1963 the cause of civil rights, as seen in activities such as the Freedom Rides and the Birmingham protests, enjoyed widespread sympathy in the white community outside of the Deep South and was gaining ground legislatively. With his ascension, Johnson elevated civil rights within the federal government from a vice presidential issue—something that had largely been fobbed off by Eisenhower onto Nixon's portfolio, and by Kennedy onto Johnson's—to a truly presidential matter. And it was that leadership—presidential leadership—that helped make possible the groundbreaking Civil Rights Act of 1964, the most comprehensive and important piece of civil rights legislation since Reconstruction. Then, in 1965, President Johnson embarked on a truly revolutionary course, defining affirmative action as the key to equal employment opportunity and telling his beleaguered nation that "we shall overcome."

Officers of the federal government's civil rights machinery took their cues from the statements and direction of President Johnson. He set a tone and established a mood—Great Society liberalism—and as a result, officials like Ed Sylvester and Vince Macaluso understood the importance of creating a society where the experiences of men such as James Ballard (who never did become a sheet metal worker) would be the exception rather than the rule.[91] Through trial and error, and amid a more traditional, inert bureaucratic culture, they set about fulfilling the president's promises to the nation.

But at the very moment Johnson was achieving personal success as the civil rights president, the nation reached a turning point in race relations—and not for the better. Civil rights without economic results bred resentments, and all the new laws, executive orders, and regulations were not reversing the alarming trends in unemployment. As white unemployment decreased, black unemployment increased, and the economic gap of de facto segregation replaced the older social divide of de jure segregation. And with tensions high over the escalating war in Vietnam and an unfair national draft policy, the nation's slums erupted into violence, from Watts in Los Angeles to Hough in Cleveland to Newark, Detroit, and Chicago.[92]

The momentum of the civil rights movement, which had achieved its greatest successes with the sympathy and support of liberal whites, began to lose steam, threatened as much by a northern white backlash against urban violence as by unreconstructed southern racists. As one summer followed the next and riot followed riot, each seemingly worse than the last, the backlash threatened to derail all the precious achievements of the previous decade.

As labor secretary for the NAACP, Herbert Hill was outspoken in his criticism of segregated unions, especially the skilled building trades. Francis Miller/Time & Life Pictures/Getty Images.

AFL-CIO president George Meany walked the line between the status quo and the need to integrate the building construction trades. George Meany Memorial Archives/ SN37.

A. Philip Randolph, president of the Brotherhood of Sleeping-Car Porters and vice president of the AFL-CIO, fought to suspend racist unions from the federation and organized the 1963 March on Washington for Jobs and Freedom. Library of Congress, Prints & Photographs Division, FSA/OWI Collection, NYWTS—BIOG—Randolph, A. Philip—Labor.

NAACP executive director Roy Wilkins worked with Vice President Richard Nixon and President Lyndon B. Johnson to integrate the skilled building trades. Photograph by Yoichi R. Okamoto, White House Press Office.

President John F. Kennedy addressed the nation on television from the White House on June 11, 1963, after violence in Birmingham, Alabama, and Philadelphia, Pennsylvania, prompted him to invigorate his policy on civil rights. Photograph by Abbie Rowe, National Park Service, John F. Kennedy Presidential Library and Museum, Boston.

As OFCC assistant director for construction, Vincent Macaluso oversaw the area coordinator program and the development of the San Francisco, Cleveland, and Philadelphia plans. Courtesy of Vincent J. Macaluso.

As secretary of labor for Presidents John F. Kennedy and Lyndon B. Johnson, W. Willard Wirtz spearheaded the drive to develop and implement affirmative action programs in the skilled building trades. Francis Miller/Time & Life Pictures/Getty Images.

In May 1963 Philadelphia blacks protested the construction of a school in a predominantly black neighborhood using only white skilled workers. Temple University Libraries, Urban Archives, McDowell Collection.

President Lyndon B. Johnson (second from left) consulted with civil rights leaders (from left) Martin Luther King of the Southern Christian Leadership Conference, Whitney Young of the National Urban League, and James Farmer of the Congress of Racial Equality before his first State of the Union address in 1964. Within the year the president would sign the 1964 Civil Rights Act. Photograph by Yoichi R. Okamoto, LBJ Library photo archives #W425–21.

Frustrated by the slow delivery of jobs promised by the Civil Rights Act of 1964, inner-city blacks responded to continuing police violence and racism with riots. The most famous was in the Watts section of Los Angeles in 1965. But rioting only made the situation worse, turning white public opinion against the civil rights movement and hurting the work prospects of local residents such as Charles Steppes (shown here in front of a riot-destroyed store near his home). Los Angeles Times Photographic Archive, Department of Special Collections, Charles E. Young Research Library, UCLA.

The San Francisco Plan, which followed integration of the St. Louis Memorial Arch job site, included such major construction projects as the Bay Area Rapid Transit system (BART). Courtesy of Bigge Construction Inc.

Implementation of the Philadelphia Plan in 1968 at the site of the new U.S. Mint sparked a walkout by skilled white workers. National Archives and Records Administration, College Park, MD.

As assistant secretary of labor under President Richard M. Nixon, Arthur Fletcher revised the Philadelphia Plan and fought for its implementation. Stan Wayman/Time & Life Pictures/Getty Images.

President Richard M. Nixon (left) and his first secretary of labor, George Shultz, fought congressional enemies of the Philadelphia Plan. Nixon soon abandoned affirmative action to woo support from white building trades workers. Hulton Archive/ Stringer/Archive Photos/Getty Images.

Elmer Staats declared the original Philadelphia Plan illegal under procurement law, then declared the revised plan illegal under the Civil Rights Act of 1964. Courtesy of U.S. Government Accountability Office.

As Lieutenant Uhura on the television program *Star Trek,* Nichelle Nichols served as a public demonstration to black youngsters that they could attain skilled employment—and a reminder to whites that blacks could perform on an equal basis. National Aeronautics and Space Administration Recruiter—GPN 2004-00017.

Chapter 4

Pushing the Envelope

The Philadelphia Plans, 1967–1969

The name of the game is to put some economic flesh and bones on Dr. King's dream.

—Arthur Fletcher, December 20, 1969

In the spring of 1968, white electricians John Melleher, Joe Quinn, and John Kennedy filed a complaint with the Philadelphia Commission on Human Relations, claiming they had been "denied work at the United States Mint" construction site "because of their race." These union men felt they had been passed over by Nager Electrical Company, a subcontractor on the project, for nonunion black electricians in violation of Title VII of the Civil Rights Act of 1964. The commission dismissed the case, noting that the mint project was federally financed and that such discrimination complaints were therefore out of its jurisdiction.

At the heart of the complaint was the men's sense that the affirmative action program used by the contractor, under the federal government's Philadelphia Plan, gave an unfair advantage to nonunion, and therefore inadequately trained, black workers. Further, they noted that there were significant numbers of black workers already on the mint job who were bona fide union members (although none were electricians, and the "significant" numbers were members of the unskilled laborers' union). On May 7, after Nager Electrical hired its second nonunion black electrician, twenty-one whites walked off the job in protest.[1]

The Philadelphia Plan was the federal government's latest solution to the problems of discrimination in the building trades. It evolved out of the Cleveland Plan of 1967, and the OFCC developed the program with the specific intent of avoiding racial violence in a city on the brink. The majority of federal construction dollars was being spent in the city's black neighborhoods, but these dollars were ending up in the pockets of skilled white union construction workers.

The Philadelphia Plan differed from previous affirmative action plans in the construction industry, in that it was developed in tandem with the local Federal Executive Board (FEB), which ensured top-level coordination among the federal contracting agencies. President Kennedy had established the FEBs in 1961 by executive order "to coordinate better the disjoint programs of federal agencies in the field." The Philadelphia FEB consisted of senior local officials from each of the federal departments with a major presence in the city."[2]

By the end of 1968, the plan was on the verge of making significant progress in integrating the skilled trades in the Philadelphia area. But its similarity to racial quotas, and the burdens it placed on contractors, brought increasingly intense challenges—first from the unions, as at the mint site; then from individual members of Congress; and finally from the General Accounting Office (GAO). The ostensibly nonpartisan GAO had been established by Congress in 1921 as an independent agency to analyze and supervise federal expenditures under the leadership of the comptroller general of the United States. During the 1960s the comptroller general had been attempting to expand the authority of the GAO, and in 1968 he challenged the Philadelphia Plan on the grounds that it violated procurement law. The Philadelphia Plan did not survive the presidential transition.

Bowing to increased pressure from civil rights advocates and local grassroots organizations, President Nixon's Labor Department issued a revised version of the Philadelphia Plan in the summer of 1969. But the revised plan also came under attack—and this time, the comptroller general was joined by powerful southern conservative senators. With renewed protests and violence at construction sites around the country, and with a presidential administration perceived as hostile to civil rights, the Nixon White House took up a spirited defense of the Philadelphia Plan at the intersection of race and politics.

Prior historians discussing the Philadelphia Plan have used it as unambiguous evidence of a positive civil rights agenda in the Nixon administration. This chapter, building on the discussion of the San Francisco and Cleveland plans in chapter 3, shows decisively that the Philadelphia Plan was developed and implemented by Johnson-era officials; that the changes between the original plan and the Nixon-era plan were minimal, dealing only with the comptroller general's concerns about procurement law; and that Nixon's motive for pursuing the plan was to enlarge his own political power by attempting to split two important Democratic constituencies: organized labor and the civil rights movement.

The Operational Plan for Philadelphia

An overview of the construction industry in Philadelphia in 1967 reveals a mixed picture of the status of African Americans in the skilled trades. According to the local plumbers' union, 6 out of 60 apprentices—or 10 percent—were black; given the national trends at the time, that represented a modestly positive figure (although the Labor Department's Bureau of Apprenticeship and Training disputed the number). The electricians were taking positive steps to increase the percentage of black journeymen (at the time, only 14 out of 1,400, or 1 percent); they admitted 11 nonwhite apprentices. Typical of the existing apprentices was Henry Clayton Lee. A graduate of the integrated Mastbaum Vocational Technical School (where he had majored in industrial electricity), Lee had served in the U.S. Navy as an electrician's mate on the USS *Saratoga* from 1955 to 1957. Employed as an electrician on nonunion residential construction jobs for years after his naval service, Lee was admitted to the Local #98 apprenticeship program only after the violence at the Thirty-first Street and Susquehanna Avenue school construction site in 1963 (see chapter 2).[3]

Other trades were slower to integrate, to say the least: the sheet metal workers, for instance, had no black or Hispanic journeymen out of a total membership of 1,200. After losing a lawsuit in the summer of 1967, the union accepted two black journeymen (thus bringing nonwhite representation in the union to one-sixth of 1 percent) and three black apprentices, admitted (like electrician Lee) after the 1963 school site protests. One of the apprentices, Judge Budd Jr., said his experience was "rougher than I expected," and he wished "more people realized the opportunity was there." But with blacks accounting for about 30 percent of the population of Philadelphia (approximately 600,000 out of 2.06 million), these figures constituted clear evidence of historically racist patterns and continuing discriminatory practices.[4]

The unions could not blame their reluctance to admit blacks on a shortage of work. The 1967 federal construction allocation to the city—more than $300 million—was 52 percent higher than it had been in 1966. What's more, nearly two-thirds of that was being spent by HUD, and the single largest category of HUD spending—$144.5 million, or nearly half the city total—was for urban renewal, a category that disproportionately included construction in predominantly black neighborhoods. HEW came in second, at $53 million, mostly for school construction, followed by the GSA at $49 million, which included construction of the new U.S. Mint. Construction at the navy yard was part of the $12 million Department of Defense allocation, and the Federal Aviation Administration (FAA) was constructing a new airport for $1 million.[5] In short, at least half of the growing federal construction budget for Philadelphia was being spent on building sites in predominantly black neighborhoods, but the vast majority of the skilled workers on those job sites were white.

National leaders in the building trades agreed that the skilled trades needed to work harder to integrate, but they placed more of the blame on apathy among prospective black apprentices than on institutional discrimination. One BAT official said that despite the apparent willingness of the Philadelphia building trades to accept black applicants, he couldn't find "a dozen qualified Negroes" to apply for apprenticeship positions.[6] As we have seen, the issue of qualification was itself contentious, and the unions' discriminatory application methods ensured that few blacks appeared qualified.

To increase the number of qualified black applicants, union leaders favored "apprenticeship outreach" programs such as those developed by the Workers' Defense League in Brooklyn, New York, under the leadership of Ernest Green; Chicago's Jobs Now program; and the NUL's on-the-job training programs, funded in several cities by the Department of Labor. (The Workers' Defense League had been founded in 1936 as a legal aid society to assist laid-off employees in obtaining unemployment insurance.) In Philadelphia the apprenticeship outreach program was organized by the local branch of the Negro Trade Union Leadership Council (NTULC), an organization founded in 1959 by A. Philip Randolph in New York to promote the interests of blacks in organized labor. As Grace Palladino tells us, the Philadelphia NTULC "used government funds to employ five black recruiters to visit schools, conduct interviews, select trainees, and prepare them to apply for apprenticeships . . . accompanied recruits to local union interviews and tests, all to ensure that they were treated fairly." And although the business manager of the Philadelphia Building Construction Trades Council—citing statistics from both skilled and unskilled unions—claimed that this had resulted in the admission of eighty-three minority youths to apprenticeships, the result in the skilled trades was little better than that seen when the Cleveland Urban League supplied applicants for IBEW apprenticeships in 1966. By March 1969, after more than two years in operation, the Philadelphia NTULC apprenticeship outreach program had failed to significantly break through unions' discriminatory practices; it had succeeded in placing only two electricians, two ironworkers, and seven plumbers or pipefitters in union-sponsored apprenticeships.[7]

As deindustrialization brought more unemployment to the North, national black unemployment increased faster than that of whites, and the summer of 1967 proved to be a tinderbox for violent outbreaks in the nation's cities. The worst riots took place in June in Tampa and in July in Newark and Detroit—where forty-three people died (thirty killed by police officers) and 2,509 buildings were burned. In Philadelphia, brief outbreaks of racial violence were suppressed by a rapid community and police response, but the city remained on edge throughout the summer.[8]

To maintain the relative calm in Philadelphia, Mayor Tate announced a major plan to avert racial violence, including the creation of 500 new city jobs (applicants would fill out paperwork in one of several "jobmobiles" patrolling black neighborhoods), increased municipal services in the ghetto (including garbage collection and expanded hours of operation for playgrounds), and reassignment of the best police officers to riot-prone areas. Operating on the theory that riots were the result of unemployment and a sense of abandonment by the wider society, Tate's plan had the two-pronged effect of creating jobs and increasing the overall municipal presence in areas where both had been sorely lacking.[9]

By late summer, there were more applicants—and with higher skill levels than expected—than there were jobs available. To meet the increased demand for jobs, Tate asked the local FEB to meet with 250 employers and develop additional solutions to avert the pending racial crisis. In Philadelphia the FEB members were senior local officials from each of the pertinent departments; federal officers of a somewhat lower rank generally filled the FEB's committees, which focused on areas of acute concern to the board.[10]

The Philadelphia FEB was led by HUD regional director Warren Phelan. Born in 1910 in the small town of Havre, Montana, Phelan graduated from the University of Montana in 1934. He worked as a public welfare officer for the state of Montana for the rest of the Great Depression, enlisted in the navy, was commissioned an officer in 1944, and served in the Pacific theater during World War II. After the war, Phelan took a master's degree in social administration at Western Reserve University in Cleveland, working part-time for the Cleveland Housing Authority. He then spent a year working in the juvenile court system of the District of Columbia, whereupon he was hired by HEW. In 1951 Phelan transferred to the Housing and Home Finance Agency (HHFA), and in 1955 he became an HHFA Philadelphia field representative for urban redevelopment. In 1961 he was promoted to regional administrator for Philadelphia, and he retained that title when the agency was folded into the new federal department, HUD, in 1966. Having witnessed the 1963 protests over segregated employment in the building trades, Phelan felt that a major area of importance for the Philadelphia FEB was integration of the construction industry, and in 1967 he reached out to OFCC construction area coordinator Bennett O. Stalvey Jr. to work toward that end.[11]

In 1962 Bennett Stalvey was an advertising director from Chicago living with his growing family in a white, segregated neighborhood in Omaha, Nebraska. When his wife became involved in a failed drive to integrate the neighborhood with the family of a local African American doctor, the Stalveys were forced to relocate. They chose Philadelphia, where Stalvey took a federal job. In the summer of 1966, Philadelphia had already been through two construction area coordinators in just over a year of the program's operation, and Vincent Macaluso tapped Stalvey for the position.[12]

When Phelan of the FEB reached out to Stalvey of the OFCC, he asked a question that temporarily stumped Stalvey: how did the OFCC handle situations in which multiple federal agencies were working on the same equal opportunity problem? In other words, how did the area coordinator—usually a junior federal officer—coordinate the compliance activities of senior federal officials?[13]

What Phelan had inadvertently stumbled upon with this question was the source of the problem that had plagued area coordinators since the beginning of the program. But Phelan was also offering a solution that had not been previously considered: using the local FEB to assist the area coordinator. Phelan and his fellow FEB members were senior federal officials in the city, and together they could manage a coordinated effort. Without their help, Stalvey might well fall short.

The Philadelphia FEB's Critical Urban Problems Committee analyzed and acted on matters such as discrimination in the local building trades. Stalvey arranged for Macaluso to attend a meeting of this committee in February 1967, and at Phelan's urging, it established a subcommittee comprising junior federal officers to focus explicitly on developing an areawide affirmative action plan for construction to be coordinated by the FEB. Phelan appointed Stalvey chairman of this Federal Contract Construction Compliance Subcommittee (FCCCS) and tasked him with developing an operational plan for construction integration by midsummer.[14]

From April through July 1967 the FCCCS hammered out the various clauses of the document, and Macaluso and Sylvester were brought in as consultants. Macaluso explained the basic contours of the San Francisco and Cleveland plans and noted that the latter, with its tough enforcement, relatively high nonwhite employment goals, and practice of requesting manning tables from contractors, was better suited to the conditions in Philadelphia. Cleveland area coordinator Charles Doneghy spoke to the subcommittee about his experiences implementing the Cleveland Plan.[15]

The ultimate result, the Operational Plan for Philadelphia (OPP), built on the successes of the Cleveland Plan but bore the mark of the more ambitious FEB coordination program. The OPP required low bidders for federally funded (or federally assisted) construction projects within the five-county metropolitan area (Bucks, Chester, Delaware, Montgomery, and Philadelphia counties) to submit pre-award affirmative action plans that contained goals for nonwhite hiring. These affirmative action plans were intended to emphasize outreach recruitment operations aimed at local black and Hispanic communities and include the maximum possible number of apprentices (to encourage the unions and contractors to admit more blacks into their apprenticeship programs). Low bidders would also be required to attend a pre-award equal opportunity meeting with the contracting agency's local compliance officer and area coordinator Stalvey and to submit up-to-date manning tables twice a month, wherein they would be encouraged to "blow off steam" in the hope that these reports would identify contractors' frustrations with the unions and other problems in implementing their hiring goals, allowing the FCCCS to focus on particular problem areas as the plan was implemented. Unlike the Cleveland Plan, under which Doneghy and Macaluso ultimately set specific goals for each contractor, the Philadelphia Plan would be "voluntary," in that the contractors would develop their own goals (but Stalvey would ensure that each contractor's goals were significant).[16]

The drafting of the OPP caused a great deal of excitement at the OFCC, where Sylvester called the FEB coordination component "a prototype for the future." But coordination at the local level also needed support at the national level. To that end, Sylvester and Macaluso organized a meeting in

Washington, D.C., on August 30, 1967, where Phelan and Stalvey would explain the OPP to the heads of the contracting agencies, including two cabinet members: Secretary Robert C. Weaver of HUD (which represented nearly two-thirds of all federal construction spending in Philadelphia), and their boss, Secretary Wirtz. (That the newest federal department—HUD—should contract so much construction spending was itself revolutionary. In addition, Weaver, who had previously served as an undersecretary in the Department of the Interior during the Roosevelt administration, was now the first black cabinet member.) The meeting and subsequent follow-up by Sylvester and Wirtz resulted in approval of the OPP by all agencies except the Department of Defense (whose representatives stated that the nature of their construction programs required a national affirmative action program rather than a series of local programs). The chairman of the U.S. Civil Service Commission went so far as to send copies of the OPP to all local FEBs around the country, urging them to consider developing similar programs. Phelan announced that the OPP would officially go into effect on November 30, 1967.[17]

Even before that date, contracting agencies began informing bidders that any projects scheduled to begin after November 30 would be subject to the rules of the OPP. In short, this meant that the OPP was already in effect as it pertained to the bidding process, pre-award meetings, and affirmative action plans (including manning tables).

At least one agency, the FAA, took its own interpretation of the OPP even further than the plan's specifications. When Latrobe Construction Company, general contractor for a new local airport, submitted an acceptable affirmative action plan at the end of October 1967, a local FAA official told Latrobe that his agency would "move on to the next low bidder" unless Latrobe integrated its workforce on a completely unrelated project 400 miles away in Ohio. The FAA determined that with 101 white and 0 black operating engineers currently employed on its Ohio project, Latrobe was unworthy of a contract, regardless of the company's promise to integrate its workforce in Philadelphia.[18] By refusing a Philadelphia contract to a company engaging in discrimination elsewhere, the FAA compliance officer was both extending the OPP beyond the five-county area and demonstrating the power of the midlevel federal bureaucrat—and how that power, when placed in the hands of a Great Society liberal, could be brought to bear forcefully on behalf of African American workers. This case also demonstrated the dynamic use of the bureaucracy that made the OPP different from previous plans, through FEB coordination.

The Federal Highway Administration (FHWA) also proved it would brook no argument when it came to enforcing the OPP. In February 1968 the Pennsylvania Department of Highways was set to open bidding for a project to build a bridge for Interstate Route 95 at Girard Point on the Schuylkill River when it was told by the FHWA engineer that federal funds would be provided only if the contractors were prepared to meet the conditions of the OPP. The Associated General Contractors of America complained that this provision was being inserted into the process less than two days before the formal opening of bids, but to no avail. The FHWA would not budge, and the state of Pennsylvania agreed; contractors had by now been aware of the OPP for several months, and the project would go forward only under its provisions.[19]

The AFL-CIO weighed in quickly. As the OPP went into effect, the AFL-CIO's Building Construction Trades Department (BCTD) was holding its annual convention in Bal Harbour, Florida. In response to the Cleveland, St. Louis, San Francisco, and Philadelphia plans, all of which had been implemented during 1967, the delegates issued a public resolution in opposition to the OPP. Calling the OFCC "overzealous" and "intemperate," and charging that the programs had resulted in "unwarranted delays on . . . construction projects," the resolution condemned the "use of such formulas as 'minority representation in every craft and every phase of work' on every federal and federally-assisted project, which formula is often impossible of fulfillment and destructive of established working conditions and performance standards." The delegates to the BCTD convention felt that their own policies were nondiscriminatory and that the programs being put forward by the OFCC were unfair to whites, would result in a decrease in the quality of work, had already resulted in a slowdown of construction, and, in any event, were illegal under the 1964 Civil Rights Act.[20]

Secretary of Labor Willard Wirtz, addressing the convention, defended the policies of the OFCC and said that these programs were not preferential toward any particular race; rather, they sought to address the effects of previous discrimination. He noted that he would be opposed to any sort of quota system and looked forward to working with the BCTD leadership to develop additional policies to increase nonwhite employment in the skilled trades, and he said that the Labor Department would continue to subsidize the local apprenticeship outreach programs.[21]

The BCTD position was not shared by mainstream civil rights organizations, which disagreed with the notion that the OPP was unfair to white workers. The local NAACP and NUL both came out in support of the plan in May 1968, just as the first contracts with pre-award affirmative action plans began to get approval from the contracting agencies.[22]

But clearly the most important external support for the OPP came from the city of Philadelphia, which announced in February 1968 that it would adopt the OPP for its own contracts, regardless of whether they received federal assistance. As monitored by the city's Commission on Human Relations, city contracts began to pass over low bidders unwilling to implement affirmative action goals similar to those contained in the OFCC plan. The city was followed in its decision by the local Catholic archdiocese in August and the quasi-public utilities in September. These moves represented a major expansion of the OPP as it went beyond federal and federally assisted contract construction.[23]

In June, with the first ten projects approved under the OPP, Stalvey could project the employment of 50 to 60 black workers in the seven critical trades (electricians, sheet metal workers, plumbers, roofers, ironworkers, steamfitters, and elevator constructors), or approximately 30 percent of the total number of workers, estimated at between 170 and 190. Contractors promised to make good-faith efforts to recruit black or Hispanic workers in each trade equal to or greater than the goals stated in their manning tables, hiring from outside the unions if necessary. As figure 4.1 demonstrates, the numbers of blacks projected to be employed in the critical

Figure 4.1. Projected Critical Trades Employees in Federal Contract Construction under the OPP, June–December 1968 (According to Pre-Award Affirmative Action Plans)

	Jun	Jul	Aug	Sep	Oct	Nov	Dec
■ Minority Employees	60	100	100	100	100	195	225
□ Total Employees	190	400	400	400	400	795	900

Source: Bennett O. Stalvey Jr., monthly reports, June, August, September, October, November, and December 1968 and January 1969, Records of the Department of Labor, Papers of the OFCC, Collection of the OFCC Assistant Director for Construction, box 24, "Monthly Reports, 1968–9" folder, National Archives and Records Administration, College Park, MD.

trades under the OPP continued to climb through December 1968, when approved affirmative action plans projected 225 blacks out of 900 workers in the critical trades—a more modest but still ambitious 25 percent. If these projected figures were actually implemented—and, based on his knowledge of the contractors and the number of skilled blacks in the community, Stalvey believed they would be—this would mean a major change for black employment in the critical trades.[24] According to these numbers, the OPP represented the beginning of the end of institutional racism in the Philadelphia building trades.

Whereas figure 4.1 represents the ambitions of the affirmative action plans approved under the OPP, figure 4.2 represents the reality. The OPP construction projects got off to a slow start because of a summertime rod setters' strike, which slowed ongoing projects and delayed new ones. Projects continued to be approved under the OPP between June and October, but no OPP-approved construction project actually broke ground until November 1968, a year after the official implementation date. That month, Stalvey reported that five of the six commenced projects were meeting or exceeding their affirmative action goals; the sixth was not yet employ-

Figure 4.2. Project Approval and Start Rate under the OPP and Number of Projects Meeting Pre-Award Projections for Nonwhite Hiring, June 1968–January 1969

	Jun	Jul	Aug	Sep	Oct	Nov	Dec	Jan
■ Approved	10	12	17	21	25	31	38	38
□ Started						6	36	38
■ Meeting Pre-Award Projections						5	7	8

Source: Bennett O. Stalvey Jr., monthly reports, November and December 1968 and January 1969, Records of the Department of Labor, Papers of the OFCC, Collection of the OFCC Assistant Director for Construction, box 24, "Monthly Reports, 1968–9" folder, National Archives and Records Administration, College Park, MD.

ing the critical trades. Each project employed different trades at different stages of construction, and the critical trades usually began work later in the life of a project.

In December and January, as the remaining approved projects broke ground, only about 15 percent of them met or exceeded their nonwhite hiring goals. If not for the delay caused by the rod setters' strike, the percentage likely would have approached 100 by that date, as the contractors increased their use of employees in the critical trades. Stalvey was confident that despite the delays caused by the strike, all OPP project contractors would meet or exceed their goals by late spring or early summer 1969.[25] In short, the OPP was only just beginning to work in January 1969, and it appeared to be headed toward success, despite ominous political rumblings in opposition.

Stalvey's conviction that the OPP was on the verge of success was based on the situation in Philadelphia; it did not account for politics in Washington. The OPP—like Macaluso's entire area coordinator program—had been developed in response to a bureaucratic "mood" on civil rights pervasive in the Johnson administration, inspired by the president's own rhetoric at his 1965 Howard University commencement address (and, from a legalistic standpoint, based on the imprimatur of Executive Order No. 11246). However, the OPP did not enjoy the explicit political backing of the White House. The Johnson administration saw no political gain in pitting two of its most important constituencies—civil rights leaders and sympathizers on the one hand, and organized labor on the other—against each other. Johnson himself had always trod lightly when it came to unions, seeing labor as critical to his political future; for example, as chairman of the PCEEO, he had allowed George Meany virtually unchecked authority in drafting the Union Programs for Fair Practices. Related programs that received more publicity—and explicit administration support—were the DOL's apprenticeship outreach and HUD's model cities, which together resulted in a nationwide deal in which the building trades agreed to train ghetto residents in construction skills while rebuilding the neighborhoods where they lived. This seemed to satisfy all interested parties except Herbert Hill of the NAACP, who pointed out that the program's "trainees" weren't actually apprentices and were given no guarantee of union membership upon completion of the program. But the OPP, with its resemblance to a quota system, was too much of a political hot potato for Johnson. The White House did not oppose the program, but it did not explicitly endorse it either.[26]

The OPP and Macaluso's other construction plans did not lack for antagonists. As we have seen, the unions opposed the plan as a quota system at the leadership level and walked off the job at the local level—at the construction site for the U.S. Mint. (Incidentally, the general contractor for the mint job, McCloskey & Co., and the contracting agency, GSA, were the same as in Washington's Area B construction project discussed in chapter 1.) Contractors also opposed the plan, not only because of the danger it posed to their fragile relationships with the unions but also, and more importantly, because the program's deliberate vagueness on the number of blacks to be employed led to potential obstacles in the bidding process and the possibility of increased costs after low bids had been accepted. Bidders had difficulty estimating such costs accurately and worried that over-estimating employee costs would result in the loss of bids. In other words, whereas unions opposed the OPP's goals for their resemblance to quotas, contractors worried that the goals were too vague and would have preferred outright quotas. With no outspoken allies in the White House and large, powerful enemies in the industry, it was only a matter of time before the OPP faced serious challenges in the political arena.

It was on the issue of vague bidding requirements that the plan came under attack in May 1968, even before the first contract had been signed. The attack came from an obscure government office, the GAO, and its even more obscure director, the comptroller general of the United States.

Comptroller General Elmer Staats presided over an incredibly powerful office with an accomplished professional's touch. Hugh Davis Graham called him "a gray bureaucrat of vintage invisibility." Staats had been hired by the GAO in 1939, not long after completing a PhD in public administration at the University of Kansas. In 1958 he became its deputy budget director, and in 1966 President Johnson appointed Staats to the top job.[27]

As powerful as it was, the GAO's authority was extraconstitutional. Although the office of comptroller general dated from the creation of the Treasury Department—part of the executive branch—in 1789, Congress created the GAO in the Budget and Accounting Act of 1921. The GAO had physical responsibility for the disbursement of government funds, in the sense that the office actually cut the checks to federal contractors—clearly an executive power. And the comptroller general—like Johnson's cabinet members—was nominated by the president and confirmed by the Senate. But as Congress's taxpayer watchdog, the GAO was an arm of the legislative branch and engaged in oversight of the executive departments, a task usually reserved to the legislature. In addition, by issuing written opinions on procurement legislation—opinions that had the force of common law—the comptroller general and his office functioned as a quasi-judiciary—at least as far as the federal purse was concerned.[28]

The GAO and government contractors made strange bedfellows indeed. Since the function of the GAO was to regulate government contracts on behalf of Congress and to rule on matters relating to procurement law, contractors usually feared the office of the comptroller general as a potential impediment to their securing of lucrative contracts; they tended to forge close relationships with officers of the contracting agencies instead. But now, with the FEB's involvement making the contracting agencies cold to any arguments against the OPP, the contractors and their congressional allies turned to Staats, who had already gained a reputation for taking on the executive branch on matters pertaining to individual contracts (an expansion of his jurisdiction over procurement law). Staats had set a precedent in 1966 by ruling on an individual case involving a small contract, but in 1968 he was ruling on the validity of major defense contracts, provoking a polemical battle with the attorney general that lasted until the end of the Johnson administration.[29]

In the winter of 1968, as the first OPP bids were moving into the pre-award phase, contractor complaints reached the ears of the ranking Republican on the House Committee on Public Works, William Cramer of Florida. A pro-business conservative, Cramer asked the comptroller general to investigate, and Staats looked into the matter. In May 1968 Staats warned Secretary Wirtz that the OPP failed to clearly set out hiring requirements in the invitations to bid. The requirement of a pre-award conference at which the low bidder could be disqualified from the contract, Staats maintained, constituted a post-bid hurdle that was antithetical to the bidding process whereby the government ensured that taxpayer dollars were efficiently spent. In short, the comptroller general felt that keeping costs down was more important than securing equal employment opportunity. Staats asked Wirtz to include concrete hiring requirements—quotas—in the official contract regulations issued through his office before the OPP went into effect.[30]

Staats's warning—a further example of his attempt to expand the powers of the GAO—seems important in retrospect, as shall become clear. But Wirtz did not see these concerns as particularly important, and the secretary was loath to include a quota system in official federal contract regulations. Title VII of the Civil Rights Act of 1964 explicitly forbade the preferential hiring of nonwhites to bring an employer's workforce in line with the racial makeup of the local community. The OPP did not in fact require preferential hiring; it required only that the contractor take affirmative steps to increase the nonwhite proportion of the workforce. Although this was a fine distinction, it was a valid one. Nevertheless, Wirtz did not make the affirmative action required under the OPP an official part of the federal labor regulations, and Staats's warning went unheeded.[31]

Staats wasn't finished with the OPP. Confident of the legality of his position, on November 18, 1968, the comptroller general took the extraordinary step of declaring the OPP illegal under procurement law and warned Wirtz that the GAO would not release funds for any additional contracts signed under it unless the DOL issued regulations. "Although it may be true that the present lack of specific detail . . . permits the utmost in creativity . . . it is equally true that it permits denial of a contract to a low bidder to be based on purely arbitrary or capricious decisions."[32] These discrepancies left too much discretion to individual federal officers like Bennett Stalvey, and without a formal appeals process, Staats believed the OPP was unfair to bidders.

To pro-OPP figures like Phelan, Sylvester, and the NAACP's Hill, this was a familiar obfuscation, reminiscent of the official attitude of the AFL-CIO. What the disingenuous Staats failed to remember was that federal contracts had never automatically gone to the lowest bidder; rather, they had gone to the lowest bidder that *met the requirements of the contract.* Staats was really saying that racism was not an important enough problem to warrant sanctions. This was similar to what Meany had told A. Philip Randolph before their public confrontation in 1959—that racism in individual unions, unlike communism or corruption, was not an important enough problem to warrant suspension from the federation. In Staats's opinion, the nondiscrimination clause in federal contracts did not carry the same value as other clauses pertaining to the contractor's fitness for the work, and he believed the federal government could disqualify potential contractors for other deficiencies (such as a poor record of on-time completion, failure to make budget, or simple lack of detail in the bid) but not for racial discrimination.

Although instigated by a southern congressman, this was ultimately a confrontation between two types of federal bureaucrats. On the one hand were Great Society liberals like Macaluso, Phelan, and Stalvey, who viewed social equity as the "third pillar" of public policy and believed that taxpayer dollars should be spent on programs that helped achieve racial (and later gender) equality. On the other hand were the traditional bureaucrats, represented by Staats. His school of thought held that public servants' only responsibilities were to ensure efficiency and economy—the first and second pillars of public policy. For Staats, the bureaucrat's role was to ignore the ends and concentrate on the means—to remove values and morals completely and focus on rules for the sake of rules.[33]

One might reasonably ask at this point exactly how much leeway bureaucrats had to act beyond the specific instructions of elected and appointed officials. In fact, they had much; elected and appointed officials were the bureaucrats' supervisors, but they had neither the time nor the ability to provide more than guidance. Although bureaucrats could be disciplined or even terminated for "cause," which included insubordination and failure to act, acts of outright insubordination were rare. The reality was that top-down policies were implemented with a speed and effectiveness determined (consciously or not) by the bureaucrats, and where specific policies did not exist, bureaucrats either took initiative or avoided independent thinking, based on their individual proclivities. Ultimately, therefore, bureaucrats had a considerable amount of leeway in terms of when, where, and how to interpret official policies. This had been a major part of the problem in the 1950s, when layers of bureaucracy prevented the PCGC from enforcing the nondiscrimination clause in federal contracts, and it was a major part of the solution in the 1960s as the OFCC staff developed and implemented the area plans. One important reason for the different behavior of these elements of the bureaucracy was Macaluso himself. Originally a Kennedy appointee, and therefore not a bureaucrat per se, Macaluso became something of a stealth bureaucrat when, during the Johnson administration, he joined the federal civil service (a "demotion" that would allow him to keep his job through the Ford administration). From within the bureaucracy, Macaluso was able to find creative bureaucratic ways to implement President Johnson's policy.[34]

Wirtz did not fight Staats's ruling. He did not have the explicit support of the White House; the attorney general was still fighting Staats on defense procurement; and, in any event, the Johnson administration had only eight weeks remaining in office. Following Graham, Nancy MacLean contends that the Johnson administration "ultimately shelved the idea for fear of clashes with unions, construction contractors, and conservative critics alike." But OFCC area coordinator Stalvey's reports show no such "shelving"; contractors continued to comply with the OPP (as revised) until March 1969, when Staats published his opinion, at which point they abandoned their affirmative action plans and the OFCC was back to square one. But as a new presidential administration took over, the OFCC—and other civil rights–related entities within the government—would face a number of other challenges.[35]

The Nixon Administration and Civil Rights: Mistakes and Setbacks

In 1968, while Phelan and Stalvey were implementing the OPP in Philadelphia, the nation experienced much tumult, centering on—but not limited to—the battle for the presidency. On March 31, facing increasingly sharp attacks from within his own party on his prosecution of the war in Vietnam, including a credible challenge from New York senator Robert F. Kennedy, President Johnson announced that he would not seek reelection, saying that the nation's concerns were too great for him to spend time campaigning. Four days later, civil rights activist and Nobel Peace Prize winner Martin Luther King Jr. was shot to death outside his hotel room in Memphis, Tennessee, where he had been advocating for the rights of black sanitation workers. Two months after that, on June 5, as he was claiming victory in the California Democratic primary, which likely would have swept him into the nomination and possibly the presidency, Senator Kennedy was shot to death. The Democratic nomination ultimately went to Vice President Hubert Humphrey, a key sponsor of the 1964 Civil Rights Act and Johnson's onetime civil rights czar. But Humphrey faced a backlash from working-class and southern whites who were incensed over what they saw as the administration's milquetoast response to the seemingly annual summertime urban riots, and he narrowly lost the White House to former vice president Richard M. Nixon.[36]

The Nixon administration quickly set a different tone on civil rights issues. Elected by a thin majority that included strong support in the white South among former Democrats such as South Carolina senator Strom Thurmond, Nixon understood that he would have to walk a fine political line between maintaining that support and following his own personal belief—inherent in his Quaker background and demonstrated by his vice presidential activities as PCGC chairman—in equal opportunity.[37] To keep this balance, he would have to choose his battles carefully, but in 1969 he stumbled—three times. The president's first political blunder came in the spring when a flap developed in a Senate committee over a decision by the EEOC and its young, Johnson-appointed chairman, Clifford Alexander.

The EEOC was created by act of Congress under Title VII of the Civil

Rights Act of 1964, which went into effect on July 2, 1965. Although the new commission should have supplanted the PCEEO, Congress failed to give the commission any real power—no authority to issue orders to recalcitrant employers or unions or even to sue in federal court under its own imprimatur. When conciliation—the commission's only real authority—failed to produce results, the EEOC would have to depend on the Department of Justice (DOJ) to sue under the "pattern or practice" section of the law. And so the EEOC—branded by critics a "toothless tiger"—focused on investigation, mediation, and referral—to either the OFCC or the DOJ.[38]

To ensure that the government did not give up any existing authority in the area of civil rights—the PCEEO could cancel contracts, debar contractors, and enforce fair employment in the civil service—President Johnson moved contract compliance to the OFCC in the DOL, and he moved fair employment in the federal government to the Civil Service Commission. The EEOC accepted private-sector complaints of unfair hiring and employment practices, engaged in conciliation activities to attempt to convince and cajole employers and unions to integrate, recommended in extreme cases that the attorney general bring suits against discriminating employers, and advocated—especially after White House aide Alexander took over in 1967—for Congress to amend the law so that the commission could issue cease-and-desist orders to segregated unions and employers and sue in federal court to have those orders enforced.[39]

With the advent of the Nixon administration, Clifford Alexander announced that he would not resign his position as chairman of the EEOC, arguing that the commission was by statute independent of any political party, with a fixed number of Democrats and Republicans. He vowed to remain until the end of his term in 1972, but in late March 1969 he was challenged on the commission's recent request that the OFCC debar three southern textile firms from defense contracts. The challenge came from Senator Everett Dirksen, an Illinois Republican who had played a key role in extracting important concessions from the sponsors of Title VII during debate in 1964. Dirksen felt that the EEOC was overstepping its authority, said that Alexander was harassing businesses, and threatened to go "to the highest office in the land to get somebody fired." Later that day the White House press secretary announced that the president would soon nominate a new chairman, and on April 8, reasoning that he would be incapable of doing his job effectively without White House support, Alexander submitted his resignation. News stories, editorials, and cartoons publicly blasted Nixon as having fired Alexander for "doing his job." The overwhelming—

and incorrect—opinion of black newspapers was that Dirksen was doing Nixon's bidding and that the president should not have interfered in the operations of the EEOC. Dirksen's motives were in fact based on a genuine concern that the EEOC's zeal to integrate was interfering with the prerogatives of free enterprise. Of course, Alexander's resignation would have little effect on equal employment opportunity; the EEOC was largely toothless, as we have seen. Alexander's most important contribution was his advocacy (stemming from his political savvy as a former White House aide) of a legislative amendment to Title VII that would give the EEOC certain sanctions and empower the agency to bring suit on its own. But by 1969, Congress had gotten the point and was moving in that direction already. Indeed, Congress had failed to do so in 1968 only for logistical reasons: the text of the amendment had been prepared too late for consideration on the calendar, and most observers believed it would be passed in one form or another in 1969 or 1970. Nonetheless, by removing Alexander and alienating the black press, Nixon had made his first political mistake on civil rights.[40]

Nixon's second political mistake came in midsummer, when his administration backed a bill to reform the EEOC. The administration's bill was at odds with the prevailing—and more ambitious—bill that had been delayed in the previous Congress. The extant bill would have given the EEOC cease-and-desist authority, meaning that the commission could order employers to hire complainants and award back pay and other damages, and it would have transferred the OFCC, with its contract cancellation and debarment authority, from the DOL to the EEOC. The administration's bill, in contrast—defended in the press and in congressional testimony by Nixon's new EEOC chairman, William H. Brown III—contained neither of these provisions. Both bills would have given the EEOC the ability to sue employers in federal court without going through the DOJ.[41]

Arguably, President Johnson had felt the same way about federal contract enforcement. Like Nixon, Johnson had opposed giving contract compliance to the EEOC, and he had created the OFCC in the DOL for that purpose. But in 1969 the situation was different. In 1965, faced with an EEOC without any real authority, Johnson had placed contract compliance in an executive department so that the staff could continue to act with executive imprimatur. By opposing a merger of contract compliance and the EEOC in 1965, Johnson had allowed the contract compliance staff to retain real power—to revoke contracts and debar contractors. Had he merged the two, Johnson would have effectively removed the authority to revoke and debar from the contract compliance staff, placing them under the control of a toothless tiger. But in 1969, the bill under consideration would give the EEOC actual powers for the first time—cease-and-desist authority, hiring and back-pay sanctions, and the ability to bring lawsuits. Such an agency would be perfectly appropriate for contract compliance, with the power to revoke and debar.

Nixon's new EEOC head, William Brown, had been nominated to fill one of the designated Republican seats on the EEOC by President Johnson in October 1968, but Senator Dirksen had placed a hold on his appointment. When Alexander announced his resignation—from the chairmanship but not the commission—President Nixon nominated Brown as his successor. Dirksen withdrew his hold on the nomination, and Brown was confirmed on May 10, 1969, "by a voice vote with a few audible nays."[42]

During his confirmation hearings, Brown had stated that he favored giving cease-and-desist powers to the EEOC. But as soon as Nixon's intent became clear, the new chairman went on record supporting the administration's version of the EEOC amendment, which would give the commission no such powers. And Nixon's status on civil rights was not helped when, during the flap over Brown's flip, an article appeared in the *Philadelphia Evening Bulletin* "estimating that of the 175 [EEOC] staffers in Washington more than 100 are thinking of leaving" over the perceived "incompetence" of the new chairman. Ultimately, neither bill would pass during the Ninety-first Congress, but the press picked up on Brown's apparent about-face, marking Nixon's second political mistake on civil rights after less than a year in office.[43]

The problem with not granting the EEOC cease-and-desist authority, but expecting it to rely on the power to sue in federal court, was not merely a matter of institutional procedure. Former chairman Alexander, who resigned his EEOC membership before the year was out, worried that without cease and desist, the fate of the commission's decisions on equal employment would be in the hands of southern judges, who presumably would not look favorably on attempts to integrate at the expense of immediate productivity, corporate profits, and the segregationist ethos. One such judge would soon deal yet another blow to Nixon's delicate balancing act: Clement F. Haynsworth Jr. of the federal appeals court in Virginia. The president nominated Haynsworth in the summer of 1969 to replace disgraced Supreme Court justice Abe Fortas, who resigned after a scandal involving questionable honoraria.[44]

Nixon came into the White House owing a debt to white southern conservatives, and early in his tenure in the Oval Office his staff developed what became known as the "southern strategy"—the deliberate courting of southern white (and reliably Democratic) votes to strengthen his tenuous support in Congress in the 1970 midterm elections (he was the first president in the twentieth century to enter office with both houses under the control of the opposition party) and ensure his own reelection in 1972. The Nixon administration, therefore, saw its political mistakes over the handling of the EEOC chairmanship and the proposed expansion of the commission's powers as ultimately less important than embarrassments that might harm the president among the growing Republican constituency in the white South.[45]

Senator Strom Thurmond's support of Nixon had marginalized a potential third-party spoiler among unreconstructed southerners, former Alabama governor George Wallace. To repay Thurmond, Nixon made a White House adviser of one of the senator's chief lieutenants, Harry Dent, and vowed to appoint a "strict constructionist" conservative judge to the Supreme Court, ostensibly to give the Court ideological and regional balance after fifteen years of its leaning northern and liberal. The Haynsworth appointment's connection to Thurmond was so overt that one NAACP correspondent called it a conspiracy and went so far as to file an unsuccessful lawsuit in civil court against the president and the South Carolina senator.[46]

Haynsworth himself was the fourth-generation scion of a plantation-owning North Carolina family. His record of trial decisions was generally antilabor and anti–civil rights, and many had been overturned on appeal. The nomination immediately garnered opposition from the AFL-CIO, the NAACP, and both the mainstream and the black press. Nevertheless, the American Bar Association gave Haynsworth its approval, the nomination was reported out of the Judiciary Committee (i.e., the committee approved the nomination for review by the full Senate), and it seemed likely that Haynsworth would be confirmed. But when reports surfaced that the nominee had presided over civil cases in which his wife's company was a litigant, this conflict of interest appeared too similar to the reasons for Justice Fortas's resignation, and Haynsworth's nomination was rejected by the Senate on November 29, 1969, by a vote of fifty-five to forty-five (making him the first Supreme Court nominee to be rejected since 1930). By failing to nominate a conservative southerner who could withstand public scrutiny, Nixon suffered a blow to his southern strategy and an embarrassment before his southern white conservative constituents.[47]

With his first year in office drawing to a close, Nixon had alienated the mainstream civil rights leadership and organized labor and suffered a major embarrassment in his campaign to bring the white South over to the Republican banner. And although the Haynsworth nomination had been defeated mainly because of a potential conflict of interest, the lesson of the three-month debate over the judge's qualifications was clear: the AFL-CIO and the NAACP represented a unified front against Nixon's southern strategy. When a fighter is on the ropes, he really has only two choices: get out of the ring, or come back swinging. Hardly the retiring type, Nixon sought a way to strike a blow. He found it in the Revised Philadelphia Plan.

The Revised Philadelphia Plan

As a civil rights agency, the OFCC was not immune to the adverse changes to the federal civil rights regimen that came with the new administration. The office endured personnel cutbacks, especially in the construction area coordinator program; the twenty area coordinators were decreased to ten regional coordinators, and their responsibilities were increased to cover all federal contracts, not just those involving construction. As one of Macaluso's key local officers, Stalvey made the cut and became OFCC regional coordinator for the mid-Atlantic region, including all of New Jersey, Pennsylvania, and Maryland.[48]

Stalvey's primary focus remained Philadelphia, where grassroots organizations were incensed over cancellation of the OPP. Stalvey worriedly reported that renewed protests at construction sites had the potential to become civil disorders as the summer approached. Further, without the OPP, the city's own plan was now in jeopardy, since it had relied on the OFCC and FEB for enforcement. And the Philadelphia Board of Education—which had been at the center of the 1963 protests—was conducting hearings on the use of its facilities by discriminatory construction unions. The abandonment of the OPP by contractors after Staats's published opinion put the outcome of those hearings in doubt, and Stalvey found that most of his job that spring involved—quixotically, for a federal official—working to maintain and expand the local government's affirmative action plans.[49]

What Stalvey needed to take the pressure off the local government's OPP "spin-offs" was help from his superiors in Washington. Macaluso would have liked to give Stalvey more support, but he had a number of increased responsibilities due to the cutbacks in his program. In any case, as a Democrat appointed during the Kennedy administration, Macaluso was doing his best to keep his political head down in what had nominally become a civil service position (and thus theoretically secure, despite the change of administration).[50] Sylvester had been promoted out of the OFCC by President Johnson in 1968 and was no longer in the federal service; the interim director would soon be replaced by the Nixon administration. The transition was not giving Stalvey the help he needed.

This changed on March 14, 1969, when President Nixon nominated Arthur Fletcher, a black Republican from Washington State, as DOL assistant secretary for employment standards. With the primary responsibility of establishing working relationships with local government officials around the nation, and with the OFCC falling under his portfolio, Fletcher quickly evaluated the various OFCC programs and decided that Stalvey, Macaluso, and Phelan had been on the right track with the OPP. On June 12, 1969, he announced that the Philadelphia Plan would be rewritten to address the objections of the comptroller general and that the revised version would be implemented forthwith.[51]

Arthur Fletcher was born in 1924 in Arizona, the son of a soldier in a black cavalry unit of the U.S. Army. His family moved from one army base to another for most of his childhood, finally settling in Junction City, Kansas, where Fletcher graduated from the local integrated high school after organizing a boycott of the segregated yearbook. He joined the army and was sent to Europe during World War II, where he was wounded while serving under General George Patton. Fletcher returned to Kansas and attended Washburn University in Topeka on the GI Bill. A college football career resulted in his becoming a defensive end for the Los Angeles Rams in 1950, and he went on to become the first black player for the Baltimore Colts. During his brief football career, Fletcher donated some of his income to the plaintiffs in the antisegregation case against the Topeka School Board (later known as *Brown v. Board of Education*).

Fletcher returned to Kansas again in 1954 to campaign among black voters for liberal Republican gubernatorial candidate Fred Hall. When Hall won, he made Fletcher deputy highway commissioner. But two years later Hall lost his reelection bid, and Fletcher couldn't find work. He and his young family followed the ex-governor to California in 1958, where Fletcher became a schoolteacher in Oakland. In 1965 he was chosen to head a Great Society education program in Washington State. He turned that into the East Pasco Self-Help Cooperative. *That* organization's success won Fletcher a seat on the Pasco City Council in 1967, and its tenets corresponded with "black capitalism," Nixon's proposal to mesh the achievements of the civil rights era with the corporatist ideology of the Republican Party. In 1968 Nixon tapped Fletcher for service on a special minority advisory committee for the presidential campaign. This served Fletcher's *own* political ends: he won the Republican nomination for lieutenant governor of Washington, winning primaries in every county—a particularly remarkable feat considering that less than 2 percent of the party electorate was black. Although Fletcher narrowly lost the general election, the Nixon administration did not forget his early support or the role his self-help civil rights theories would play in the new administration.[52]

Upon confirmation by the Senate, Fletcher shared the mantle of senior black official in the Nixon administration with former CORE director James Farmer, now an assistant secretary at HEW. With that mantle came a moral responsibility. Fletcher's political beliefs may have differed from more left-leaning leaders of the civil rights movement, but his appointment represented continuity with the black officials of the Johnson years, during which the civil rights movement had seen its greatest successes. As assistant secretary of labor, Fletcher represented the drive for integration in federal contract employment. And since the most blatant discrimination in contract employment was occurring in the skilled building trades, Fletcher resolved to go to work in that area. With the permission of Secretary of Labor George P. Shultz, he took the OFCC into his portfolio.[53]

Fletcher had done his homework well. Under the Revised Philadelphia Plan (RPP), contracting agencies would include detailed nonwhite hiring goals or percentage ranges in the invitation to bid, thereby precluding the possibility that contractors would face additional costs as a result of post-bid negotiations. And he ensured that the terms of the RPP had been cleared by the solicitor of labor, who ruled that the plan was legal under procurement law, thereby obviating any further challenge from the comptroller general's office.[54]

Like the OPP, the RPP covered the same five counties in the Greater Philadelphia area—Bucks, Chester, Delaware, Montgomery, and Philadelphia—as well as five skilled trades—ironworkers, plumbers, steamfitters, sheet metal workers, and electrical workers. Dropped from the revised plan were the operating engineers, with whom the DOL was then working on a nationwide integration agreement; added to the new plan were the roofers (who had excluded blacks by canceling their apprenticeship program) and elevator constructors (whose relatively small membership excluded blacks altogether).[55]

Released on June 27, 1969, the RPP did not state specific goals, but after public hearings held in July by Macaluso and Stalvey (attended by representatives of the plumbers but none of the other affected trades, who stayed away in protest) and in August by Fletcher, the OFCC released the details of the program. On average, they expected the covered trades to be approximately 7 percent black or Hispanic by the end of 1970, rising to about 25 percent by the end of 1973. These goals were significantly lower than those of the OPP, at least for the first three years; Fletcher called those higher goals an unrealistic public relations ploy by the previous administration. "There are differences between this administration and the last," Fletcher said. "We're not running a P.R. program; we're running a program that will have results."[56]

Another important difference between the RPP and the OPP was the "good-faith" clause, which Fletcher pointed to as evidence that the goals were not, in fact, synonymous with "quotas." If a contractor failed to meet its agreed-upon goals for nonwhite hiring, it need only show that it had exercised "good faith" in attempting to do so for funding to continue (as long as such "good faith" was not limited to simply asking the union for workers). The term was deliberately left undefined so as to give contractors that exercised affirmative action as much leeway as possible should their efforts fail to produce results.

The RPP also contained a training component that the OPP had lacked. The RPP called on the DOL's Manpower Administration Office to provide funding for nonwhite training programs (independent of the unions, if necessary) that would select youths from Philadelphia's black community to receive on-the-job training on federal projects at no additional cost to the contractor.[57]

After being declared legal by the solicitor of labor, the RPP quickly earned the endorsements of two key players within the administration. A senior Justice Department official said, "We find [the plan] to be consistent with the executive order [No. 11246] and with the Civil Rights Act of 1964." And unlike his predecessor Wirtz, who had never publicly endorsed the OPP, Secretary of Labor Shultz called the RPP "a fair and realistic approach, not an arbitrary imposition, in the pursuit of goals I believe are reasonable." The editors of the *New York Times* also endorsed the plan and speculated that the Shultz and DOJ endorsements indicated that support for the program reached all the way up to the White House.[58]

In the civil rights community, support came quickly from such longtime advocates of construction integration as Herbert Hill and Philadelphia

NAACP president Cecil B. Moore, who were happy to see the government finally taking what appeared to be aggressive action to enforce the non-discrimination clause and integrate the trades. And the RPP received a big boost from the construction industry when the Mechanical Contractors Association of Philadelphia endorsed the plan as well. Fletcher personally visited the executive director of the Philadelphia Urban League and NAACP chief Roy Wilkins to promote the plan.[59]

The NUL and NAACP were officially leery of quotas owing to their restrictive nature as well as their propensity to inflame white sentiment against civil rights causes, and these organizations had to be convinced that the specific goals of the RPP represented the minimum, not the maximum, numbers expected to be hired. Similar plans had been attempted during the Great Depression, when Interior Secretary Harold Ickes had first used the weight of the federal government in the construction market to effect equal opportunity. The result had been to set quotas at the proportion of blacks employed in the construction industry before the Depression, which mitigated the worst effects of the economic downturn but relegated blacks to discriminatory 1930 employment levels.[60]

The organizations also worried about how their endorsement of a government-sponsored quota system would affect their support in the white liberal community, particularly among Jews. Quotas had been used to exclude Jews from elite colleges such as Harvard, and they had been a common restriction on Jews in Europe going back to the Middle Ages. The establishment of Brandeis University, a secular Jewish college, on a strictly nonquota basis in 1948 had been meant as a strike against quotas in any form.[61] The endorsement of the RPP by leaders of the NUL and NAACP was qualified with the caveat that the plan not engage in any firm quota system.

The endorsement of the RPP by administration officials and civil rights leaders meant little to Elmer Staats, however. On August 5, 1969, disregarding the opinion of the solicitor of labor, the comptroller general found the RPP to be illegal.[62] His ruling was based not on procurement law but on section 703(j) of Title VII of the Civil Rights Act of 1964, which held:

> Nothing in this title shall be interpreted to require any employer, employment agency, labor organization, or joint labor-management committee subject to this title to grant preferential treatment to any individual or to any group because of the race, color, religion, sex, or national origin of such individual or group on

account of an imbalance which may exist with respect to the total number or percentage of persons . . . admitted to membership . . . by any labor organization, or admitted to . . . any apprenticeship or other training program, in comparison with the total number or percentage of persons of such race, color, religion, sex, or national origin in any community, State, section, or other area, or in the available work force.[63]

In other words, Title VII did not support quotas or preferential treatment to remedy the discrimination for which Title VII had been passed.

Staats found, in particular, that the RPP could easily be used to discriminate against whites. Posing a hypothetical situation, he asserted: "if . . . a contractor requires 20 plumbers and is committed to a goal of employment of at least five from minority groups, every nonminority applicant for employment in excess of 15 would . . . be [discriminated against] in his opportunity for employment, because the contractor is committed to . . . employ five applicants from minority groups." This requirement that whites be rejected after their quota had been filled, Staats felt, constituted discrimination under Title VII, which afforded the same protections to whites as it did to blacks.[64]

Further, in citing Title VII in his ruling against the RPP, Staats revealed that the true nature of his opposition to the Philadelphia Plan (and that of his congressional allies such as William Cramer) was abhorrence of racial quotas rather than genuine concern for the cost to contractors, which had been his complaint about the OPP. Without any evident violation of procurement law, he reached out to other legislation. In doing so, Staats was again attempting to extend his authority. Few in the executive branch would begrudge the comptroller general his right to pass on procurement law; that was, after all, one of the main functions of the GAO. But by declaring the RPP illegal under the Civil Rights Act, he was stating that he had the authority to interpret laws having nothing to do with procurement.[65]

What's more, Staats was now reversing his earlier opinion. In 1968, by arguing that the vagueness of the OPP goals was unfair to contractors, Staats had implied that he would have preferred firm quotas. Now, in 1969, he was condemning the RPP for precisely that solution.

In any event, Staats was joined in his opposition to the RPP by the *Philadelphia Bulletin,* which, as the voice of the city's commercial interests, decried the plan's "quotas" as potentially damaging to community relations by pitting whites against blacks for the same jobs. (Of course, the black community had already been "damaged" by the withholding of those jobs in the first place.) The *Bulletin* argued that the interests of the black community would be better served by more federal funding of the local apprenticeship outreach program, wherein the NTULC trained local youths for apprenticeship examinations. In this opinion they were joined by AFL-CIO president Meany, as well as the leaders of the local Building Construction Trades Council.[66]

With Staats asserting his authority to rule on laws unrelated to procurement, the Nixon administration had to either fight Staats's interpretation or allow the comptroller general, in essence, to set up the GAO as a coequal branch of government. Attorney General John Mitchell chose to fight, and on September 22, 1969, he issued his formal response to Staats's opinion. He conceded that the comptroller general could opine on procurement issues related to other laws, such as the 1964 Civil Rights Act, but stated that such opinions, unlike those limited strictly to procurement law, were not final. On this matter, the comptroller general could be overruled by the attorney general, Mitchell claimed, and only an act of Congress or concurring federal court decision could result in Staats's opinion having the force of law.

In response to Staats's specific objections, Mitchell said, "The obligation of nondiscrimination . . . does not require and, in some circumstances, may not permit obliviousness or indifference to the racial consequences of alternative courses of action which involve the application of outwardly neutral criteria." In other words, nondiscrimination and "color-blindness" were not always compatible; race could be considered to implement the nondiscrimination clause in contracts and comply with Title VII. He said that if Staats's hypothetical plumbing contractor indeed made a good-faith effort to recruit black workers, such situations as Staats feared would rarely arise, and if they did, a good-faith effort would inoculate the contractor from charges of discrimination and would allow the hiring of the sixteenth white if he were best qualified.[67] The RPP did not establish quotas, which would have required the hiring of a fixed number of black workers. Rather, the RPP set minimum goals for minority hiring, assuming that a good-faith attempt to meet the goals would generally assure a workplace of more equal opportunity for all.

Interestingly, neither Mitchell's interpretation nor any other legal interpretation at the time (nor any historians from Hugh Davis Graham in 1989 to Terry Anderson in 2004) considered the fact that section 703(j) did *not* outlaw quotas. Taken literally, the opening clause—"Nothing in this title shall be interpreted to require"—meant only that Title VII did not *authorize* quotas. The subsection did not explicitly declare quotas illegal, stating only that they were not *required* for compliance with Title VII. Authorities operating outside of Title VII—such as the OFCC, which operated pursuant to Title VI—could mandate quotas, as long as such quotas were based on authority held outside of Title VII.[68]

This was the case with the RPP. The plan drew its authority not from Title VII but from Title VI, which governed federal expenditures, and from Executive Order No. 11246, which gave the OFCC the power to cancel contracts. Officers of the OFCC could not file a complaint with the EEOC for a contractor's failure to comply with a quota because the EEOC handled complaints of discrimination under Title VII; nor could they ask the DOJ to file a lawsuit under Title VII, for the same reason. But they could certainly withhold federal funds from such a contractor. What's more, the RPP did not require quotas per se; rather, it allowed contractors with stated goals for minority hiring to obtain federal contracts. To be clear: when the OFCC threatened to revoke a contract or debar a contractor for failure to comply with the nondiscrimination clause, the office was not violating Title VII because that title did not apply. The OFCC was acting pursuant to its authority outlined in Title VI (and Executive Order No. 11246). In 1979 the Supreme Court addressed this question in *United Steelworkers v. Weber,* finding that section 703(j) assumed, by stating that Title VII did not allow quotas, that quotas were otherwise legal.[69]

Staats's objections also relied on the fact that the authors of the civil rights law did not intend to establish quotas—the "legislative intent" argument—and it seems quite clear that this is the case. In June 1964, according to Hugh Davis Graham, "when Humphrey was . . . defending the Senate's compromise with Dirksen, he explained that Section 703(j) on racial balance was added to 'state the point [that] Title VII does not require an employer to achieve any sort of racial balance in his work force by giving preferential treatment.'"[70] But what scholars of legislative intent fail to remember is that two senators—or ten, or even thirty—does not a law make. Legislative intent beyond the letter of the law is in fact impossible to ascertain. To truly understand legislative intent, one would have to divine the intent of each person who voted aye—an insurmountable task, even if all were alive, willing to speak on record, and truthful. The authors of a bill and its amendments often want something more or less than what is reflected in the language, but ultimately, the only evidence we have of *real* legislative intent is the language of the law itself—which is the only thing the majority actually approved. And the law disallows quotas only for employment governed by Title VII.

A quick example illustrates the point. The legislative history of the inclusion of protection against sex discrimination in the Civil Rights Act of 1964 is well known. Virginia Democrat Howard Smith introduced an amendment to add the word "sex" to Title VII in the hope that it would scuttle the bill. While feigning seriousness, he made it quite clear on the floor of the House of Representatives that he not only opposed protecting women from sex discrimination but also opposed the entire bill. The amendment passed; the word "sex" was added to Title VII, and the bill was signed into law. Were the federal government to respect legislative intent in this case, it might be obligated to ignore complaints of sex discrimination (and for a few years, the EEOC basically did just that). But the modern women's workplace rights movement traces its origins to Title VII, because by adding that word to the bill and passing it into law—whatever Representative Smith's intentions—Congress declared sex discrimination illegal.[71] Legislative intent is not law; statute is.

Despite the comptroller general's ruling, Fletcher signed an order on September 23, 1969—the day after the release of Attorney General Mitchell's opinion—implementing the RPP. One month later, on October 23, the first RPP contract was signed between HEW and Bristol Steel and Iron Works of Richmond, Virginia, to build "an addition to a children's hospital and a child guidance center" in Philadelphia. By the end of 1969 Stalvey was able to report that there were already seven contracts under the RPP, with a value of more than $30 million (although none of the projects had broken ground due to cold weather).[72]

With the comptroller general and the attorney general at an impasse over the legality of the RPP, the question would have to be decided by Congress, the federal courts, or both. And for the proponents of the RPP to prevail, they would need the political support of the White House. Nixon's White House, however, had thus far not demonstrated any particular zeal for civil rights issues. To secure White House support for the RPP, Fletcher and Shultz had to demonstrate the program's political value, and their efforts received a boost in the fall of 1969 as protests broke out at construction sites in Pittsburgh, Chicago, and elsewhere in the nation—protests far more potent and widespread than those seen at sites in Philadelphia and Newark in the spring of 1963.

According to an EEOC report, blacks constituted more than 16 percent of the population of Pittsburgh, while the percentage of blacks in the skilled building trades in the city stood at only 1 percent. On August 28, 1969, claiming that although its apprenticeships were "promoted extensively" it had "not been able to recruit enough [blacks] into the construction industry, try hard as we have," the Western Pennsylvania Master Builders' Association—the Pittsburgh construction contractors' umbrella organization—refused to participate in the extension of a black-controlled apprenticeship outreach and training program designed to increase the number of black youths in construction apprenticeships. The association claimed that it had participated in an extensive outreach program and listed a series of actions it had taken to integrate in response to being "singled out" by local black activists. But the association's claims fell short, rooted as they were in statistics that included the integrated—but unskilled—laborers, the largest union listed.[73]

In response, mass protests broke out at several major construction sites around the city. Clashes between protesters and police resulted in the injury of 45 people (including 12 policemen) and 180 arrests. Two days later, as negotiations resulted in the temporary halting of work at several job sites, angry white construction workers organized a protest of their own at Pittsburgh's city hall. Undeterred, black community activists organized weekly "Black Monday" protests at construction sites, demanding not only an extension of the apprenticeship outreach program but also integration at the journeyman level. Negotiations with the contractors continued throughout September and October.[74]

The concept of "Black Mondays" proved transferable. In Chicago, NUL statistics estimated the building trades' overall nonwhite component—including both skilled and less skilled trades—at 3 percent, whereas the local building trades council estimated it to be 10 percent but would not break that figure down by individual craft. In August protests shut down twenty building sites, and HUD threatened to delay all contracts in the city until the industry could work out the tensions. Consciously recalling the late Martin Luther King's "Letter from a Birmingham Jail," the Reverend Jesse Jackson, who had been arrested while protesting at a Chicago building site, wrote a letter of his own from jail: "We do not seek to take white jobs. But neither do we intend to allow whites to keep Black jobs while we are passively quiet and docile." The letter continued, "there will be no more rest and tranquility until our just pleas are heeded. Many of the whites are employed upon the prerogatives of discrimination and exclusionary procedures."[75]

With similar protests erupting in Seattle, Los Angeles, and Buffalo and still more planned for San Francisco, Milwaukee, Cleveland, and Boston, Fletcher announced that he would hold hearings on the building trades in Chicago on September 24, 1969, in anticipation of issuing an affirmative action program for Chicago similar to the RPP. But instead of orderly proceedings in the Chicago federal building, Fletcher was forced to postpone the hearings and move the location to the better-secured customs house when thousands of white construction workers blocked the entrance and chanted, "Blacks, yes! Gangs, no!" (One of the organizations that had organized the protests at the Chicago job sites was the Conservative Vice Lords, a local street gang.)[76]

The construction workers quickly turned to violence, pummeling a black motorist's car (as well as a police officer who intervened). When four black youths were surrounded by the mob, one brandished a gun and fired several warning shots into the air. After being beaten by the crowd, the four were arrested for gun possession. A small group of white women, holding placards in favor of union and job site integration, were surrounded and threatened by the "cursing, flag-waving, beer-drinking white construction workers," as the *Philadelphia Tribune* called them. But by then it was the third day of such protests, and the police had become better organized. The women were protected, and Fletcher was able to hold his hearings, which resulted in the contractors, unions, and community groups agreeing to a voluntary plan to admit as many as 4,000 more blacks into the construction unions by the end of 1971. The OFCC was able to gather enough information to put seventeen contractors on notice that they would be debarred unless they complied with the nondiscrimination clause of their federal contracts.[77]

If the botched handling of the EEOC chairmanship, the failed nomination of a conservative southerner to the Supreme Court, and the massive demonstrations at construction sites around the country weren't enough to convince the White House to support the RPP, rising inflation would be. The escalating cost of the war in Vietnam had led to rapidly rising inflation rates, and Nixon's cutbacks of domestic programs had not been sufficient to curb it. Unable (or unwilling) to make good on his campaign promise to decrease American involvement in (and therefore American costs related to) the war in Vietnam, Nixon needed another area where he could attack inflation. Rapidly rising construction wages seemed to be an obvious target and, with the trades' bad press for discrimination, an easy one. At the president's urging, Secretary Shultz studied the skilled construction workers' union-mandated wage increases. The administration was determined to reassign blame for the nation's economic woes.[78]

The Construction Users' Anti-Inflation Roundtable, an organization of very large contracting companies, wholeheartedly agreed that union wages were a prime culprit for rising inflation. Of course, they knew that the union case for high wages was based on the seasonality of construction employment; high wages were necessary to help workers keep up with the rising cost of living. But with the White House analyzing wages as a problem leading to inflation, the roundtable seized the opportunity to strike a blow against union power.[79]

In addition to its desire to take positive action on civil rights after the EEOC debacle, the White House had found a way to scapegoat the construction unions for the war-induced rising inflation. The RPP served that purpose and provided a convenient wedge issue with the potential to split the organized labor–civil rights coalition that had defeated the Haynsworth nomination. In the fall of 1969 President Nixon and his staff committed themselves to supporting the RPP against the comptroller general and his congressional allies.

The notion that Nixon used the Philadelphia Plan for the political purpose of dividing the civil rights leadership from organized labor has been repeated by copious outside analysts and three White House insiders. Stephen Clapp first posited it in 1971. In "Divide and Rule," Clapp notes, "What the hiring plans have done is increase animosity between blacks and the labor movement, which has been used to political advantage by [Republican] mayors and governors" such as New York's Governor Nelson Rockefeller and Mayor John Lindsay (as discussed in greater detail in the next chapter). As evidence for his thesis, Clapp interviewed Bayard Rustin, George Meany, Clifford Alexander, and Herbert Hill. Historians have generally drawn similar conclusions. Graham, in *The Civil Rights Era,* sees Shultz's subsequent promotion to head the White House Office of Management and Budget as a political payoff for hitting labor with the RPP, and he adds that the inclusion of Hispanics, specifically Cubans, to affirmative action coverage by the RPP was crassly political. J. Larry Hood, in "The Nixon Administration and the Revised Philadelphia Plan for Affirmative Action," sees the RPP as an exercise in the expansion of presidential power at the expense of Congress (addressed later). Joan Hoff's *Nixon Reconsidered,* meanwhile, is largely an attempt to view Nixon beyond the prism of Watergate. Nevertheless, she admits that Nixon used the RPP to draw attention to the civil rights issues of the

North and away from the South, as part of the southern strategy. Judith Stein, in *Running Steel, Running America,* finds that Nixon pushed the RPP to break unions' control over wage levels. Nancy MacLean in *Freedom Is Not Enough,* Grace Palladino in *Skilled Hands, Strong Spirits,* and Terry Anderson in *The Pursuit of Fairness* concur with Graham. Kevin Yuill disagrees in *Richard Nixon and the Rise of Affirmative Action,* noting that the RPP threatened to split useful constituencies in the southern strategy as much as it threatened to split the civil rights–labor coalition. Although Yuill's is a compelling argument, it falls short based on the accounts of White House insiders. In 1971 presidential civil rights aide Leonard Garment confirmed that the administration expected contractors to use the Philadelphia Plan as "leverage" against the power of the unions, and Fletcher made similar public statements. Finally, senior White House aide John Ehrlichman, in his 1982 memoir *Witness to Power,* specifically states that Nixon fought the battle to save the RPP to split the civil rights–labor coalition.[80]

Congressional debate over the conflict between the administration and the comptroller general began in early August. After Republican senator Paul Fannin of Arizona publicized Staats's rebuttal to Shultz's statement on the legality of the RPP, Democratic senator John McClellan of Arkansas, chairman of the Appropriations Committee, rose before the full Senate on August 13, 1969, to tell his colleagues about what he considered an "act of defiance" on the part of the secretary of labor.[81]

Fannin and McClellan were strange bedfellows. As a corporate-minded Republican, Fannin opposed the RPP for the same reason his colleague from Illinois, Everett Dirksen, had opposed Clifford Alexander's activities at the EEOC: he saw it as governmental intrusion in the prerogatives of business. McClellan, in contrast, was a southern Democrat who opposed the RPP for traditional racist reasons: if Congress were to allow the Nixon administration to force construction contractors in the North to integrate, the administration's next focus might be on the southern workplace or—even worse—on the still very segregated public schools. A public challenge to an integration program in a northern city might serve to deflect the press's attention from the slow pace of integration in the South.[82]

When it became clear over the following months that the administration would not back down in its promotion of the RPP, Democrat Sam Ervin of North Carolina resolved that his Subcommittee on the Separation of Powers (a subcommittee of the Senate Committee on the Judiciary) would hold hearings and solicit written opinions on the matter, which it

did during October and November 1969. EEOC chairman Brown submitted a brief in which he supported the RPP as a legitimate and necessary plan for affirmative action. Secretary Shultz submitted a lengthy
legal justification of the plan, in consultation with the solicitor of labor.
In public testimony before the committee, Staats reiterated his opposition
to the plan, stating that Shultz and Mitchell, in their zeal to implement
the program, failed to understand the truly coercive nature of the RPP. He
explained that although the plan itself did not call for quotas, he believed
that contractors, desperate not to lose contracts, would impose hard quotas to avoid the wrath of the OFCC. Quotas in fact, if not in intent, were
quotas nonetheless, and they rendered the RPP illegal, he said, under the
Civil Rights Act.[83]

Staats upped the ante on November 9, 1969, when he wrote a letter to
all contractors in Philadelphia stating that he would not disburse funds to
them for any contracts signed under the RPP. This was not a move against
the contractors themselves, most of which would not request funds for
RPP contracts for several months, but rather a warning shot at the administration. Staats was flexing his muscles. He followed this letter with another
to Shultz, along with a copy of his Senate testimony, saying, "the General Accounting Office will regard use of the Plan as a violation of the
Civil Rights Act of 1964 in passing upon the legality of matters involving
expenditures of appropriated funds for federal or federally-assisted contracts incorporating the Plan."[84] Between the activities of the Ervin committee and these threats from Staats, the comptroller general and his allies
had thrown down the gauntlet. Just how far the Nixon White House would
go to take it up remained an open question.

But it would not be the Ervin committee that took formal action
against the RPP. During his testimony, Staats recommended that Congress
uphold his ruling by passing an appropriations law. Staats was only seeking to protect what he saw as the prerogatives of his office, and senators like Ervin were uninterested in a drawn-out debate over affirmative
action. And so it was the Senate Appropriations Committee, chaired by
notorious segregationist Richard Russell, a Democrat from Georgia, that
led the attack. On December 2, 1969, Staats wrote to Senator Robert Byrd,
a Democrat from West Virginia and a member of the committee, requesting that he attach a rider to an appropriations bill that would establish
Staats's authority to rule on the legality of all matters related to procurement, regardless of which laws he drew from in drafting his opinion.[85]

In December 1969 the Senate Appropriations Committee was considering a supplemental appropriations bill, H.R. 15209, which had already been approved by the House of Representatives. On Wednesday, December 17, the committee was prepared to vote on the bill, and most observers expected it to be ready for the president's signature before the Christmas break. Just prior to the vote, Senator Byrd introduced the following rider:

> Sec. 904. In view of, and in confirmation of, the authority vested in the Comptroller General of the United States by the Budget and Accounting Act of 1921, as amended, no part of the funds appropriated or otherwise made available by this or any other Act shall be available to finance, either directly or through any Federal aid or grant, any contract or agreement which the Comptroller General of the United States holds to be in contravention of any federal statute.[86]

The Byrd rider would give the opinions of the comptroller general the force of law on any matter dealing with the federal budget, explicitly lifting the limitation of his authority to procurement law. Were the Byrd rider to pass, Staats's opinions on matters outside of procurement law would be final, and the RPP would be illegal. In short, the GAO would become a virtual fourth branch of government in charge of the federal treasury. And Byrd—that great senatorial upholder of the Constitution—would sublimate his sense of the constitutional right to his sense of the segregationist right.

The choice of the supplemental appropriations bill for inclusion of the Byrd rider was ingenious. H.R. 15209 had been passed by the House of Representatives to provide federal support to the survivors of Hurricane Camille and to address other pressing matters. Once it had been approved by the committee, it was expected to be approved pro forma and quickly by Congress as a whole, with few senators or congressmen willing to oppose disaster relief. For the same reason, the bill was unlikely to receive a presidential veto. The enemies of the RPP—Staats, the AFL-CIO, southern segregationists, and construction contractors—had chosen their plan of attack carefully, and the committee approved the Byrd rider for inclusion in the bill and unanimously reported it to the full Senate.[87]

Senate proponents of the RPP got their chance to attack the Byrd rider the next day, on Friday, December 18, when the full Senate considered the supplemental appropriations bill. New York senator Jacob Javits and

Hawaii senator Hiram Fong, both Republicans, argued that the RPP would be helpful to blacks and Hispanics and that its legality should be challenged in the courts, not in Congress. Javits worried that the Byrd rider would give far too much power to the comptroller general. Their efforts to have the Senate declare the rider "not germane" and strike it from the bill failed. The Senate approved the bill, with the rider attached. Since the Senate bill now differed from the House bill, the House-Senate conference committee met on Saturday, December 20, to reconcile the two versions. The conference committee approved the Senate version with the Byrd rider. This left the fate of the Byrd rider—and therefore the legality of the RPP—to the House of Representatives, which scheduled a vote on the Senate version for Monday, December 22. If the House members voted to recommit the bill to the Senate, rejecting the Byrd rider, they would run the risk of not approving an important disaster relief bill before the holiday break, a political faux pas.[88] Things did not look good for the Philadelphia Plan, and it appeared that the administration had suffered yet another setback on civil rights.

When news of the Byrd rider and its passage by the Senate reached the White House, Nixon held a meeting in the Oval Office with Shultz, Fletcher, press secretary Ronald Ziegler, civil rights aide Leonard Garment, and House minority leader Gerald Ford to strategize their response. Immediately the group swung into action. Fletcher pressed the NAACP and NUL to actively lobby Congress, while Shultz worked to get the industrial unions—many of which were already significantly integrated, and whose leaders were resentful of the craft unions' continued recalcitrance—to repudiate AFL-CIO president Meany's statements in opposition to the RPP. Ford, for his part, worked to ensure that every Republican in the House of Representatives voted against the Byrd rider.[89]

The president told the press that the RPP had his full support, noting that "the Philadelphia Plan does not set quotas; it points to goals." Giving three press statements on the subject over four days, he urged the House to reject the Byrd rider and threatened a veto, saying that he might ask Congress to return immediately after Christmas, if need be, to pass a relief bill that didn't nullify the RPP:

Nothing is more unfair than that the same Americans who pay taxes should by any pattern of discriminatory practices be deprived of an equal opportunity to work on federal construction contracts. . . .
    The Attorney General has assured the Secretary of Labor that

the Philadelphia Plan is not in conflict with Title VII of the Civil Rights Act of 1964. I, of course, respect the right and duty of the Comptroller General to render his honest and candid views to the Congress. If in effect we have here a disagreement in legal interpretation between the Attorney General and the Comptroller General the place for the resolution of this issue is in the courts.

However, the Rider adopted by the Senate last night, would not only prevent the federal departments from implementing the Philadelphia Plan; it could even bar a judicial determination of the issue.

Therefore, I urge the conferees to permit the continued implementation of the Philadelphia Plan while the courts resolve this difference between Congressional and Executive legal opinions.[90]

With the president vigorously and publicly backing the Philadelphia Plan, Ziegler took the offensive, announcing that if the Byrd rider were ultimately defeated and Staats continued to refuse to disburse funds under the RPP, Attorney General Mitchell would sue the GAO. Shultz and Fletcher held two press conferences at the White House to explain why the RPP was important and how it would be nullified if Congress passed the rider. Deliberately playing on a growing national consensus for fair play (long inherent in liberal beliefs and now becoming an important tenet of racially conservative thought, ironically, as a means of combating affirmative action) and invoking the name of a slain civil rights leader and imagery from his days as a football player, Fletcher told reporters that "the name of the game is to put some economic flesh and bones on Dr. King's dream."[91]

In the House, Ford circulated comments written by Shultz in opposition to the Byrd rider called "Why Vote to Recommit," which explained that the rider gave sweeping, unprecedented authority to the comptroller general. Ford urged his colleagues in the House to recommit the bill to the Senate, thereby insisting on the reinstitution of the original, House-approved, version—without the rider.[92]

Their work paid off. On Monday, December 22, the House voted 256 to 108 to recommit the bill to the Senate without approval. The following day the Senate reversed itself rather than run the risk of not passing the relief bill before Christmas, accepting the House version—without the Byrd rider—by a vote of 39 to 29. The Byrd rider had been stricken from the supplemental appropriations bill, Congress had failed to uphold

Staats's opinion on the RPP, and the Nixon administration—after a year of blunders—could claim a major victory in the field of civil rights.[93]

In 1967 Vincent Macaluso's construction area coordinator program reached maturity. Building on the successes and failures of St. Louis, San Francisco, and Cleveland, area coordinator Bennett Stalvey worked in tandem with Warren Phelan's FEB to produce the Philadelphia Plan. Stalvey believed the early reports on affirmative action under the plan foreshadowed its success, but just as integrated construction jobs were breaking ground, Comptroller General Elmer Staats declared the plan illegal under procurement law. On their way out of office, and with a number of successful civil rights achievements under their belt, Willard Wirtz and the Johnson administration did not argue with the GAO, and when the Staats opinion was published the following spring, the contractors ignored their affirmative action agreements forged under the plan. When Nixon appointee Arthur Fletcher revised the Philadelphia Plan soon after, and the comptroller general again challenged it—this time under the Civil Rights Act of 1964—the White House met the challenge. It fought Staats's allies in Congress and won.

Unlike the Johnson administration, the Nixon White House badly needed a successful civil rights initiative. Both Nixon and Johnson had somewhat lackluster civil rights records as vice presidents. But whereas Johnson clearly identified himself early in his presidency with the surging civil rights movement, Nixon's first year in the Oval Office was spent cutting social programs and firing the EEOC chairman for political reasons. With protests and violence erupting at construction sites throughout the country, the RPP seemed to be a way for Nixon to take up the mantle of the civil rights presidency.

If the mood of the country demanded a positive civil rights policy, politics demanded careful consideration. The AFL-CIO and NAACP had scored a major victory in defeating Haynsworth's nomination to the Supreme Court, even if the nomination's demise had more to do with the southern conservative judge's personal ethics than his record on civil rights or labor. The RPP was supported by civil rights groups but opposed vigorously by organized labor, which preferred voluntary affirmative action programs such as apprenticeship outreach and negotiated integration plans like the one forged in Chicago in the wake of the hard-hat riots there. Nixon's successful backing of the Philadelphia Plan was a blow against the AFL-CIO and would help him drive a wedge between organized labor and civil rights leaders.

With hostile majorities in both houses of Congress, the battle over the Byrd rider also struck a blow against Democratic control of the government. Allowing Staats the power to interpret laws unrelated to procurement would have represented a major concession of the executive authority. By forcing Congress to pass the supplemental appropriations bill before the Christmas break, Nixon exercised political and executive power and showed the Democratic leaders that despite Republican minorities in Congress, his would be a dynamic presidency.

As 1969 drew to a close, a seat on the Supreme Court remained vacant, and the civil rights–labor alliance seemed to be in flux. Flush with victory from the Byrd rider battle, and still playing by the rules of his southern strategy, Nixon resolved to appoint another white southern conservative to the Supreme Court, but one without a record hostile to labor. The rights-labor coalition would be tested again.

And as Philadelphia contractors began implementing the affirmative action goals of the RPP, the program faced yet another challenge. The Contractors' Association of Eastern Pennsylvania filed suit against the DOL in federal district court under the Civil Rights Act of 1964. Meanwhile, the complaints of men like Melleher, Quinn, and Kennedy—the three white electricians who claimed to be the victims of reverse discrimination—only grew louder. Were the mandatory affirmative action goals of the RPP legal, or were they illegal quotas—racism in reverse? The fate of contract compliance—and the Nixon administration's only civil rights initiative—hung in the balance.

Chapter 5

Constructing Affirmative Action, 1970–1973

These "home-town solutions," which are being substituted for the
Philadelphia Plan, are a meaningless hodgepodge of quackery and
deception, of doubletalk and doublethink.
—Herbert Hill, June 30, 1970

In 1970 three trained steamfitters—George Rios, a Puerto Rican, and
Eugene Jenkins and Eric O. Lewis, both African American—were rebuffed
when they attempted to obtain "A Branch" journeyman membership in
New York City Steamfitters Local #638. The union refused to refer them
to work, and they were refused jobs by all members of the local Mechanical Contractors' Association (MCA). Wylie B. Rutledge, another African
American, was rejected by the local JAC when he applied for apprenticeship as a steamfitter.[1]

Local #638 maintained two grades of steamfitters: "A Branch," whose
members were referred to lucrative, specialized jobs in construction, and
"B Branch," whose members worked primarily in repair shops, performing routine maintenance. The union's A Branch admitted its first black
steamfitter in 1967, but only after a probe by the New York City Human
Rights Commission. The union did not maintain a hiring hall per se, since
the MCA, an organization of steamfitting contractors in the city, maintained fairly stable work crews, moving them from job to job. The union
and the MCA had a generally good relationship, and together they ran the
JAC to the detriment of black applicants like Rutledge. Rios, Jenkins, and
Lewis claimed that "employment was denied . . . because of the many barriers to membership and employment [which] included age and residence
requirements, unnecessary long periods of apprenticeship and institutional
training, tests which were not in any way related to the work to be per-

formed, formal educational requirements and artificial restrictions on the size of union membership."[2]

As the steamfitters' JAC received increasing pressure from the Bureau of Apprenticeship and Training to admit blacks during the late 1960s, it agreed to establish an affirmative action plan. What this meant in practice, as Rutledge discovered in 1970, was that the JAC would advertise the formation of each new apprenticeship class in a local black newspaper, the *New York Amsterdam News,* and then promptly reject any black applicant on whatever grounds the committee found most convenient. For instance, if most of the white applicants were residents of Staten Island and the blacks were residents of Harlem or Bushwick, the union would call it a Staten Island steamfitters' apprenticeship class, exclude black applicants for failure to meet residency requirements, and grant a waiver to white applicants who resided elsewhere. If the black applicants lacked high school diplomas, the union would make high school graduation a requirement for admission and grant a family waiver to any white nongraduate who had a father or an uncle in the trade (indeed, George Meany had received such a waiver decades earlier). If the black applicants were all older than twenty-five years, the union would create an age limit and admit only the younger whites. Or if the blacks were under twenty-one and the whites were older, it would do the opposite. Meanwhile, the lie of the "Steamfitters Accepting Apprentices" advertisement blared out of the *Amsterdam News,* luring unwitting black youths into what usually amounted to little more than a waste of time.[3]

But not this time. Rios, Jenkins, Lewis, and Rutledge sought help from two organizations: Harlem's Fight Back and Columbia University's Employment Project. The brainchild of James Haughton, a local black activist, Fight Back was dedicated to fighting for fair employment in the New York construction industry. Haughton was a veteran of earlier successful pushes to get skilled blacks employed in the construction of the Downstate Medical Center in Brooklyn, the Harlem State Office Building (later renamed the Adam Clayton Powell Jr. State Office Building), and the World Trade Center, and he had recently denounced the New York Plan, a union-devised knockoff of the Philadelphia Plan, as a "perpetuation of racism . . . not worth the paper on which it is written." In 1964 he had founded the Harlem Unemployment Center, and by 1971, having renamed the center Fight Back, Haughton spent his mornings at job sites cajoling shop stewards and foremen to hire more blacks and his afternoons at his office on 125th Street in Harlem registering skilled black construction workers who were looking for work and willing to picket. Fight Back worked with the Employment Project at Columbia University's Center on Social Welfare Policy and Law, melding a grassroots organization with a prestigious academic institution.[4]

Together with Fight Back and Columbia, the four workers brought a class-action lawsuit against the union, the MCA, and the JAC, and on March 25, 1971, a federal district judge found that the New York City steamfitters' union "has followed a course of racial discrimination over the years." The judge ordered the union to admit Rios, Jenkins, and Lewis to A Branch journeyman membership as a preliminary injunction based on its violation of Title VII of the Civil Rights Act of 1964. The case was then consolidated with other cases against Local #638 being brought by the DOJ, and on January 3, 1972, another federal district judge ordered the union to admit "some 169 qualified non-white workers to membership" and enjoined it from striking a contractor for laying off black and white workers in equal numbers.[5]

The union did not appeal; the worm had clearly turned. But the courts were still not finished with the case, now known as *Rios et al. v. Enterprise Association Steamfitters.* Still to be considered were compensatory damages for the plaintiffs and injunctions to ensure fair employment practices in the future. In 1972 Congress gave the EEOC the power to sue on its own authority, and the commission joined the plaintiffs in *Rios.*

The union signed a city-based affirmative action program called the New York Plan in an attempt to avoid major financial penalties or court-imposed quotas. The New York Plan, a union-industry knockoff of the Revised Philadelphia Plan, did little to integrate unions or job sites, and the union's signing of it failed to impress the court. On June 21, 1973, it ordered the union to hold regular examinations for members of its B Branch who wished to be upgraded to the A Branch. For three months, the union could admit only graduates of its apprenticeship class and qualified nonwhites. The JAC was required to admit a total of 400 new apprentices during 1973, "of whom 175 should be non-white, indentured into a program not to exceed four years." And all these provisions would be overseen by a court-appointed administrator, to whom the defendants were ordered to submit acceptable affirmative action plans by the end of the year—plans that would result in 30 percent black and Puerto Rican union membership and contract employment by 1977. Again and again, in decisions that continued through the 1980s, the court reaffirmed its judgment, eventually citing the Supreme Court's 1979 decision in *United Steelwork-*

ers v. Weber that the imposition of such a quota was not a violation of the Civil Rights Act of 1964, and changing only the specific quota and the timeline for its fruition.[6]

The initial decisions in *Rios* were part of a developing trend as the federal government, organized labor, and civil rights organizations continued to grapple with the question of affirmative action and fair employment during the early 1970s. In the RPP the federal government had developed a program with the potential to force the skilled construction unions to finally open their doors to African American workers. A series of favorable court decisions and a committed team of Labor Department officials appeared to be the perfect combination for full implementation. But White House support, predicated on the political dynamic, remained tenuous. For the proponents of fair employment, much depended on the decisions made by President Nixon, who soon showed that he would sacrifice his civil rights ideals if it brought him political advantage. The president quickly faced a series of choices that put the long-term viability and efficacy of affirmative action programs in doubt.

The Nixon administration came under renewed attack from organized labor when the president attempted for a second time to appoint a conservative white southerner to the U.S. Supreme Court. Unable to use the appointment to drive a wedge between the unions and civil rights organizations, the White House resolved to play to the patriotism and anticommunist sentiment of white workers while simultaneously undermining the Philadelphia Plan.

Chapters 3 and 4 show that development of the Philadelphia Plan was a Johnson administration initiative and that the Nixon administration pushed the program for political rather than egalitarian purposes. This chapter shows how Nixon abandoned support of the plan as soon as it became politically inexpedient. As we will see, however, the plan survived administration apathy and court challenges alike and ultimately succeeded in integrating the skilled construction unions. Nevertheless, changes in the industry—from a sharp decrease in federally funded jobs to the ceding of control over hiring to contractors and job site foremen—resulted in continued employment discrimination in the skilled trades.

The Labor–Civil Rights Coalition in a New Political Paradigm

Fresh from his victory in Congress over the Byrd rider, President Nixon resolved to put to the test the breach created between the leaders of the civil rights movement and organized labor. Meanwhile, Nixon still felt obligated to repay his electoral debt to Strom Thurmond. Hoping to turn a courting of the white South to his advantage in the 1970 midterm elections and his own 1972 reelection bid, the president sought a southern conservative candidate to fill the still vacant Supreme Court seat (owing to Haynsworth's rejection the preceding summer). But he would need to find a nominee without any personal skeletons in the closet that would frighten the senators. He thought he had found that candidate in Florida judge G. Harrold Carswell of the U.S. Court of Appeals, and on January 19, 1970, Nixon sent his nomination of Carswell to the Senate.[7]

The Senate considered the Carswell nomination for three months, during which time no allegations of financial impropriety or professional misconduct surfaced. What did surface, however, was a checkered history with regard to race relations. Although he presented himself as favoring equal opportunity and an eventual end to segregation, Carswell had been one of Thurmond's avid supporters during the 1948 Dixiecrat insurgency; had run (unsuccessfully) for office that same year, giving a speech that overtly appealed to white racism; had participated in the privatization of a segregated public golf course to avoid its integration; and had ruled from the bench in such a manner as to allow the perpetrators of lynchings to escape prosecution on technicalities. Within eleven days of the nomination, the leaders of six major civil rights organizations had written to the president asking him to withdraw Carswell's name.[8]

For all his past attacks on civil rights, what Carswell did not have was a record of decisions antagonistic to the interests of organized labor. For Nixon, this represented the perfect political triangulation: the Philadelphia Plan was supported by civil rights leaders and opposed by organized labor; the Carswell appointment, reasoned White House strategist Harry Dent, would be opposed by civil rights activists but supported by the AFL-CIO. Regardless of whether the Senate confirmed Carswell, his appointment would endear Nixon and the Republicans to white southerners and drive deeper the wedge he had placed through the heart of the rights-labor coalition.[9]

But then something happened that the administration did not expect. For the first time in the history of the AFL-CIO or its predecessor the AFL, the federation opposed a Supreme Court nomination on grounds other than a record of decisions considered hostile to labor. On January 31, 1970, AFL-CIO president Meany publicly labeled the nomination "a slap in the face to Negroes," and the next week the AFL-CIO executive board urged the Senate to reject Carswell.[10]

Of course, observers in the civil rights movement were not surprised; Meany in particular and other leaders of the AFL-CIO in general had long espoused racial egalitarianism, and the Carswell nomination represented a fairly safe way for Meany to put his money where his mouth was, as it were. But the importance of Meany's stance cannot be overstated. Here was the widely respected leader of an advocacy organization for labor rights—an organization that had yet to fully integrate its own ranks—challenging the president of the United States on a matter that, on its face, had little or nothing to do with labor rights. But by the end of the 1960s, Meany had come to understand civil rights as a human rights issue—irretrievably linked to labor rights—and if Carswell was hostile to civil rights, he would not get the support of organized labor.[11]

In the end, the Senate rejected the Carswell nomination—not for his civil rights or labor record but for something else entirely. Whereas Haynsworth's rejection had been based on impropriety, for Carswell, it was based on mediocrity. The judge's decisions had been overturned so many times that his record brought into question his intellectual acumen. And it didn't help when Nebraska Republican Roman Hruska pleaded Carswell's case by saying—in a manner that indicated the senator either thought the Jewish justices had been the smartest or was just plain anti-Semitic—"So what if he is mediocre? There are a lot of mediocre judges and people and lawyers. They are entitled to a little representation, aren't they? We can't have all Brandeises, Cardozos, and Frankfurters and stuff like that there." In any event, on April 8, 1970, the Senate rejected the nomination by a vote of fifty-one to forty-five. Ostensibly bowing to the Senate's insistence that Fortas not be replaced by a conservative white southerner, Nixon shortly named Harry Blackmun of Minnesota to fill the seat, an appointment the Senate quickly confirmed.[12]

President Nixon had been defeated in his desire to use the Supreme Court vacancy to drive a wedge between the civil rights movement and organized labor. If he was looking for another opportunity to accomplish the same goal, he found it the next month when white construction workers—the very group cast as villains in the battle over the Philadelphia Plan—rose up in violent support of the president and his Vietnam policies and in opposition to the antiwar sentiment of the Left. The president realized that his long history as an anticommunist could net him a more valuable constituency than could his lackluster record on civil rights.

On May 8, 1970, approximately 1,000 college students and other protesters gathered at Federal Hall on Wall Street in New York City to mourn the four students killed days earlier at Ohio's Kent State University while protesting the Nixon administration's ongoing involvement in Vietnam. The rally continued peacefully and without incident throughout the morning, but around noon some 200 counterprotesters, mostly construction workers wearing hard hats, converged on the site. Held off for a time by a thin line of policemen, the hard hats soon rushed the antiwar protesters, reportedly reserving their greatest ferocity for the men with the longest hair. Some then marched north to City Hall Park, where they engaged in a rock-throwing fight with students at Pace University and stormed city hall itself, demanding that the building's flag—which was at half-mast out of respect for the victims at Kent State—be raised to full staff. By about 2:00 P.M. the riot had ended. For the rest of the month, construction workers engaged in mostly peaceful counterprotests in support of the president and his war policy, but individual acts of violence continued against those who appeared to represent the counterculture of the 1960s.[13]

The spectacle of the proletariat bludgeoning leftists was, as Peter Levy tells us, a product of the Vietnam War. During the 1930s labor was reliably Democratic, and most white workers were at least tolerant of the left wing; some rising union leaders flirted with communism, and Walter Reuther of the United Auto Workers was famously employed at the Gorky Works in the Soviet Union. By the end of World War II, both the rank and file and union leaders had become staunchly anticommunist (indeed, some had been so in the 1930s); however, for the most part, they remained part of the liberal New Deal framework and usually supported Democratic politicians. During the early and mid-1960s labor supported civil rights bills as well as Johnson's escalation of the war in Vietnam; labor leaders attended civil rights rallies such as the March on Washington. Many in the rank and file could even support civil rights from the conservative viewpoint, which accepted Great Society programs as a form of rehabilitation for the poor. With Johnson in the White House waging anticommunist war in Vietnam, white workers might gripe about a lackluster response to inner-city riots, but they largely remained in the Democratic fold. But as the summertime riots grew worse, traditional civil rights and liberal groups began to lose ground to more radical organizations such as the Black Panthers and Students for a Democratic Society, and rising Democratic Party leaders from Robert Kennedy to George McGovern embraced entitlement solutions to race and poverty questions. White workers increasingly viewed the civil rights and antiwar Left with revulsion, and when Johnson refused to run for reelection, their connection to his party grew tenuous. This backlash helped propel Nixon into the White House, and the pro-war demonstrations at Wall Street were only the latest (and most violent) iteration of an increasingly divergent movement.[14]

The hard hats were behaving like Brownshirts, according to one columnist,[15] and like any right-wing demagogue, Nixon took full advantage. Where he had failed with Supreme Court appointments, he would succeed with patriotism.

Hugh Davis Graham sees Nixon's decision to court the hard hats as simply more in line with his political ideology, and Terry Anderson concurs. But Marc Linder and Nancy MacLean see the decision as stemming from Nixon's genuine affection for any person or group that would support his decision to expand the Vietnam War into Cambodia, something much more important to the president than equal employment opportunity. Jefferson Cowie notes that Nixon was naturally attracted to the hard hats because of their widespread patriotism and obvious masculinity.[16]

President Nixon had a tough row to hoe in order to garner political support from the construction unions and their workers. In addition to supporting the RPP, the president had made construction workers the whipping boy for his economic policy. Rather than blaming federal spending on the war for spiraling inflation and the economic recession at home, Nixon blamed the rising wages of skilled construction workers. In any event, dealing with the seasonality of employment and regular layoffs, most construction workers needed what appeared to be excessively high wages just to keep up with the rising cost of living.[17] What the president needed was an ally within the trades, and he found it in Peter Brennan.

Peter Brennan was born in 1918 and attended Commerce High School in New York City, after which he became an apprentice painter and took classes at City College. At the start of World War II Brennan was a journeyman painter, active in union organizing. During the war he served in the U.S. Navy on a submarine in the Pacific, and shortly thereafter, in 1947, he became business manager of his local painters' union. In 1951 Brennan was named director of the New York City Building Trades Maintenance Division, and in 1957 he was elected president of the New York City Building Construction Trades Council. He soon began to serve concurrently as head of the Building Trades Council of New York State.[18]

By 1970, Brennan had added the vice presidencies of the New York City and New York State AFL-CIO to his portfolio, and as a close adviser to AFL-CIO president Meany, Brennan was considered a likely future head of the AFL-CIO's Building Construction Trades Department. Although he quickly disavowed any responsibility for the riots that followed the counterprotest at city hall, it was Brennan who organized the (mostly) peaceful rallies that followed nearly every day for the rest of the month. The lifelong Democrat and dynamic union leader caught Nixon's attention at a meeting with other building trades leaders at the White House in March, and soon he and the president were meeting regularly. Nixon was cultivating a powerful ally in a traditionally Democratic constituency.[19]

With burly construction workers attacking gangly college students in the streets of New York, the White House response was purely political. Mindful of alienating the "silent majority" on which the president's political fortunes rested, the White House treated the hard-hat riots quite differently from the student antiwar demonstrations. Whereas the president had made a habit of scolding student protesters, admonishing them to remain peaceful, the hard hats received no such admonishment from the White House. For all Nixon's calls for "law and order" when the potential lawbreakers were on the Left, actual lawbreaking by possible political allies was greeted with invitations to the White House.[20]

To cement his growing friendships with the leaders of the building trades, especially Brennan, the president stopped talking about the Philadelphia Plan after the hard-hat riots: presidential statements made in person or reported by press secretary Ziegler after May 26, 1970, did not mention the Philadelphia Plan until the president was pressed to do so during his 1972 reelection campaign. At the DOL, Arthur Fletcher grew concerned that the hard-hat riots were designed to deflect national and White House attention from union policies of racial exclusion. If that were the case, they were succeeding. By September, the NAACP's labor secretary warned that the Nixon administration had abandoned the Philadelphia Plan and in fact all major civil rights initiatives. If he couldn't use affirmative action to split the labor-rights coalition, Nixon would simply appeal directly to the patriotism of the larger constituency.[21] And labor was clearly a larger constituency than black people. In any event, by mid-1970 the Philadelphia Plan and other affirmative action programs for construction had begun to take on a life of their own.

A Proliferation of Plans

In 1970, under pressure from the AFL-CIO and contractors, the Labor Department presided over the creation of a dual system for contract compliance in local building construction. The mandatory plans, modeled after and building on the Philadelphia Plan, were imposed by the OFCC in cities where civil rights groups, labor, and contractors could not work out voluntary plans—also called "hometown solutions"—whereby the parties agreed to their own affirmative action training and hiring programs.

The defeat of the Byrd rider may have cowed Congress into grudging acceptance of the Philadelphia Plan, but not so the AFL-CIO. In a speech at the National Press Club on January 12, 1970, Meany blasted the plan as a political ploy, and he charged that the "good-faith" clause allowed contractors to ultimately hire few or no blacks. By contrast, he held up the Chicago Plan—a voluntary agreement among contractors, unions, and community organizations forged out of the Black Monday demonstrations the previous fall—as eminently superior. The Chicago Plan promised at least a thousand new construction jobs for nonwhites over four years and, coupled with the DOL-funded apprenticeship outreach program, sought to significantly increase nonwhite union membership.[22]

Secretary Shultz agreed that—at least in principle—such hometown solutions were preferable to the mandatory approach of the Philadelphia Plan. But the White House—in the wake of its victory in the Byrd rider fight, and before the hard-hat riots—saw the Philadelphia Plan as the model, and it increased the OFCC's 1970 budget to that end. In consultation with Leonard Garment, the president's special assistant on civil rights, Shultz and Fletcher resolved to use the threat of the imposed plan to push unions and contractors to develop voluntary hometown plans of their own. The OFCC would implement local versions of the mandatory Philadelphia Plan in cities that failed to develop satisfactory hometown plans. This served the dual purpose of satisfying the unions—which were, after all, the DOL's primary constituency—while pushing them inexorably toward integration. To demonstrate that he was earnest, on May 16, 1970, Shultz announced that the DOL would spend nearly half a million dollars on nonwhite recruitment in Chicago, and he transferred thirty staffers to the OFCC to help the regional coordinators implement other hometown plans.[23]

The construction unions complained that they had been singled out, that discrimination was no worse in the building trades than in other fields. It was true that they had been singled out by the OFCC, but with good reason: whereas other unions discriminated, the record of the skilled construction trades was particularly bad; furthermore, this discrimination was most visible in the black community and therefore a more constant affront.

Nonetheless, the OFCC introduced Order No. 4, a version of the Philadelphia Plan that required all government contractors, not just those in construction, to submit affirmative action programs.[24]

For his work in defeating the Byrd rider, pacifying the construction unions, and enlarging the power of the president in the face of a hostile Congress, Nixon rewarded Shultz by naming him the first director of the White House Office of Management and Budget. Undersecretary James D. Hodgson, who had worked closely with Shultz and Fletcher on the Philadelphia Plan, became the new secretary of labor.[25]

Over the next two years, the OFCC approved voluntary hometown plans in twelve cities. In California, Governor Ronald Reagan proposed a statewide voluntary plan. This may have been an attempt to limit the impact of integration on California job sites, since nonwhites constituted more than 20 percent of the population in California's big cities but only 10 percent of the statewide population, and the plan's goals were based on the state's population. Nevertheless, the OFCC ultimately approved it. And although each of the other twelve hometown solutions posed its own problems, none generated as much controversy as the New York Plan.[26]

In March 1970 Peter Brennan began touting a plan to train local blacks and Hispanics for union membership. Dubbed the New York Plan, Brennan's program soon won the support of his fellow union leaders and the local contractors' associations. What the Brennan plan lacked, however, was support from the local black community—a critical factor in the OFCC's approval of the Chicago Plan and other hometown plans. The reason for this lack of support soon became clear as community leaders tore Brennan's plan apart in print and protested it at job sites. The plan was simply an apprenticeship training plan and did not make any provisions for journeyman union membership, let alone actual paying jobs. But what made the New York Plan truly abhorrent to community leaders was Brennan's proposal to establish a separate training center for blacks recruited under the plan. Sixteen years after *Brown v. Board of Education*, a New Yorker was proposing the establishment of a segregated training facility![27]

To be fair, Brennan had a history of seeking integration. In 1963 he had appointed a committee to find and refer black applicants for apprenticeship in the New York building trades, urging the local JACs to accept all qualified applicants—defined as those possessing a high school diploma and two years' residence in the city. He later worked with Ernest Green of the Brooklyn Workers' Defense League, encouraging apprenticeship outreach programs. But Stacy Kinlock Sewell sees Brennan's 1963 committee as a ruse, claiming that it was designed to prove that "capable minority applicants could not be found." Further, "unlike most outreach and recruitment efforts, the Brennan committee had no ties to the organized black community," and "not surprisingly, few nonwhites ever saw jobs as a result of the endeavor."[28]

We must also distinguish Brennan's plan to establish segregated training facilities from the goals of the RPP. Whereas the RPP was an attempt to force segregated organizations to integrate by admitting blacks into existing apprenticeship programs and hiring skilled blacks to work at segregated job sites, the New York Plan would create a new segregated institution—a black and Hispanic training center—out of whole cloth, ostensibly to eventually achieve integration at the job site.

The opposition of local black leaders might have been sufficient to scuttle the New York Plan, but thanks to Nixon's rigorous courting of the hard hats, Brennan was becoming a powerful and respected figure in the highest circles of government. The New York Plan quickly garnered the support of two prominent Republicans: Governor Nelson Rockefeller and Mayor John Lindsay. On January 30, 1971, Lindsay quietly made it law in New York City by including the plan in an executive order.[29]

The controversy over the New York Plan was loud enough to attract the attention of the U.S. Commission on Civil Rights, which held hearings on the matter in March. While Brennan and other union leaders testified in favor of the plan, Herbert Hill and other representatives of civil rights and nonwhite labor organizations presented a solid front in opposition. Although the commission had no formal power, its recommendations and findings often drew the close attention of compliance officials. But Brennan had an ace up his sleeve. In June he met one-on-one with President Nixon, and shortly thereafter the president ordered the OFCC to approve the New York Plan as an acceptable hometown solution and thereby exempt the city's construction contractors and unions from the threat of an imposed affirmative action plan.[30]

Other cities had neither the union and contractor goodwill nor the political clout of a Peter Brennan, and in these cases, the OFCC implemented mandatory plans without first trying hometown solutions. In Washington, D.C., this strategy met with marked success: the Washington Plan, implemented around construction of the district's Metro (rapid transit) system, forced contractors into compliance even for their nongovernmental construction work, and it brought nonwhite representation in the skilled trades in that city from virtually nil in 1970 to 16.1 percent by mid-1971. Other cities receiving mandatory plans were Seattle, where protests by black and Hispanic workers at construction sites at the University of Washington forced government action, and St. Louis, where, sadly, the achievements in integrating the plumbers and pipefitters following the Memorial Arch walkout of 1966 had not been sufficient to bring those unions into long-term compliance.[31]

By the summer of 1971 it was clear that the hometown solutions were not working as well as the mandatory plans. Although Indianapolis's voluntary plan was meeting with some success in all skilled unions except the carpenters, other voluntary plans were failing abysmally to meet their stated goals. Contracting agencies had all but stopped signing construction contracts in the Pittsburgh area because of contractors' failure to submit acceptable affirmative action plans, and the OFCC was forced to replace the Atlanta and Rochester voluntary plans with mandatory ones. Worse still, the Chicago Plan—the showpiece of the hometown solutions and touted by Meany in his attacks on the Philadelphia Plan—had virtually no chance of meeting the AFL-CIO president's prediction that its labor unions would be fully integrated by Labor Day 1971. One local black leader, calling for the Chicago Plan to be replaced with a mandatory plan, charged Chicago contractors with shuttling their few black hires from one site to another to make their numbers seem greater. And the *New York Times* reported that "nonwhite leaders in 12 cities in every section of the country" felt that the voluntary hometown plans had failed and that "massive action by . . . the Federal Government"—the imposition of mandatory plans—was required.[32]

Meanwhile, the White House continued to make it clear that the president's support of the Philadelphia Plan had been but a blip on a radar screen that showed no other major civil rights policy. Nixon and EEOC chairman Brown stuck to their guns on the reorganization of the commission, favoring the proposed amendment to the Civil Rights Act of 1964 that would give the EEOC the power to sue in federal court but not cease-and-desist authority nor jurisdiction over the OFCC. By the end of 1970 one of the two top-ranking blacks in the administration, former CORE director James Farmer, had resigned from his post as assistant secretary of HEW. When the Congressional Black Caucus threatened to boycott the president's 1971 State of the Union address, even the loyal Arthur Fletcher—now alone as the highest-ranking black in the administration—could not help but comment, resorting to his old football metaphors: "Blacks would like for the president to be on the offensive early in the third quarter in order to have a good fourth quarter. We are entering the third quarter."[33]

As the 1972 presidential election approached, President Nixon came under increased pressure to disavow policies that smacked of racial preference. Labeling such policies "reverse racism," antagonists such as the American Jewish Committee worried—as Staats had in 1969—that race-conscious government programs violated the Civil Rights Act of 1964. White House aides grew concerned that the growing white backlash against the perceived excesses of the 1960s and the civil rights movement, which had helped topple the Johnson administration, might take a bite out of Nixon's reelection bid. In the summer of 1972, when the American Jewish Committee asked both major-party nominees to publicly state their position on quotas—which Jews traditionally abhorred for their restrictive qualities—both Nixon and Democratic nominee George McGovern replied that they opposed quotas.[34]

The president now came under fire for the continued implementation of the Philadelphia Plan. If he opposed quotas, could he justify goals and timetables for nonwhite hiring in the construction industry? In the event, Nixon went in the opposite direction entirely, rhetorically abandoning the Philadelphia Plan in a Labor Day speech before construction workers. This made EEOC chairman Brown furious, and he circulated a memo to his staff stating that discrimination cases against construction unions and employers would be prosecuted with the same vigor as before. White House aide Garment, trying to staunch the bleeding, noted publicly that the Philadelphia Plan was based on contractors' good-faith attempts to bring their job sites into compliance; meeting the goals within stated timetables would not only alleviate the effects of past discrimination but also constitute evidence of such good faith. But it was a very fine point.[35]

The Nixon administration's ambivalence regarding the Philadelphia Plan, coupled with the president's fastidious courting of Brennan, paid off in spades. On September 26, 1972, worried that McGovern represented the excesses of Great Society liberalism (and that his position on Vietnam indicated a softness on communism), nine of the seventeen traditionally Democratic presidents of the international building trades unions endorsed Nixon's reelection. The Building Construction Trades Department of the AFL-CIO, and even Meany himself, declared their official neutrality in the election—a major coup for the White House.[36]

But Nixon's victory in November 1972 was cheered by one hard hat more than any other: Peter Brennan. On November 29, 1972, President

Nixon accepted the resignation of Labor Secretary Hodgson and appointed Brennan as his replacement. Brennan quickly declared the Philadelphia Plan a failure, indicating (not surprisingly) that he would favor programs like his own segregated New York Plan.[37] The future of integration in the building trades lay in doubt.

The Philadelphia Plan in Practice: The 1970s and Beyond

Almost immediately after the defeat of the Byrd rider, which effectively ended congressional opposition, the RPP faced one additional hurdle: a challenge in the courts. Ultimately, the federal courts decided that the RPP was consistent with the Civil Rights Act of 1964. In the meantime, OFCC director John Wilks, assistant director for construction Vincent Macaluso, and regional coordinator Bennett Stalvey went about implementing the plan in Philadelphia. When it came to integrating the skilled construction unions, they met with marked success, but the gains were short-lived as the declining economy, a major decrease in government-funded construction, and the end of union control of the hiring process resulted in few real gains in black employment in skilled construction.

The Last Hurdle: Contractors' Association v. Shultz

In January 1970 the Contractors' Association of Eastern Pennsylvania filed suit against the Department of Transportation to change the terms of a contract to build a highway in Chester County, Pennsylvania, one of the five counties covered by the Philadelphia Plan. The plaintiffs contended that the requirement to implement the Philadelphia Plan on the highway job constituted illegal enforcement of a quota system. Title VII of the Civil Rights Act of 1964 required that they hire workers on a nondiscriminatory basis, and the Philadelphia Plan, they concluded, ordered otherwise. The contractors feared that complying with the plan would subject them to equal employment opportunity lawsuits from frustrated white job seekers. The lawsuit was combined with a similar suit filed by the same plaintiffs against the Department of Agriculture, naming Shultz, Fletcher, and Wilks as codefendants.[38]

Having won the support of the White House in 1969 and defeated opposition in Congress, Fletcher was not perturbed. He predicted that the Philadelphia Plan would survive court challenges and that it would ultimately do for equal employment what the *Brown* decision had done for school integration. His opinion was shared by the city of Philadelphia, which filed a brief asking that the case be dismissed.[39]

In the event, the proponents of affirmative action were glad the case was not dismissed, for it resulted in a series of favorable court decisions and produced a record of case law establishing the legality of the RPP. In March 1970 a Philadelphia federal district judge found for the defendants, ruling that the goals and timetables listed in the Philadelphia Plan did not constitute quotas and deadlines. The Contractors' Association appealed, and a year later, in April 1971, the U.S. Court of Appeals for the Third Circuit upheld the decision. The association then appealed to the Supreme Court, which refused to hear the case the following October. The Philadelphia Plan was now, for all intents and purposes, the law of the land.[40]

It was unsurprising that the Supreme Court denied certiorari (i.e., refused to hear the appeal) in the RPP case, because earlier that year it had upheld similar case law in its unanimous ruling in *Griggs v. Duke Power Company.* At issue in *Griggs* was the right of an employer to administer ostensibly neutral hiring tests despite their potentially disparate impact on nonwhites when they examined skills unrelated to job performance. For instance, the requirement of a high school diploma for unskilled or semi-skilled labor in a paper mill would have a disparate impact on the black community because limited, segregated educational facilities resulted in a disproportionately low number of black high school graduates, and completion of a high school education was unnecessary to demonstrate fitness for such jobs.[41]

Paul Moreno sees the *Griggs* decision as the completion of a shift in emphasis from individual rights to group rights, an upholding of the EEOC's interpretation of Title VII of the Civil Rights Act of 1964 over congressional intent. In other words, *Griggs* allowed employers to use quotas to meet their obligations under Title VII, in that quotas recognized membership in a nonwhite ethnic or racial group as a hiring factor outside of other qualifications. But it was the Court's subsequent decision to deny certiorari to the RPP appeal in *Contractors' Association of Eastern Pennsylvania* that had the greatest effect on the integration of government contract employment. In the building trades, which relied so heavily on federal contracts, it was this decision that made the most difference. Nancy MacLean also emphasizes *Griggs* and finds that equal employment opportunity advocates, after what she calls a failure of direct action, went directly to the courts for redress under Title VII. In fact, as we saw in chapter 2, direct action (such as at Philadelphia construction sites in 1963) led to a renewed commitment from the executive branch to implement affirmative action through programs at the OFCC. In short, *Griggs* ratified the EEOC's understanding of Title VII, which governed private employment; *Contractors' Association* ratified the OFCC's interpretation of Title VI, which governed federal expenditures. Further, the denial of certiorari in *Contractors' Association* upheld the use of the manning table—an earlier compliance shortcut that led to quotas. It was the conclusion of both these cases—not *Griggs* alone—that resulted in the legalization of de facto quotas to meet equal employment obligations.[42]

The defeat of attempts to render the Philadelphia Plan illegal, along with the imposition of mandatory city-based construction compliance programs, did not instantly translate into full integration of the skilled building trades. Although the AFL-CIO Civil Rights Committee claimed significant strides toward integrating the trades, an EEOC report in May 1970 showed that 75 percent of all blacks in the building trades were still in the laborers' union, the least skilled (and usually lowest paid) of the trowel trades.[43] By including the laborers, the federation was using a metric that had always made its record on integration look better than it actually was. The skilled trades remained highly segregated, and the RPP would require aggressive implementation.

Implementation, 1970–1973

Largely as a result of the lawsuit, implementation of the RPP got off to a rocky start in 1970. Although eleven jobs had commenced and five had reached the 10 percent completion point by May, OFCC director Wilks reported that none of the contractors were in full compliance with the program, and there was no evidence that the RPP had resulted in the hiring of even one new black employee. Regional coordinator Stalvey admitted to the *New York Times* that "there is no question that compliance is lagging." By July it was clear that at least part of the problem had to do with contracting agencies' failure to submit reports. Inertia reigned as the lawsuit worked its way through the courts. With no pressure to show compliance themselves, the contracting bureaucrats failed to apply pressure to the contractors. And despite the initial March ruling that found the RPP to be legal, the contractors and unions hoped for better luck with their appeal; in the meantime, they dragged their feet, all the while drawing $7 million in federal funds for their work on RPP jobs.[44]

With the Nixon administration cozying up to the hard hats, civil rights leaders saw the RPP's sluggish start as indicative of its abandonment. The NAACP's Herbert Hill and Roy Wilkins both called the plan a failure, and Wilkins exasperatedly admonished existing black construction workers to set a good example and show contractors that they were just as capable as whites, since government enforcement of equal employment opportunity, he felt, would not be forthcoming. Hill condemned the administration for abandoning the Philadelphia Plan, calling the hometown plans "a meaningless hodgepodge of quackery and deception, of doubletalk and doublethink." The director of the Philadelphia NUL called the RPP "a flop" and said that apprenticeship outreach remained the best method for integrating the skilled trades.[45]

In response to the criticism and the reality of early difficulties in implementing the RPP, Wilks, Fletcher, and Secretary Hodgson resolved to crack down on recalcitrant contractors and push the contracting agencies to submit more timely reports. With some eighteen contractors in noncompliance, the OFCC pushed the agencies to issue "show-cause notices"—warning letters requiring the contractor to show probable cause that it had exercised good faith in attempting to integrate or face the loss of the contract.[46]

For once, the crackdown was little carrot and lots of stick, including the threat of debarment—a step never taken in the past for noncompliance with the equal opportunity clause. One contractor, Edgely Air Products of Levittown, failed to adequately integrate or show good faith. Edgely was a sheet metal subcontractor on a University of Pennsylvania job partially funded by HEW. At OFCC urging, HEW agreed to make an example of Edgely and canceled the contract. The message was clear: the OFCC had the power to revoke and debar and was willing to use it.[47]

By the end of the summer of 1970, blacks constituted 22.7 percent— nearly one in four—of the skilled workers on RPP projects, up from just 2 percent at the outset of the program, and the DOL credited the RPP for the employment of forty-one new skilled black construction workers in the five-county area. Hodgson even noted that in some crafts, compliance was significantly above 1970 expectations and had reached the full integration promised by the end of the plan, still three years away. Although white construction workers continued to voice concerns about safety, and black workers continued to report incidents of discrimination, only eight months after the defeat of the Senate rider, it was clear that the RPP had succeeded in integrating affected projects.[48]

Some criticism of the RPP continued, especially from unlikely bedfellows George Meany and Herbert Hill. Arguing the superiority of the hometown plans, Meany accused the DOL of fudging the numbers, allowing RPP contractors to get away with what the *Wall Street Journal* called "motorcycle compliance"—that is, contractors' shuttling black workers from one project to another to fool inspectors into thinking their numbers were greater than they actually were. And in the summer of 1971 Hill got into a public argument with Fletcher over the RPP at the NAACP convention. Pointing out that Edgely Air Products—whose contract had been canceled—was only a minor subcontractor, Hill accused Fletcher of letting the bigger contractors with larger pieces of the federal pie merely pay lip service to the notion of "good faith." Fletcher rebutted that the RPP had already succeeded in meeting its 1971 goals and that although Edgely was small, the message of contract cancellation had not been lost on the other contractors. The OFCC, in fact, had taken the extraordinary step of debarring Edgely from future bidding until the company could show sufficient integration in its nonfederal construction work. And to show that it wasn't just frying the small fish, the OFCC debarred Russell Associates Inc., a noncompliant Philadelphia plumbing contractor.[49]

By the end of 1971, in any event, the OFCC and contracting agencies had gotten wise to such techniques as "motorcycle compliance." They were conducting surprise inspections at all RPP job sites and recording the names of individual black workers. The overall results were slightly below the goal for that year, with some crafts not quite in compliance and a few crafts ahead of the game. Of the 743 workers employed in the critical trades, 102 were nonwhites, or 13.7 percent. These included 34 of 270 electrical workers (12.6 percent), 18 of 103 sheet metal workers (17.4 percent), 22 of 181 plumbers (12.2 percent), 9 of 93 steamfitters (9.6 percent), 17 of 83 ironworkers (20.5 percent), and 2 of 13 elevator constructors (15.4 percent). The average for these trades had been 2 percent in 1969, with some trades employing no blacks or Hispanics at all. By the end of 1972, all contractors had met the goals of the RPP except for sheet metal work, which nevertheless came close at 13.5 percent nonwhite employment. Average skilled black and Hispanic representation at RPP job sites was 16.6 percent, and union membership was approximately 15 percent.[50]

Apprenticeship provided additional cause for hope. Thanks to the DOL's apprenticeship outreach program, administered in most cities by the NUL, there were some 8,000 black youths in construction apprenticeships in 1970, constituting 11 percent of the national total; about half of those were training for membership in the skilled unions. In 1971 that number had swelled to 10,000. "The kids are there and anybody that says you can't teach them is lying," said the black business agent of the Atlanta cement masons. Clearly, blacks were applying, being accepted, and remaining enrolled in skilled construction apprenticeship programs. One EEOC researcher predicted that this would translate into the slow but steady integration of the trades at the journeyman level during the 1970s.[51]

Indeed, these predictions gained traction when the EEOC released a 1972 study comparing nonwhite representation in the skilled trades in that year with comparable figures for 1969. As figure 5.1 demonstrates, of the four nonwhite groups considered, only Asians declined, and the fastest increase was among African Americans. The study covered boilermakers, electrical workers, elevator constructors, ironworkers, plumbers/pipefitters, and sheet metal workers. Total nonwhite representation in these trades increased from 6.2 percent in 1969 to 6.9 percent in 1972—a small but significant increase. Nonwhite representation among the skilled trades was slowly increasing, and the Philadelphia Plan and other such programs were meant to ensure that the percentages of nonwhites on building sites—if not their actual numbers, because of a decrease in construction starts during the 1970s—would increase.

Paul Frymer, in *Black and Blue: African Americans, the Labor Move-*

Figure 5.1. Changes in Percentage of Nonwhite Representation in Skilled Building Trades Membership, 1969 and 1972.

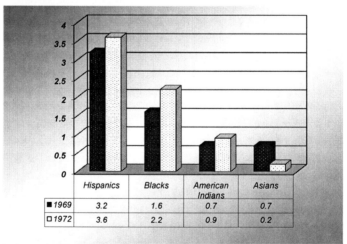

	Hispanics	Blacks	American Indians	Asians
■ 1969	3.2	1.6	0.7	0.7
□ 1972	3.6	2.2	0.9	0.2

Source: "Blacks Made Slight Progress between 1969 and 1972 in Entering Building Trades," *Construction Labor Report* 978, July 10, 1974.

Table 5.1. Changes in Percentage of Black and Spanish-Surnamed Representation in Skilled Building Trades Membership, 1968 and 1983.

Union	1968	1983	% Change
Asbestos workers	0.1	10.1	+10
Boilermakers	7.6	15.9	+8.3
Carpenters	4.9	12.6	+7.7
Electrical workers	5.1	10.5	+5.4
Elevator constructors	2.5	7.8	+5.3
Operating engineers	4.3	11.8	+7.5
Painters	12.0	19.3	+7.3
Plasterers	25.4	37.1	+11.7
Plumbers/pipefitters	2.1	8.0	+5.9
Sheet metal workers	2.6	11.0	+8.4
Teamsters	16.0	26.5	+10.5
Average	7.5	15.5	+8.0

Source: Paul Frymer, *Black and Blue: African Americans, the Labor Movement, and the Decline of the Democratic Party* (Princeton, NJ: Princeton University Press, 2008), 93.

ment, and the Decline of the Democratic Party, argues that the RPP was a failure, noting that the real number of blacks at construction sites dropped between 1971 and 1973: "OFCC statistics of the plans in five major cities found that thirteen of the sixteen targeted craft unions had fewer minority workers in 1973 than in 1971, and two of the others had an increase of only five workers." If the purpose of the RPP had been strictly to create jobs for blacks in the wake of the inner-city riots of the 1960s, these figures would indeed represent failure. But the RPP's purpose was to integrate unions and job sites so that blacks could enjoy equal employment opportunity, and Frymer belies his own argument by presenting an even more comprehensive picture of black gains in union representation between 1968 and 1983, as demonstrated by table 5.1. In the context of declining construction starts and decreased federal funding, an increase in the percentage of skilled minorities at job sites—including an increase in the real numbers of blacks in two targeted unions—represents success.[52]

But despite the increases in percentages, Frymer's use of the real numbers makes a different—albeit no less important—point. For all its success in integrating the unions, the OFCC's efforts were not resulting in increased overall employment for blacks. To accomplish that would have required a different White House economic policy, and the OFCC, as a bureau in the executive branch, was in a position to directly lobby the president from within the administration.

What the OFCC needed was an advocate in the upper levels of the administration, and if anyone was on the civil rights offensive, it was Arthur Fletcher. The problem was that the policies he was pursuing no longer held any political advantage for the Nixon White House. And although he wasn't personally antiunion, he wasn't exactly pro-union either. In March 1971, in a speech at the annual convention of the Associated General Contractors, Fletcher insinuated that integration would serve to weaken the power of the unions, going so far as "to announce the end of . . . the era of union dominance in the construction industry." This was a poor choice of words, considering that unions were the DOL's primary constituency. The president of the sheet metal workers' union publicly called for Fletcher's resignation, and a high-ranking White House aide concurred, noting that Fletcher's continued presence in the DOL would "antagonize millions of union members and George Meany."[53]

Here again, Nixon was faced with what another president might have seen as a tough choice. Since the defeat of the Byrd rider, Fletcher's aggressive implementation of the mandatory plans and hometown solutions had made him something of a star among civil rights advocates. And again, as in 1969, the Philadelphia Plan and its satellite programs represented Nixon's sole civil rights policy of any merit. The NAACP's Roy Wilkins postulated that Nixon could actually win the black vote in 1972 if he could provide significant new jobs for blacks, and as a start, he and others recommended that Fletcher be appointed to head the Office of Economic Opportunity. But Nixon was not another president, and for him, the question was merely one of political expediency. Nixon played to his growing support in organized labor. By the end of the summer of 1971, Fletcher was out.[54]

After a brief stint on the United Nations delegation, Fletcher became executive director of the United Negro College Fund (UNCF), where he replaced Vernon Jordan (who had taken over the NUL after the untimely death of Whitney Young). At the UNCF, Fletcher helped coin the phrase "A Mind Is a Terrible Thing to Waste." But he couldn't stay out of government work for long, returning in 1975 as civil rights adviser to President Gerald Ford. In 1978 Fletcher was the Republican nominee against Marion Barry in the first open election for mayor of Washington, D.C. Although Republicans constituted only 10 percent of the electorate, Fletcher garnered an impressive 37 percent of the vote. Fletcher later chaired the U.S. Commission on Civil Rights for President George H. W. Bush, and he ran for the 1996 Republican presidential nomination to protest the party's move away from civil rights, which had ironically started during Nixon's presidency.[55]

Long-Term Impact, 1973–1995

As the unions were forced to integrate, they gave up one of their most important prerogatives—control over the hiring process. Illegal under the Taft-Hartley Act, this vestige of the closed shop had been a convenient practice for contractors and a cherished right for unions. But in the 1970s and 1980s, as the federal government gradually withdrew from its position as the primary user of the construction trades, building trades leaders were facing increased pressure from nonunion contractors, the antiunion Business Roundtable, major corporations with building projects such as Monsanto and Brown and Root (now Halliburton), and Republican machinations. A letter-writing campaign forced President Ford to veto an important union-based amendment to Taft-Hartley, despite the president's earlier support and evident distress. Union business agents, eager to convert nonunion job sites, agreed to accept nonunion men as card-carrying journeymen; other unions allowed nonunion men to work at union job sites after paying for a permit. The result was a glut in the employment market. Individual union members decided that their job prospects would be better served by foremen they knew, who could reasonably claim to base hiring decisions on previous knowledge of a worker's skill and talent, rather than a hiring hall required to dole out jobs fairly to a membership that increasingly included nonwhites and even newer faces—women. One local at a time, union members voted to cede control over hiring to job site foremen. This proved ominous for the employment prospects of new black union members, because the compliance activities of the government under the Nixon and Ford administrations, notwithstanding the occasional contract revocation, were more zealous against unions than against contractors.[56]

The decrease in construction starts also proved ominous. As black and Hispanic apprenticeships increased very quickly, and journeyman membership increased more slowly, a longtime EEOC consultant worried that equal employment, freed by the 1964 act and sympathetic court decisions, would nevertheless face bureaucratic hurdles at the OFCC. Indeed, by 1973 the agency was losing its vision and cohesion, with the Nixon administration gutting its staff and forcing a reorganization that resulted in stunted leadership and poor field communication. Although nonwhite membership in the skilled trades did reach 15 percent during the 1970s—

largely as a result of the RPP and other mandatory plans—reduced construction employment and a weakening of union control over the hiring process meant that for many blacks, union membership was no longer the guarantee of steady or even fair employment it had once been. Judith Stein makes a similar argument, noting that "both the number of blacks earning more than $50,000 and those earning less than $5,000 grew at the expense of the middle."[57] In effect, skilled blacks were finally being admitted to unions with little hindrance, but they were not earning what they would have earned with union membership in the 1960s.

In 1973, with the RPP in its fourth and final year of scheduled operation, the OFCC should have undertaken a systemic evaluation of the program's successes, failures, and projections in anticipation of possible extension or modification. This was especially important in light of the earlier debate over quotas. Strong, positive leadership could have used the RPP's successes to support a public relations campaign differentiating between goals and quotas and making the moral argument that mandatory compliance programs like the RPP were still necessary to achieve integration and equal employment opportunity.

Instead, Peter Brennan made it clear early in his tenure as labor secretary that he considered the RPP a failure, at least in comparison with his own voluntary New York Plan (which covered only training—and segregated training, to boot). Throughout 1973 Brennan increased funding for the New York and other remaining hometown plans to the detriment of the RPP and other mandatory plans, eventually going so far as to instruct contractors to disregard any elements of mandatory plans that weren't also found in the voluntary hometown plans. Yet the New York Plan had already been declared a failure by no less an authority that the city's Republican mayor, John Lindsay. In a news release on April 17, 1973, city hall declared, "No juggling of statistics can hide the fact that the Plan fell far short of [its] goal. And besides . . . that goal was not nearly adequate."[58]

Brennan's antipathy to the RPP did not fully dislodge it or even prevent its titular extension; as President Nixon's only successful civil rights initiative and the subject of a concerted campaign by civil rights leaders, the program was extended for an additional four years.[59] But without dynamic cabinet-level leadership, the RPP stagnated, and the goal ranges plateaued at 1973 levels. No innovations were made, the training component never fully took off, and contractors discovered that cancellations and debarments could be avoided with "good-faith" lip service.

The decline in construction—caused by an economic downturn, as well as the Nixon administration's cuts to programs such as model cities—was resulting in an increase in overall unemployment, and as usual, the black community was most acutely affected. Whereas the overall unemployment rate increased between 1970 and 1972 from 4.5 percent to 5.2 percent, for blacks, the jobless rate rose from 8.2 percent to 10.2 percent in the same period. The black unemployment rate—already double that of whites—was increasing more than twice as quickly as the overall rate. And as the decade continued, black joblessness went from bad to worse, reaching 10.9 percent by 1975, with the NUL figuring that as many as 3 million blacks—more than one in four—were likely out of work (when one included those who had given up the job search).[60]

Congress attempted to alleviate unemployment by passing an emergency housing bill to fund more construction work. Meany pleaded with President Ford to sign the bill, to no avail. Ford had an antipathy to federal spending on social programs, and he used a slight uptick in the housing market as an excuse to veto the measure (remaining true to form, later that year he would also veto a school lunch bill and ignore the pleas of an insolvent New York City). Continuing a precedent set by Nixon, the Ford administration would intervene in theoretical fair employment matters, stepping in to address specific complaints of discrimination or to push individual affirmative action programs, but it would not get involved in actual job creation. The gains that had been made by federally imposed affirmative action plans were derailed by the economic downturn and federal refusal to help.[61] A receding tide grounds all boats.

In 1976 the U.S. Civil Rights Commission announced that all the federal laws and programs had failed to fully integrate employment in the building trades. Economists Roger Waldinger and Thomas Bailey later painted a similarly bleak picture: "though . . . years of protest over discrimination in construction have produced progress, the gains are disappointing and severe barriers remain in place . . . the history of affirmative action policies in construction bears witness to the unions' ability to control those policies to meet their ultimate ends."[62] By turning over control of employment to the contractors' foremen, the unions had again circumvented responsibility for integration. In the 1950s and 1960s contractors had blamed unions for the segregated workforce. Now the integrated unions blamed the contractors. In any case, the skilled workers at job sites remained disproportionately white.

With the election of Ronald Reagan to the presidency in 1980, the two critical agencies for equal employment opportunity came under renewed scrutiny by the White House and by Congress. The EEOC, under the leadership of Clarence Thomas, saw a budget cut of 12 percent and abandoned "pattern or practice" investigations and class-action lawsuits. At the OFCC—now called the Office of Federal Contract Compliance Programs (OFCCP)—the budget was cut by 34 percent; contractor debarments fell from thirteen in the four years of the Carter administration (totaling twenty-six when the Johnson, Nixon, and Ford administrations are included) to zero during Reagan's first term and only two during his second. In Congress, Senator Orrin Hatch attacked the EEOC, calling its requests that companies show evidence of nondiscrimination "burdensome, governmental repression."[63]

Nonetheless, by this time, large companies like those represented by the National Association of Manufacturers and the Business Roundtable had become so accustomed to the equal opportunity and affirmative action regulations—and their ability to use shortcuts such as manning tables to meet them—that they opposed any major changes. The Reagan and George H. W. Bush administrations, like those of Nixon and Ford, demonstrated mixed feelings toward affirmative action. Electorally they opposed it all the way to three terms in office, with Reagan winning the votes of large numbers of working-class whites and Bush winning a "solid South." But because equal employment opportunity goals and timetables had the support of big business, Reagan and Bush maintained the status quo.[64] The result was a combination of a bad plan—using quotas as shortcuts to equal employment opportunity—and the weakening of the unions working to make such opportunities meaningful in the long term.

When the skilled unions relinquished control over hiring, the growing ranks of trained black Philadelphia construction workers found their hard-won union membership but an empty promise. In 1995, when the *New York Times* examined the Philadelphia Plan as part of a series on affirmative action, membership in the skilled unions remained steady at an average of 15 percent black and Hispanic and 85 percent white, but black workers spent significantly fewer days on the job than their white counterparts. "I have often wondered whether I don't last on jobs because I don't work hard enough or I lack skill," said one Philadelphia ironworker. "I have concluded that the problem is I am Black."[65]

The Philadelphia Plan, an experiment in the racial integration of one of the most segregated and publicly visible areas of the American economy, was successful when implemented by dynamic, active leaders with little external (read political) interference. The original plan, under the leadership of Warren Phelan, Vincent Macaluso, and Edward Sylvester, showed signs of incipient success before being scotched by a comptroller general who was more interested in the prerogatives of his own office than in fair hiring practices and by the unwillingness of a lame-duck labor secretary and president to fight for it.

In contrast, the revised plan appeared to have much more promise, earning White House support at a critical moment when challenged by Congress and quickly winning the support of the federal courts. But its support from the White House was always thin, based on the president's political need to demonstrate a minimal commitment to civil rights and a similarly political desire to split two traditionally Democratic constituencies—organized labor and mainstream civil rights organizations. When Nixon discovered that he could gain the political support of the larger of those two constituencies simply by continuing to rattle the anticommunist saber—even though federal spending in Vietnam ultimately contravened the interests of both—he abandoned the Philadelphia Plan and embraced building trades leaders such as Peter Brennan. Mandatory plans were de-emphasized in favor of union- and contractor-supported "hometown solutions," which quickly failed.

Nevertheless, under the guidance and leadership of John Wilks, Arthur Fletcher, and James Hodgson, the Philadelphia Plan and other mandatory plans succeeded in integrating unions and job sites alike—permanently, in the case of unions. But here again, politics intervened. Proponent Fletcher was fired for being insufficiently pro-union, and antagonist Brennan was rewarded for his political loyalty, leaving an effective program essentially leaderless. When the unions abrogated their control over hiring, and contractors realized they could keep the federal dollars flowing with mere lip service about "good-faith" efforts at affirmative action, foremen were left to make the hiring decisions on their own. And with few black foremen, white workers continued to get more work than their black counterparts. Like a car with its driver asleep at the wheel, the Philadelphia Plan pushed forward. But it couldn't avoid the bumps, the curves, or the other traffic.

Conclusion

Affirmative Action and Equal Employment Opportunity

Merriam-Webster's online dictionary defines *affirmative action* as "an active effort to improve the employment or educational opportunities of members of minority groups and women."[1] Noteworthy in that definition is the word *opportunities*. In the context of the racism that has pervaded the educational, employment, and social institutions of the United States since colonial times, equal opportunity cannot be achieved without such "active effort." As employers, government officials, and union leaders found during the 1960s, the act of establishing "color-blind" employment policies alone did not result in a significantly integrated workforce. Such policies tended to result in token integration, with employers quickly snapping up the few African Americans who had previously managed to obtain specialized training in the hostile environment. For these exceptional blacks, the "Ralph Bunches and Lena Hornes," as the NUL's Whitney Young called them, this meant a sudden increase in available employment opportunities. But for most, color-blind employment policies did not translate quickly into better jobs.

For most blacks, arrival at the job interview meant competition with whites who had benefited from generations of Jim Crow—from superior educational and social training and continued family and social connections. Decades of assimilation—as well as federal programs from the New Deal into the Cold War—had done much to eradicate the class and status differences between the various white ethnicities, but blacks continued to be socially and financially marginalized. Such programs, including the GI Bill, had little impact when it came to benefits for blacks. In such a context, color-blind employment policies would not translate into truly equal employment opportunity. At his seminal statement to the NUL on September 7, 1961, Young said, "I contend, over many protests, that as the Negro for over 300 years has been given the special consideration of exclusion, he must now be given by society special treatment, through services and opportunities, that will ensure his inclusion as a citizen able to compete equally with all others."[2]

In his November 25, 1964, "To Be Equal" column, which appeared in many black newspapers throughout the nation, Young wrote, "It's beginning to look like the sky's the limit for qualified Negro youth, at least in most states." Young postulated that the increased job opportunities for blacks had not resulted in white job displacement. Rather, by increasing black spending power, such opportunities were "creating more demand for goods and services, more jobs and higher prosperity."[3] In short, Young was arguing that employing more blacks enhanced the economy, resulting in more jobs for whites. A society that made use of the potential of all its citizens would result in an economy that provided for all its citizens.

President Johnson, at his commencement address at Howard University in 1965, said, "You do not take a person who . . . has been hobbled by chains, and then . . . bring him up to the starting line [and] say, 'You are free to compete with all the others,' and still justly believe that you have been completely fair."[4] For truly equal opportunity, employers, government officials, and union leaders needed to find other methods of leveling the playing field. They needed affirmative action.

The common usage of the phrase *affirmative action*, however, morphed during the 1980s and 1990s and came to mean "preference" and "diversity." In other words, when many Americans hear the phrase *affirmative action* today, they imagine unqualified blacks getting hired or promoted at the expense of better-qualified whites, or black students being admitted into elite colleges for the sake of campus diversity. The Reagan and Bush administrations, as Terry Anderson tells us, "changed the argument to a simplistic choice that was easy for whites to understand: quotas versus fairness." As such, a cleavage has formed between proponents of compensatory policies and diversity on the one hand and opponents of so-called reverse discrimination on the other. Meanwhile, Democrats and moderate Republicans coalesced around the substitute and warmer-sounding term *diversity*.[5]

Affirmative action was never intended to result in preference for blacks at the expense of standards, but it did comport with the Great Society ethic that the government should provide for the rehabilitation of the poor and the alleviation of poverty. W. Willard Wirtz, secretary of labor during the Kennedy and Johnson administrations, said, "An affirmative responsibility to counteract the effect of that previous policy . . . does not mean hiring or admitting unqualified applicants. It does mean," he continued, "(i) making it effectively clear that the old policy has been changed, (ii) participating in the training and preparation of people who would have been ready if it had not been for that discrimination, and (iii) accepting, when they are ready, those who would have been accepted earlier if there had not been a discriminatory policy." In short, affirmative action in employment means defining a section of the population as economically handicapped, usually for historical reasons, and taking positive steps to end that handicap as quickly as possible. Affirmative action requires responsibility for making that change. Historian Nancy MacLean agrees with this definition of affirmative action, listing the methods whereby more blacks could be recruited, hired, and promoted as the "active recruitment of potential employees through institutions and media in black neighborhoods . . . training . . . eliminating requirements and . . . tests that had no bearing on job performance, job posting . . . counseling . . . restructuring of job ladders . . . and sometimes, as in the Philadelphia Plan, hiring preferences."[6]

In 1961 Secretary of Labor Arthur Goldberg announced an affirmative action program for the personnel in his own department. Goldberg sent job announcement letters to the presidents of historically black colleges throughout the country and followed up by sending his director of personnel on a recruiting trip to those same colleges. But he was clear that this was neither a quota system nor a preference system: "members of minority groups [must] meet the same qualification standards . . . and qualify in the same examinations or evaluations as others seeking employment or promotion." When the personnel director reported that "few black students at the campuses he visited had taken the civil service examinations required for white-collar jobs," Goldberg asked the head of the Civil Service Commission to arrange for a special exam session. Whites who had missed the first exam were also free to register for the supplemental exam, but the real intent was integration of the DOL. The result? Between 1961 and 1963, 19 percent of new federal employees were black.[7]

Another example of affirmative action as it was originally intended was the integration plan of the Lycoming Division of AVCO Inc. in Connecticut. This U.S. Air Force contractor took six concrete steps in 1962 to meet Wirtz's criteria for affirmative action. As the chief of the Equal Opportunity Office of the air force's New York Contract Management District put it:

Lycoming . . . has initiated a positive program to recruit qualified minority group employees. Among the most recent activities of Lycoming are:

a. Conferring with the Apprenticeship Training Division of the Department of Labor, the Employment Division of the Commonwealth of Puerto Rico, the Human Relations Advisor to the Mayor of New Haven and others requesting their assistance in referring potential employees.

b. Mailings to Negro and Puerto Rican leaders in the Bridgeport area, citing AVCO's Equal Employment Opportunity Policy and seeking their help to locate potential employees with needed skills.

c. Employing three nonwhite engineers.

d. Participating in a pilot program with Community Progress, Inc., of New Haven to train minority group members for job openings. Community Progress, Inc., a new agency financed primarily by a Ford Foundation Grant, will establish programs with educational institutions to qualify trainees for various technical and semi-technical positions.

e. Transferring a Negro employee from the factory force to the employment information window.

f. Hiring an employment recruiter who is a native of the Negro community in Bridgeport. Part of his time is devoted to contacting schools, churches, social groups and civil organizations to stimulate the referral of potential employees.

In the past four or five months, as a result of these activities, Lycoming has hired three times the number of minority group workers it ordinarily would have employed, if the company had relied solely upon its customary recruitment and referral services.[8]

Lycoming had not given preference to unqualified blacks over qualified whites; rather, the company had invested time and money to attract qualified blacks (and other nonwhites) who otherwise would not have applied and to train unqualified blacks so that they would qualify later. It did this by reaching out to the local black community, placing qualified black employees in the personnel department, and participating in local training programs that primarily benefited blacks. The result of this affirmative action program was an increase in qualified black applicants, which, coupled with nondiscriminatory hiring practices, led to a more rapidly integrating workforce.

How different this plan was from Peter Brennan's New York Plan, which advocated segregated training facilities! By patronizing black social networks and black training organizations such as Community Progress Inc. of New Haven, Lycoming relied on existing segregated frameworks as a temporary stopgap to further the goal of integration. Brennan's plan, by contrast, sought to create new segregated facilities out of whole cloth. With the ostensible aim of progress, the New York Plan was ultimately regressive.

Part of Lycoming's strategy included diversity, as evidenced by the transfer of a black worker to the personnel window. In that case, diversity was used not as an end but as a means; not to give the white employees a "diverse experience"—a recent justification for diversity policies in higher education—but to show potential black employees that their applications would not go directly into the "circular file." As a side benefit, the visibility of qualified blacks in new positions schooled the white employees on the equal capabilities of blacks.

Diversity of this sort was important in popular culture as well. Nichelle Nichols, costar of the popular *Star Trek* television series, recounted her own experience with diversity. As an African American woman, her presence on the series was groundbreaking: her character served as a senior officer of the fictional starship *Enterprise.* (The series was also diverse in its inclusion of a Russian, a Japanese, and even an extraterrestrial as protagonists, but the moment that best typified the spirit of the show was the first interracial kiss on American television, which Nichols, as Lieutenant Uhura, shared with the swashbuckling Captain Kirk, played by William Shatner.) Yet in the first season, Nichols found her character largely shunted to the background. When she considered quitting the series in 1966, she was dissuaded by Martin Luther King Jr. Although the actress had been hired out of a desire for diversity—that is, the producers saw the social benefit of casting a black actress in a forward-thinking dramatic series—the character of Uhura, King reminded her, had not.

He said to me, "Think for a moment why Uhura was chosen above and beyond anyone else to go on this mission where no man or woman has gone before—because she was the most qualified and was chosen on that basis alone. And so it says something—you're saying something for women, you're saying something for Afri-can Americans, you're saying something for the whole race—for all of humankind." And he said, "I am very proud of the manner in which—the dignity with which—you have created your character. You must stay." And so I had to stay.[9]

Diversity in the present had resulted in a true meritocracy in the imagi-nary future and, by extension, the real future. Thanks to King's encourage-ment, Nichols remained on the show for its three-season run and went on to reprise her role in six feature films. And like the black applicants who were encouraged by the sight of a black employee in Lycoming's person-nel department, a generation of black—and female—television viewers was shown each week that they were capable of handling complex, tech-nical tasks, including leadership, just as well as whites—and men. And the side benefit—but not the primary one—was the education of whites, espe-cially young white men, on the equal potential of blacks.

A popular movement in Philadelphia brought results similar to those of Lycoming, but prompted by a source other than earnest company moral-ity or fear of losing a federal contract. In 1959 the Reverend Leon Sul-livan organized 400 black Philadelphia ministers in a campaign called "selective patronage." The campaign was run by a coordinating commit-tee that met in secret in one of their churches in the middle of the night to select employers that didn't hire blacks at all or didn't promote blacks into more desirable positions. (Sullivan claimed the selective patronage campaign had no real leadership so that the various ministers—charis-matic personalities all—would not waste precious time arguing over it; nevertheless, his organizational stamp was seen throughout the campaign, and his name appears in all records of it.) When the committee members chose a company for selective patronage, they would list a concrete set of demands, set a deadline for the company to meet those demands, and then request a meeting with personnel managers or other appropriate company authorities. The deadlines allowed sufficient time for the companies to meet with the ministers, but companies that tried to stall by delaying these meetings would not be given any additional time to comply. At the meet-ings, the ministers from the coordinating committee politely presented their demands to company officials, apprised them of their deadline, and informed them that if the demands weren't met by the deadline, the parish-ioners of 400 black churches would stop patronizing their company and stop buying their products. The demands were not open to negotiation, so the ministers kept them modest, reflective of a careful, sober analysis of each company's situation.[10]

The Tasty Baking Company "had hundreds of Negro employees" but "did not have any Negroes driving trucks or working in its office." In the summer of 1960 the coordinating committee demanded that "the company hire two Negro driver-salesmen, two Negro clerical workers, and three or four Negro girls in the icing department," and it gave Tasty two weeks to comply. Company officials refused, stating that there was no need for additional employees in those areas at the time. When the deadline passed, 400 black ministers told their congregants during their Sunday morning sermons that Tasty was practicing discrimination and that the purchase of Tasty products was, by extension, an act of discrimination. As many as 500,000 blacks boycotted Tasty products for two months, and the ministers called off the boycott only after the company had hired "two Negro driver-salesmen, two Negro clerical workers and some half-dozen Negro icers." Tasty was the second of twenty-nine companies approached by the coordinating committee between 1959 and 1963, and it was the first to be subjected to a boycott. Most of the companies approached after the Tasty boycott gave in to the ministers' demands without argument, although many tried to negotiate.[11]

How did these companies comply with the ministers' demands? The critic of affirmative action might ask if any white workers were laid off or demoted as a result of these boycotts. The answer is probably yes. Tasty had protested that it didn't need any additional drivers or clerical workers, yet to end the boycott, the company hired exactly as many blacks as the ministers demanded. Doubtless the company hired more workers than it needed; demoted several whites but maintained their previous level of pay, at a cost to the company; or demoted or terminated several white workers outright.

But the aforementioned critic would be wrong to cite this as evidence against the morality of affirmative action, since selective patronage and the targeted companies' responses were not affirmative action at all but rather a laissez-faire response to the demands of the market (or at least a racially based component of the market). The black boycotters exercised their rights as customers not to patronize businesses where their fellow blacks couldn't work (or couldn't be promoted to more desirable positions) because of the color of their skin. (Tasty and the other companies never argued that they couldn't find qualified blacks. Rather, they said that promoting blacks would breed racist resentment among white employees and that, in the case of Tasty, black driver-salesmen would be at a disadvantage trying to sell in white neighborhoods.) And the companies exercised their right to implement new hiring and promotion policies based on the changing demands of the market. Tasty and the other companies did not engage in affirmative action as a result of selective patronage, because they did not take actions to promote equality of opportunity; they merely acceded to the ministers' demands to avoid losing a significant portion of the market.

Although the results may be initially satisfying to their proponents, the danger of activities like selective patronage is that they rely on market forces to achieve integration. Selective patronage cut the market demand for particular products through boycotting, and the producers responded by meeting the new demands of the market. But market forces can easily be turned against minority groups owing to the simple fact that minority groups do not constitute a majority of the market or the population. After the Tasty boycott, it is conceivable that the whites of Philadelphia and its environs could have organized a 4,000-church/synagogue boycott of their own, ten times the size of the black ministers' boycott, to get Tasty to fire or demote the new black employees—based simply on the number of whites in the Philadelphia area at the time. Without the component of morality or government regulation, Tasty would have been forced to comply, sacrificing black workers as well as black consumers.

Self-regulation by companies such as Lycoming and Tasty jibed with the opinions of conservative economist Milton Friedman, who believed that laws securing equal employment opportunity were unnecessary because the market would, over time, correct any such deficiency. "The development of capitalism has been accompanied by a major reduction in the extent to which particular religious, racial, or social groups have . . . been discriminated against . . . there is an economic incentive in a free market to separate economic efficiency from other characteristics of the individual." Equal employment legislation, Friedman writes, "clearly involves interference with the freedom of individuals to enter into voluntary contracts with one another."[12]

There are problems with such overreliance on market forces, of course. Ray Marshall (who served as President Jimmy Carter's labor secretary) rebutted Friedman by noting that the market often moves too slowly to protect minorities, and it responds to the boycotts of racists the same way it responds to the boycotts of civil rights advocates.[13] When a majority of the community is content with discriminatory business practices, as in the

Jim Crow South, such practices are correct—at least as far as the market is concerned. In short, market protections work best for the majority, but they cannot be depended on by a minority. Such practices, in an unfettered capitalist market, can be changed in the long run only with moral suasion—a tactic the NUL had been trying for fifty years, with very limited success. The relative brevity of most advances made by blacks under Jim Crow proved that the market is a fickle friend.

Conservatives like Friedman saw employment discrimination as a "freedom" for employers that chose to engage in it; discrimination was an individual right rather than something that caused harm to a group. But even in the context of individual rights, the argument breaks down under scrutiny. Murderers and rapists might see the individual right to murder or rape as their own "freedom." Or, taking some less extreme examples, energy explorers might see the destruction of natural resources as their right to do as they wish with "their" land; factory owners might see the decision to refuse to provide safety equipment to workers as their freedom to take full advantage of the labor market. In each of these cases, it is the government's responsibility to weigh the desire for individual freedom on the part of racists, murderers and rapists, energy explorers, and factory owners against the group rights of nonwhites, victims of violent crimes, environmentalists, and factory workers—in other words, the collective good of the society. In 1964 the government decided, on behalf of that society, that it had an interest in ensuring equal employment opportunity, just as it did in preventing murder and rape, avoiding the destruction of natural resources, and ensuring the safety of workers.

But the government, like the market, can be a fickle friend, changing with the whims of the majority. MacLean cites studies showing fewer Americans expressing confidence that the federal government will "do what is right all or most of the time," falling from 80 percent in 1964 to 20 percent in 1994. She postulates that this cynicism is the result of "the war in Vietnam and the exposures of Watergate." Rather counterintuitively, midlevel federal bureaucrats like Vincent Macaluso and Bennett Stalvey, who applied good government to the purpose of good changes, also helped undermine public confidence in the federal government. When Watts, Hough, Newark, and Detroit exploded, President Johnson resolved to fight racial violence with a long-term plan to create jobs, and he set agencies like the OFCC to the task. But as Gareth Davies tells us, a significant number of the nation's whites instinctively saw a military crackdown as the best solution to the violence, and they viewed Johnson's program as an unjust reward for misbehavior.[14] Whereas in 1963 whites had sympathized with blacks when Birmingham authorities attacked children with fire hoses, now they sympathized with police and store owners in riot-torn inner cities. As agencies like the OFCC did their jobs, and did them well, and as the White House refused to meet the threat of urban violence with massive force, white support—especially white male support—for equal employment opportunity was lost. And for a generation after, politicians would win elections with veiled—and not so veiled—racist rhetoric.

So what, then, is the best solution for ensuring equal employment opportunity? Which of these fickle friends—the market or the government—can be trusted to make the moral choice and effect positive change? What we have seen is that, when its midlevel bureaucrats are inclined to produce a positive change, the government is a far more effective and reliable mechanism for ensuring the rights of minority groups. It is fortunate that at a crucial moment in history, the American people and their leaders produced a government willing—indeed, eager—to effect positive change.

The real affirmative action discussion should not be about compensatory hiring, preference, or diversity. Affirmative action comprises the series of necessary activities, to be undertaken as quickly as possible, to implement equal opportunity. In higher education, affirmative action might mean elite colleges engaging in outreach activities in inner-city schools, advocating for better government funding for at-risk teens, or hiring nonwhite guidance counselors to help black and Hispanic youngsters succeed. It might mean creating tutoring programs to help targeted youngsters score better on tests (but not assigning additional test points to such youngsters). In employment, affirmative action might mean employers and government agencies investing in community outreach and on-the-job training programs, again targeted at specific communities identified as requiring such action to level the playing field.

Union leaders periodically made the point that the dearth of black members was the result of a corresponding dearth of skilled black workers. This argument had a measure of validity, largely because few black youths were admitted into skilled apprenticeships. When pressed to explain this situation, union leaders claimed that no qualified blacks applied. We have seen that this was not the case. But in addition, the unions could have done a better job promoting apprenticeship opportunities in nonwhite neighborhoods and then following up with additional pre-apprenticeship training programs.

Federal contractors periodically made the point that awarding contracts to other than low bidders because of a failure to comply with the nondiscrimination clause was an illegal waste of taxpayer funds. But that argument has always been unsound. The principle of letting to the lowest bidder has the rather obvious caveat that only bidders capable of meeting the terms of the contract—*qualified* bidders—can be considered. For example, I could submit a bid for a federal construction contract for a new federal office building in downtown Manhattan for the cost of a New York City subway ride (presumably, I would submit it in pencil on a cocktail napkin). But because I am in no position to fulfill the terms of the contract, obviously I would not receive it. That I am incapable of fulfilling the terms because I don't know how to build a building is, at least in principle, no different from a bona fide construction contractor being considered incapable of fulfilling the terms because it doesn't hire black workers (or subcontracts hiring to unions with no black members). Ultimately, the contracting agency must eliminate from consideration bidders that are incapable of fulfilling the contract terms and award the contract to the lowest *qualified* bidder.

The activities of the federal government in its attempts to integrate the building construction trades were an example of coercion, mostly intended to force unions and contractors to engage in affirmative action activities (manning tables notwithstanding). Sylvester's equal opportunity program of 1966 was the first example, and the Cleveland, Philadelphia, and Washington, D.C., plans carried the concept to its ultimate development. Armed with the power to withhold, revoke, and debar, the OFCC required contractors to attend pre-award meetings with the equal employment officer of the contracting agency and the area coordinator to discuss methods of affirmative action to be employed on the project. Given the availability of skilled and aspiring blacks in most cities, these federal officials assumed that if the contractor engaged in affirmative action, and if the affected unions understood that fighting integration would result in lost jobs, federally funded and federally assisted construction sites would integrate and the unions would be forced to accept more qualified blacks as journeymen and more aspiring blacks as apprentices. The methods and details of implementing these programs differed from city to city, based mainly on local nonwhite unemployment levels, the availability of federal contracts, and the degree of union recalcitrance.

What is ironic about the mandatory plans is not *how* they succeeded in integrating the building trades but rather *where* they succeeded: the unions. The plans were aimed at unions only obliquely; by their own language, they were directed at the contractors. But the unions found themselves caught in a vise. On the one hand, if they failed to integrate, contractors would be forced to look elsewhere for black employees, and labor's control of the hiring process would be weakened. On the other hand, frustrated black applicants for apprenticeships and journeyman membership were increasingly seeking redress in the courts under Title VII of the Civil Rights Act of 1964. But as the unions integrated, white workers increasingly found their privileges as union members eroding, and one by one the skilled trades voted to cede hiring to job site foremen. In the end, the RPP and subsequent regulations succeeded in integrating the skilled trades at the union hall but not satisfactorily at the job site.

Following implementation of the RPP, the biggest obstacle to the full integration of job sites was the decline of the government-sponsored economy. Presidents Nixon and Ford presided over a major retrenchment in domestic spending, including federal and federally assisted construction. This resulted in a decimation of construction jobs just as affirmative action programs such as the RPP were beginning to work. As jobs became scarce, the whites who held them due to historical privilege became even more concerned about keeping them, and qualified blacks who were admitted to skilled unions as a result of government or court pressure were labeled unqualified. Contractors relied on manning tables to get contracts, and when they filled their nonwhite quotas, this bred resentment among white workers and their advocates, who now equated affirmative action with reverse racism. The resultant backlash—combined with the leaderless follow-through of Peter Brennan's tenure as labor secretary—led to the ultimate failure of affirmative action to achieve its goals in the twentieth century.

During the 1970s the impetus for enforcing equal employment opportunity passed from midlevel bureaucrats to the courts. But the courts, notwithstanding the precedent-setting potential of case law, can rule only on individual cases. Whereas Sylvester, Stalvey, and their colleagues proactively developed comprehensive programs to address historical inequality, the courts can only reward and punish individuals, unions, and companies. Further, courts do not revisit cases without an appeal. In short, the OFCC was proactive and the courts are reactive, and this system has not served the long-term needs of the nonwhite population as a whole.

Writing in opposition to affirmative action in 1975, Nathan Glazer saw the imposition of state-run programs to implement equal employment opportunity as the betrayal of a national consensus in favor of a color-blind ethos. The American people throughout their history, he said, have been overwhelmingly open and egalitarian. Slavery, anti-immigrant sentiment, and Jim Crow were aberrations to be eventually overcome.[15] But the civil rights movement, as we have seen, never adhered to a color-blind ethos; rather, it saw the achievement of equal opportunity as impossible without "color-consciousness." And the default attitude of our society, despite moments of revulsion upon witnessing the excesses of racism and discrimination, has too often been an almost tribal distrust of the "other."

Affirmative action, then, remains necessary. Comprehensive programs to address inequality based on historical (and continuing) discrimination are no less necessary today than they were in 1967. That affirmative action is still required to achieve equal opportunity four decades after its inception is evidence not of a fault in the concept but of a failure in the implementation.

Notes

Preface

1. Joan Hoff, *Nixon Reconsidered* (New York: Basic Books, 1994); Kevin L. Yuill, *Richard Nixon and the Rise of Affirmative Action* (Lanham, MD: Rowman and Littlefield, 2006).

Introduction

1. "New Challenge Seen for Labor, Rights Alliance," *AFL-CIO News,* April 5, 1969.

2. *Color-blind* was a term coined by conservatives attempting to redefine the pre-1965 objectives of the civil rights movement to undercut arguments favoring affirmative action. See Nancy MacLean, *Freedom Is Not Enough: The Opening of the American Workplace* (New York: Russell Sage Foundation, 2006).

3. Kathy Sawyer, "Affirmative Action: Birth and Life of a Bugaboo," *Washington Post,* April 11, 1982.

4. Sylvester quoted in John David Skrentny, *The Ironies of Affirmative Action: Politics, Culture, and Justice in America* (Chicago: University of Chicago Press, 1996), 135; Terry Anderson, *The Pursuit of Fairness: A History of Affirmative Action* (New York: Oxford University Press, 2004), 103; Clinton quoted in "Give All Americans a Chance," *Washington Post,* July 20, 1995.

1. Fighting Bureaucratic Inertia

1. J. Carlton Yeldell to Julius Thomas, August 8, 1958, NUL Papers, series I, box A52, "Trade Union Advisory Council, 1958" folder, Manuscripts Division, Library of Congress, Washington, DC.

2. Kevin Boyle, *The UAW and the Heyday of American Labor, 1945–1968* (Ithaca, NY: Cornell University Press, 1995), 107–31; Thomas J. Sugrue, *The Origins of the Urban Crisis: Race and Inequality in Postwar Detroit* (Princeton, NJ: Princeton University Press, 1996), 115; Grace Palladino, *Skilled Hands, Strong Spirits: A Century of Building Trades History* (Ithaca, NY: Cornell University Press, 2005), 158; Anthony S. Chen, *The Fifth Freedom: Jobs, Politics, and Civil Rights in the United States, 1941–1972* (Princeton, NJ: Princeton University Press, 2009), 43.

3. See, for instance, Elmo Roper, "Discrimination in Industry: Extravagant Injustice," *Industrial and Labor Relations Review,* July 1952; J. J. Morrow, "American Negroes—A Wasted Resource," *Harvard Business Review,* January 1957; and Jennifer Delton, *Racial Integration in Corporate America, 1940–1990* (New York: Cambridge University Press, 2009), 42–98.

4. See, for instance, Charles B. Dew, *Ironmaker to the Confederacy: Joseph R. Anderson and the Tredegar Iron Works* (New Haven, CT: Yale University Press, 1966), and *Bond of Iron: Master and Slave at Buffalo Forge* (New York: W. W. Norton, 1994); Claudia Dale Goldin, *Urban Slavery in the Antebellum South, 1820–1860: A Quantitative History* (Chicago: University of Chicago Press, 1976); Ronald L. Lewis, *Coal, Iron, and Slaves: Industrial Slavery in Maryland and Virginia* (Westport, CT: Greenwood Press, 1979); Robert S. Starobin, *Industrial Slavery in the Old South* (New York: Oxford University Press, 1970); John E. Stealey III, *The Antebellum Kanawha Salt Business and Western Markets* (Lexington: University Press of Kentucky, 1993); Richard C. Wade, *Slavery in the Cities: The South, 1820–1860* (New York: Oxford University Press, 1964); Gavin Wright, "Did Slavery Retard the Growth of Cities and Industry?" in *Reckoning with Slavery: A Critical Study of the Quantitative History of American Negro Slavery,* ed. Paul A. David et al. (New York: Oxford University Press, 1976); and Julie Winch, *A Gentleman of Color: The Life of James Forten* (New York: Oxford University Press, 2002).

5. See, for instance, Bruce Laurie, *Artisans into Workers: Labor in Nineteenth-Century America* (New York: Noonday Press, 1989); David R. Roediger, *The Wages of Whiteness: Race and the Making of the American Working Class* (London: Verso, 1991); and Robert H. Zieger, *For Jobs and Freedom: Race and Labor in America since 1865* (Lexington: University Press of Kentucky, 2007), 9–69.

6. Herman D. Bloch, "Craft Unions and the Negro in Historical Perspective," *Journal of Negro History* 43, no. 1 (January 1958); A. Philip Randolph, address to the Trade Union Leadership Council, February 7, 1959, NAACP Papers, series III, box A30, "Randolph" folder, and address to the 1959 NAACP Annual Convention, July 15, 1959, ibid., box A10, "Speeches" folder, Manuscripts Division, Library of Congress; Sugrue, *Origins of the Urban Crisis,* 117; Palladino, *Skilled Hands,* 37–38, 41, 158.

7. Randolph, address to Trade Union Leadership Council, February 7, 1959, and address to the 1956 NAACP Annual Convention, June 27, 1956, NAACP Papers, series III, box A3, "Speeches" folder; MacLean, *Freedom Is Not Enough,* 40; James N. Gregory, *The Southern Diaspora: How the Great Migrations of Black and White Southerners Transformed America* (Chapel Hill: University of North Carolina Press, 2005); Peter Gottlieb, *Making Their Own Way: Southern Blacks' Migration to Pittsburgh, 1916–1930* (Urbana: University of Illinois Press, 1987); James R. Grossman, *Land of Hope: Chicago, Black Southerners, and the Great Migration* (Chicago: University of Chicago Press, 1989); Kimberley L. Phillips, *Alabama North: African-American Migrants, Community, and Working Class Activism in Cleveland, 1915–1945* (Urbana: University of Illinois Press, 1999); Zieger, *For Jobs and Freedom,* 70–105; Paul Frymer, *Black and Blue: African Americans, the Labor Movement, and the Decline of the Democratic Party* (Princeton, NJ: Princeton University Press, 2008), 52–53, 59; Palladino, *Skilled Hands,* 96; Chen, *Fifth Freedom,* 43.

8. In Motion: The African-American Migration Experience, http://www.inmotionaame.org/migrations/topic.cfm?migration=9&topic=2 (accessed September 23, 2007); Alfred Baker Lewis, *Progress—At Very Deliberate Speed,* n.d. [circa 1962], Thelma McDaniel Civil Rights Collection, series IIC, folder 5, item 27, p. 8, Historical Society of Pennsylvania, Philadelphia. The quotations are from Lewis.

9. http://www.conservativeusa.org/eo/1941/e08802.htm (accessed September 23, 2007); Eric Arnesen, *Brotherhoods of Color: Black Railroad Workers and the Struggle for Equality* (Cambridge, MA: Harvard University Press, 2001); Herbert Garfinkel, *When Negroes March: The March on Washington Movement in the Organizational Politics for FEPC* (New York: Atheneum Press, 1959); Merl Elwyn Reed, *Seedtime for the Modern Civil Rights Movement: The President's Committee on Fair Employment Practice, 1941–1946* (Baton Rouge: Louisiana State University Press, 1991); James D. Wolfinger, "'An Equal Opportunity to Make a Living—and a Life': The FEPC and Postwar Black Politics," *Labor: Studies in Working Class History of the Americas* 4, no. 2 (summer 2007): 65–94; John David Skrentny, *The Minority Rights Revolution* (Cambridge, MA: Belknap Press, 2002), 27; Chen, *Fifth Freedom,* 32, 37.

10. Jervis Anderson, *A. Philip Randolph: A Biographical Portrait* (Berkeley: University of California Press, 1972); Paula F. Pfeffer, *A. Philip Randolph, Pioneer of the Civil Rights Movement* (Baton Rouge: Louisiana State University Press, 1990); Clarence Taylor, "Sticking to the Ship: Manhood, Fraternity, and the Religious World View of A. Philip Randolph," in *Black Religious Intellectuals: The Fight for Equality from Jim Crow to the Twenty-first Century* (New York: Routledge, 2002); A. Philip Randolph Oral History Interview I, October 29, 1969, by Thomas H. Baker, electronic copy in Lyndon Baines Johnson Presidential Library and Museum, Austin, TX (hereafter cited as LBJ Library); Paul Delaney, "A. Philip Randolph Is Dead; Pioneer in Rights and Labor," *New York Times,* May 17, 1979. The espionage case was ultimately dismissed; see Anderson, *A Philip Randolph,* 106–9.

11. Anderson, *A. Philip Randolph;* Pfeffer, *A. Philip Randolph;* Taylor, "Sticking to the Ship"; Randolph Oral History Interview I; Delaney, "A. Philip Randolph Is Dead"; Judson MacLaury, *To Advance Their Opportunities* (Knoxville, TN: Newfound Press, 2008), 138.

12. In Motion: The African-American Migration Experience; James D. Wolfinger, *Philadelphia Divided: Race and Politics in the City of Brotherly Love* (Chapel Hill: University of North Carolina Press, 2007); NAACP press release, April 16, 1959, NAACP Papers, series III, box A183, "States" folder. See also Kevin Schultz, "The FEPC and the Legacy of the Labor-Based Civil Rights Movement of the 1940s," *Labor History* 49, no. 1 (February 2008): 71–92; Executive Order No. 10308 and White House press release, December 3, 1951, NUL Papers, series I, box D15, "President's Committee on Government Contract Compliance" folder; "Truman Appoints 6 to Anti-Bias Board," *New York Herald-Tribune,* January 11, 1952; "A New F.E.P.C.," *New York Times* editorial, December 4, 1951; "Fair Employment Practices," *New York Herald-Tribune* editorial, December 5, 1951; "Statement of Clarence Mitchell, Director of the Washington Bureau, NAACP, before the President's Committee on Government Contract Compliance," June 9, 1952, NUL Papers, series I, box D15, "President's Committee on Government Contract Compliance" folder; Steven F. Lawson, ed., *To Secure These Rights: The Report of President Harry S. Truman's Committee on Civil Rights* (Boston: Bedford/St. Martin's, 2004); Anderson, *Pursuit of Fairness,* 56; Sugrue, *Origins of the Urban Crisis,* 115; Chen, *Fifth Freedom,* 40, 85.

13. MacLaury, *To Advance Their Opportunities,* 143; Skrentny, *Minority Rights Revolution,* 11; Chen, *Fifth Freedom,* 86.

14. MacLaury, *To Advance Their Opportunities,* 137–44. Chen, in *The Fifth Freedom* (50), reminds us that the argument for equal employment opportunity as a Cold War weapon dates to the 1947 Truman Doctrine.

15. MacLaury, *To Advance Their Opportunities,* 144–45.

16. "Nixon Calls Conference on Job Bias; States and Cities to Send Officials," *New York Herald-Tribune,* April 20, 1955; Thomas to Lester Granger, April 21, 1955, NUL Papers, series I, box A62, "Industrial Relations Department [IRD], Memos and Reports, 1955, January–April" folder; "Nixon Cites Bias in Job Promotion," *New York Times,* October 26, 1955; James F. Mitchell to Cleveland Urban League, January 21, 1956, NUL Papers, series I, box E31, folder M; Herbert Hill to Henry Lee Moon, July 22, 1958, NAACP Papers, series III, box A190, "PCGC 1" folder; Delton, *Racial Integration in Corporate America,* 65–67. The quotations are from the *Herald-Tribune.*

17. NUL Department of Industrial Relations Report, May 1956, AFL-CIO Papers, Records Group (RG) 1–038, box 95, folder 8, George Meany Memorial Archives, National Labor College, Silver Spring, MD; NAACP press release, May 31, 1956, NAACP Papers, series III, box A178, "B Miscellaneous 1" folder.

18. MacLean, in *Freedom Is Not Enough* (42), concurs, but with the caveat that in 1958 the NAACP largely ceded the strategic role of coordinating with organized labor to Randolph's new Negro American Labor Conference.

19. On the evolution of the NAACP from an organization that privileged fighting for equal employment opportunity and working conditions to one in which school desegregation became paramount, see Risa L. Goluboff, *The Lost Promise of Civil Rights* (Cambridge, MA: Harvard University Press, 2007). For more on the history of the NAACP, see Manfred Berg, *The Ticket to Freedom: The NAACP and the Struggle for Black Political Integration* (Gainesville: University Press of Florida, 2005), and Patricia Sullivan, *Lift Every Voice: The NAACP and the Making of the Civil Rights Movement* (New York: New Press, 2009).

20. NUL Report, February 13, 1957, NUL Papers, series I, box Q1, "Negroes and the Building Trades Unions, 1957" folder.

21. Mitchell and Granger, addresses to the National Youth Training Incentives Conference, February 4, 1957, NUL Papers, series I, box G7, "PCGC, Reports and Miscellaneous Material" folder; NAACP press release, May 2, 1957, NAACP Papers, series III, box A239, "Nixon" folder; Granger to Urban League local branches, September 26, 1957, NUL Papers, series III, box 462, folder 3; Theodore Kheel, *Report to Vice President Johnson on the Structure and Operations of the President's Committee on Equal Employment Opportunity,* n.d. [June 1962], NUL Papers, series II, box A48, "PCEEO, 1962, 2" folder, concluded in box A42, "PCEEO, 1964, 1" folder; MacLaury, *To Advance Their Opportunities,* 146, 152; Palladino, *Skilled Hands,* 157. The quotation is from Kheel.

22. Ann Taneyhill, "What's Ahead for Negro Youth?" *The Pilot* (winter 1957), NUL Papers, series I, box E30, "Taneyhill" folder; Mitchell, David Sarnoff, Boris Shishkin, Clifford Froehlich, and Granger, addresses to the National Youth Training Incentives Conference, February 4, 1957, NUL Papers, series I, box G7, "PCGC, Reports and Miscellaneous Material" folder. One famous example of this process was Malcolm X, whose talents are now obvious in retrospect. His autobiography also recounts the experiences of several acquaintances whose immense talents were squan-

dered in lives of crime, such as a Harlem bookmaker whose skills with "the numbers" might have qualified him for advanced training as a mathematician. Malcolm X, *The Autobiography of Malcolm X, as Told to Alex Haley* (New York: Grove Press, 1965).

23. NAACP resolution, July 8, 1958, NAACP Papers, series III, box A7, "Resolutions" folder; Hill to Moon, July 22, 1958, ibid., box A190, "PCGC 1" folder; Paul Jacobs, "The Negro Worker Asserts His Rights: A New Militancy Troubles an Old Alliance," *The Reporter,* July 23, 1959. Most notable among these new organizations were the Congress of Racial Equality (CORE), founded in 1942 and headed by James Farmer, and the Southern Christian Leadership Conference, founded in 1957 and headed by the Reverend Dr. Martin Luther King Jr. For more on CORE, see chapter 2.

24. Steven Greenhouse, "Herbert Hill, a Voice against Discrimination, Dies at 80," *New York Times,* August 21, 2004. Hill was a controversial figure among labor activists and scholars during his long career in the NAACP and during his even longer career as an academic. In 2006 historian Eric Arnesen led a roundtable on Hill's legacy. See Eric Arnesen, "Assessing the Legacy of Herbert Hill: An Introduction"; Nancy MacLean, "Achieving the Promise of the Civil Rights Act: Herbert Hill and the NAACP's Fight for Jobs and Justice"; Clarence E. Walker, "The Legacy of Herbert Hill"; Nelson Lichtenstein, "Herbert Hill in History and Contention"; and Alex Lichtenstein, "Herbert Hill and the Negro Question," all in *Labor: Studies in Working Class History in the Americas* 3, no. 2 (summer 2006).

25. NAACP press release, April 24, 1958, NAACP Papers, series III, box A190, "PCGC 1" folder.

26. Hill to Mitchell, May 13, 1958, ibid., box A177, "Labor, AFL-CIO, 1956–58" folder.

27. PCGC newsletter, July 1958, NUL Papers, series I, box A41, "PCGC" folder. Car cards are the rectangular advertisements familiar to riders of modern mass transit systems.

28. NAACP resolution, July 8, 1958, NAACP Papers, series III, box A7, "Resolutions" folder.

29. Hill to Moon, July 22, 1958; NAACP resolution, July 1959, NAACP Papers, series III, box A10, "Resolutions" folder; NAACP resolution, June 1960, ibid., box A11, "Resolutions" folder.

30. MacLean, *Freedom Is Not Enough,* 40; Chen, *Fifth Freedom,* 43.

31. Yeldell to Granger, January 1, 1957, NUL Papers, series I, box G7, "PCGC Correspondence" folder; "Job Bias Bill Woos Ave's OK," *New York Age,* March 23, 1957; NAACP press release, October 16, 1957, NAACP Papers, series III, box A178, "Apprenticeship Training, General" folder.

32. NUL Board of Trustees to George Meany and Walter Reuther, December 1955, NUL Papers, series I, box A41, "President's Committee on Fair Government Contracts, 1955" folder; Dean Chamberlin to Meany, December 14, 1955, ibid., box A23, "IRD, Correspondence Concerning, 1948–56" folder.

33. Hill to Milton Webster, June 12, 1956, NAACP Papers, series III, box A177, "Labor, AFL-CIO, 1956–58" folder; Jacob Seidenberg to Wilkins and Hill to Wilkins, October 31, 1956; Wilkins to Seidenberg, November 2, 1956; Frank Baldau to Seidenberg, November 15, 1956; and Wilkins to Baldau, November 27, 1956, ibid., box A190, "PCGC 1" folder.

34. NAACP press release, October 16, 1957, ibid., box A178, "Apprenticeship Training, General" folder.

35. Hill to Shishkin, October 16 and December 4, 1958, NAACP Papers, series III, box A177, "Labor, AFL-CIO, 1956–58" folder; Roy Wilkins to Meany, December 19, 1958, ibid.; A. H. Raskin, "NAACP Accuses Labor of Bias Lag; Action on Discrimination Doesn't Match Words, Association Charges," *New York Times,* January 5, 1959. The source of the leak remains unknown.

36. Archie Robinson, *George Meany and His Times* (New York: Simon and Schuster, 1981); Jerry Flint, "George Meany Is Dead; Pioneer in Labor Was 85," *New York Times,* January 11, 1980; AFL-CIO Web site, http://www.aflcio.org/aboutus/history/history/meany.cfmand (accessed September 23, 2007). The quotation is from Flint.

37. Ibid.

38. Ibid.; Chen, *Fifth Freedom,* 43.

39. Hill to Wilkins, February 2, 1959, NAACP Papers, series III, box A177, "Labor, AFL-CIO, 1959" folder. MacLean, in *Freedom Is Not Enough* (41), agrees with Hill's assessment of the AFL-CIO Civil Rights Committee under Boris Shishkin, who "spent much of his time defending craft unions from blacks' complaints and criticizing civil rights leaders." For more on the relationship between organized labor and the NAACP, see Goluboff, *Lost Promise of Civil Rights,* 222–24.

40. Wilkins to A. Philip Randolph, February 6, 1959, NAACP Papers, series III, box A177, "Labor, AFL-CIO, 1959" folder. See also Jacobs, "The Negro Worker Asserts His Rights."

41. Randolph, address to the Trade Union Leadership Council, February 7, 1959, NAACP Papers, series III, box A30, "Randolph" folder.

42. NAACP press release, March 20, 1959, NAACP Papers, series III, box A177, "Labor, AFL-CIO, 1959" folder; Hill to Shishkin, July 23, 1959, ibid.

43. "NAACP and Labor: Frost upon a Friendship," *Detroit Free Press* editorial, September 19, 1959.

44. George Meany, address at the 1959 National Urban League Equal Opportunity Day Dinner, November 17, 1959, NUL Papers, series I, box E31, folder M; Robinson, *George Meany,* 123–40; Anderson, *A. Philip Randolph,* 301–7; Pfeffer, *A. Philip Randolph,* 208–13.

45. Ibid.; Frymer, *Black and Blue,* 52.

46. Palladino, *Skilled Hands,* 53–62, 97.

47. Hill to Moon, September 24, 1959, NAACP Papers, series III, box A177, "Labor, AFL-CIO, 1959" folder; Yeldell to Granger, September 24, 1959, NUL Papers, series I, box A63, "IRD, Memos and Reports, 1959, July–December" folder; "Union Racism Hit: Randolph Attacks Bias Policies of AFL-CIO" and "Unions Are No Different" editorial, *New York Age,* September 26, 1959; Chuck Stone, "Negroes Tell Meany: You're Wrong; Unanimous Censure of His Temper" and "A Stone's Throw: We All Appointed Randolph, George; Who Appointed You to Speak for Bigots?" column, *New York Age,* October 3, 1959; Alfred Duckett, "Mr. Meany's Outburst," and M. Harris, "Apology Wanted," *New York Age* letters to the editor, October 3, 1959; NAACP Board of Trustees resolution, October 13, 1959, NAACP Papers, series III, box A30, "Randolph" folder; Frymer, *Black and Blue,* 64–65.

48. Granger, "Manhattan and Beyond" column, October 2, 1959, and Granger to

NUL Board of Trustees, October 7, 1959, NUL Papers, series III, box 462, "Granger 4" folder; Chuck Stone, "Who Gave In—Meany, Randolph or League? Tempers Calm after Labor Czar Flies In"; "Mr. Meany and the Urban League" editorial; and Anna Arnold Hedgeman, "One Woman's Opinion: Trade Unions and Negroes" column, *New York Age,* October 10, 1959; Brotherhood of Sleeping-Car Porters press release, October 10, 1959, AFL-CIO Papers, RG 1–035, box 95, folder 8; NUL press release, October 11, 1959, ibid.; Theodore Kheel to Granger, October 13, 1959, NUL Papers, series I, box A9, "President, Correspondence with, 1959" folder.

49. Meany, address at the 1959 NUL Equal Opportunity Day Dinner.

50. "NLRB Action against Union Racism Asked," *Minneapolis Morning Tribune,* April 27, 1960; Frymer, *Black and Blue,* 32.

51. "Attacking One's Friends," *Twin City Observer* editorial, May 5, 1960; Anderson, *Pursuit of Fairness,* 104; Frymer, *Black and Blue,* 28–30, 51, 56.

52. A. Philip Randolph, address to the 1960 NAACP Annual Convention, June 24, 1960, NAACP Papers, series III, box A12, "Speeches" folder.

53. California Labor Fellowship resolution, December 1958, NAACP Papers, series III, box A64, "General, 2" folder.

54. IBEW resolution, October 1958, ibid.

55. PCGC newsletter, January 19, 1959, NUL Papers, series I, box D16, "PCGC, 1956–60" folder; NAACP newsletter, January 22, 1959, NAACP Papers, series III, box A190, "PCGC 2" folder. The term *affirmative action* can be found in various government documents dating at least as far back as the Wagner Act of 1935, but it did not become the "official" phrase for government programs to address racial inequality until 1961, when White House aide Hobart Taylor inserted it into President Kennedy's Executive Order No. 10925. According to Stacy Kinlock Sewell's "Contracting Racial Equality: Affirmative Action Policy and Practice in the United States, 1945–1970" (Ph.D. diss., Rutgers University, 1999), 141, in 1947 President Truman's minority affairs liaison David Niles became the first public official to use the phrase in its current form. For more on Executive Order No. 10925 and Hobart Taylor, see chapter 2. For more on the origins of the phrase *affirmative action,* see Hugh Davis Graham, *The Civil Rights Era: Origins and Development of National Policy* (New York: Oxford University Press, 1990), 33, and Chen, *Fifth Freedom,* 210–11.

56. Luther F. Jackson, "Urban League Hears of District's Problems with Job Discrimination," *Washington Post,* September 9, 1959; "Negro Job Dispute Brings Plea to U.S.," *New York Times,* November 26, 1959; Thomas to Granger, April 19, 1960, NUL Papers, series I, box A63, "IRD, Memos and Reports, 1960, January–April" folder; Jacob Schlitt to Yeldell, March 16, 1960, NUL Papers, series II, box D27, "AFL-CIO, 1960–63" folder.

57. Granger to Richard Nixon, April 28, 1960, NUL Papers, series I, box A23, "IRD, Correspondence Concerning, 1957–60" folder; Nixon to Granger, May 2, 1960, ibid.; Jean White, "5 Negroes Unqualified for Jobs, Panels Rule," *Washington Post,* May 19, 1960.

58. NAACP press release, May 20, 1960, NAACP Papers, series III, box A190, "Labor, President's Committee on Equal Employment Opportunity" folder.

59. Thomas A. Johnson, "Lester B. Granger, 79, Is Dead; Led the National Urban League," *New York Times,* January 10, 1976; NUL Web site, http://www.nul

.org/history.html (accessed September 23, 2007); Meany to Wilkins, May 27, 1960, NAACP Papers, series III, box A177, "Labor, AFL-CIO, 1960" folder.

60. NUL press release, May 21, 1960, NUL Papers, series I, box A169, "Miscellaneous Speeches, 1957–1960, Granger" folder; "Let's Skip the Politics," *Washington Evening Star* editorial, May 21, 1960.

61. Irving Ferman to Granger, May 27, 1960, NUL Papers, series I, box A9, "Board of Trustees, Members, Correspondence with, 1960" folder; Granger to John A. Roosevelt, June 2, 1960, ibid. The quotation is from Ferman.

62. Granger to Franklin Floete, September 16, 1960, NUL Papers, series I, box A23, "IRD, Correspondence Concerning, 1957–60" folder; Thomas to Granger, October 20, 1960, ibid., box A64, "IRD, Memos and Reports, 1960, May–December" folder; *Washington Post* and *Washington Times-Herald,* October 21, 1960, as described in NUL employment clippings, NUL Papers, series I, box N90. The quotation is from Thomas.

2. Becoming the Urban Crisis

1. Art Peters, "Camera Taken, Clubbed Says Social Worker," *Philadelphia Tribune,* May 28, 1963.

2. Ibid. *Militant* in the civil rights sense means "aggressively active," as opposed to the conventional definition "engaged in warfare."

3. Malcolm Poindexter, "NAACP Leads 300 Pickets at 2 Schools," *Philadelphia Bulletin,* May 24, 1963; Art Peters, "LaBrum Admits Group's Power to Bar Building Bias," *Philadelphia Tribune,* May 25, 1963. For more on Moore, see Matthew J. Countryman, *Up South: Civil Rights and Black Power in Philadelphia* (Philadelphia: University of Pennsylvania Press, 2006); Gerald L. Early, *This Is Where I Came In: Black America in the 1960s* (Lincoln: University of Nebraska Press, 2003); Paul Lermack, "Cecil Moore and the Philadelphia Branch of the National Association for the Advancement of Colored People," *Black Politics in Philadelphia,* ed. Miriam Ershkowitz and Joseph Zikmund II (New York: Basic Books, 1973).

4. Fred L. Bonaparte, "'Average Joes' Star in Demonstrations"; Mark Bricklin, "Tempers Flare; Girl Picket Hit, Dragged by Mob"; and Lou Potter, "Commissioner Apologizes to Irate Crowd," *Philadelphia Tribune,* May 28, 1963.

5. John F. Morrison, "Protests Here Only the Start, NAACP Warns," *Philadelphia Bulletin,* May 30, 1963; "All Night Talks Reach Pact," *Philadelphia Bulletin,* May 31, 1963.

6. Nick Bryant, *The Bystander: John F. Kennedy and the Struggle for Black Equality* (New York: Basic Books, 2006), 225–42; Anderson, *Pursuit of Fairness,* 60.

7. See, for instance, Joel Seldin, "NAACP Drive on Job Rights in the Unions," *New York Herald-Tribune,* October 17, 1962.

8. U.S. Conference of Mayors, "Changing Employment Practices in the Construction Industry," November 3, 1965, NAACP Papers, series III, box A178, "1965" folder.

9. Ibid.

10. Ibid.; Vincent G. Macaluso to Edward C. Sylvester, November 4, 1965, Records of the Department of Labor, Collection of the OFCC Assistant Director for

Construction, box 26, "Correspondence, 1965–1966" folder, National Archives and Records Administration, College Park, MD (hereafter cited as OFCC ADC); Bennett O. Stalvey Jr. to Macaluso, August 9, 1966, ibid., box 3, "Philadelphia—Correspondence" folder.

11. "Jim Crow's Sweetheart Contract," *Greater Philadelphia Magazine,* February 1963; U.S. Conference of Mayors, "Changing Employment Practices"; Howard G. Foster, "Nonapprentice Sources of Training in Construction," *Monthly Labor Review,* February 1970.

12. Ibid.; Palladino, *Skilled Hands,* 141–42.

13. U.S. Conference of Mayors, "Changing Employment Practices"; Macaluso to Sylvester, November 4, 1965; Stalvey to Macaluso, August 9, 1966, OFCC ADC, box 3, "Philadelphia—Correspondence" folder; Marc Linder, *Wars of Attrition: Vietnam, the Business Roundtable, and the Decline of Construction Unions* (Iowa City: Fănpìhuà Press, 2000).

14. Ibid.; Palladino, *Skilled Hands,* 7.

15. DOL Bureau of Labor Statistics Report, April 1961, NUL Papers, series II, box A53, "Washington Activities, Department of Labor" folder; Joseph Alton Jenkins to Lyndon Baines Johnson, January 2, 1961, Records of President Lyndon Baines Johnson, Vice Presidential Papers, Civil Rights file, box 8, "Correspondence Relating to Drafting of Executive Order" folder, LBJ Library; Gerald W. Siegel to LBJ, January 3, 1961, ibid.

16. John F. Kennedy, Executive Order No. 10925, NUL Papers, series II, box A3, "B, 1961" folder; Anderson, *Pursuit of Fairness,* 60–61; MacLaury, *To Advance Their Opportunities,* 170–76; Palladino, *Skilled Hands,* 159.

17. George E. Reedy to LBJ, February 28, 1961, LBJ Vice Presidential Papers, Civil Rights file, box 8, "Correspondence Relating to Drafting of Executive Order" folder; MacLaury, *To Advance Their Opportunities,* 177–87.

18. Doris Kearns, *Lyndon Johnson and the American Dream* (New York: Harper and Row, 1976), 162; Graham, *Civil Rights Era,* 38–43; Dennis C. Dickerson, *Militant Mediator: Whitney M. Young, Jr.* (Lexington: University Press of Kentucky, 1998), 245–46; Robert Caro, *The Years of Lyndon Johnson, Master of the Senate* (New York: Knopf, 2002), 31–32; Robert Dallek, *Lyndon B. Johnson: Portrait of a President* (New York: Oxford University Press, 2004), 125–26, 133–36; Randall B. Woods, *LBJ: Architect of American Ambition* (New York: Free Press, 2006), 394–95.

19. NAACP press release, March 10, 1961, NAACP Papers, series III, box A175, "Kennedy Miscellany 2" folder; "Tucker Lauds U.S. Move on Job Bias," *Washington Post,* March 17, 1961.

20. For more on Kennedy, Johnson, and the PCEEO, see Graham, *Civil Rights Era,* 38–39, 43, and Kearns, *Lyndon Johnson and the American Dream,* 162.

21. PCEEO press release, October 31, 1961, AFL-CIO Papers, RG 1–038, box 78, folder 12; Anderson, *Pursuit of Fairness,* 64; MacLaury, *To Advance Their Opportunities,* 189–94.

22. PCEEO press releases, August 8 and October 31, 1961, AFL-CIO Papers, RG 1–038, box 78, folder 9.

23. John G. Field to LBJ, October 6, 1961, LBJ Vice Presidential Papers, Subject file, box 85, "PCEEO, July–December, 2" folder; "Kennedy Aide Warns on Job Dis-

crimination," *Chicago Sun-Times,* October 12, 1961; PCEEO press release, October 31, 1961, AFL-CIO Papers, RG 1–038, box 78, folder 12.

24. Robert Troutman Jr. to LBJ, November 1, 1961, LBJ Vice Presidential Papers, Subject file, box 85, "PCEEO July–December, 2" folder; MacLaury, *To Advance Their Opportunities,* 195–96.

25. Richard C. Wells to Sterling Tucker, December 20, 1961, NUL Papers, series II, box D31, "PCEEO 1961–2" folder. Chen, in *Fifth Freedom* (213), concurs that Plans for Progress was largely a method whereby companies could voluntarily take a few actions that would keep the heavier regulatory hand of the government off their backs; Sewell, in "Contracting Racial Equality" (150), calls Plans for Progress a "publicity venture."

26. MacLean, *Freedom Is Not Enough,* 44; Anderson, *Pursuit of Fairness,* 65.

27. PCEEO Report, March 30, 1962, LBJ Vice Presidential Papers, Subject file, box 139, "Labor, PCEEO, January–April" folder.

28. Statement of Herbert Hill to the PCEEO, April 6, 1962, NAACP Papers, series III, box A184, "Herbert Hill, Statements" folder; MacLaury, *To Advance Their Opportunities,* 204.

29. Wirtz quoted in MacLaury, *To Advance Their Opportunities,* 215, 324; Delton, *Racial Integration in Corporate America,* 184–85.

30. PCEEO press release, November 15, 1962, LBJ Vice Presidential Papers, Civil Rights file, box 12, "Press Releases" folder.

31. List of signers of Union Programs for Fair Practices, November 15, 1962, ibid., box 13, "Union Programs for Fair Practices" folder; Hobart L. Taylor to LBJ, February 27, 1963, LBJ Vice Presidential Papers, Subject file, box 198, "Labor, PCEEO, March–May" folder; Frymer, *Black and Blue,* 32; MacLaury, *To Advance Their Opportunities,* 215–19; Palladino, *Skilled Hands,* 162.

32. Herbert Hill to LBJ, June 27, 1962, NAACP Papers, series III, box A190, "R Miscellaneous" folder; John D. Pomfret, "U.S. Plans Drive for Job Equality," *New York Times,* July 29, 1962; PCEEO press release, October 1962, NUL Papers, series II, box A42, "PCEEO, 1962, 1" folder; PCEEO press release, November 16, 1962, LBJ Vice Presidential Papers, Collection of George E. Reedy, box 22, "Press Releases, 1962" folder (hereafter cited as Reedy Collection).

33. Peter Braestrup, "U.S. Panel Split over Negro Jobs," *New York Times,* June 18, 1962; *New York Times* editorial, June 19, 1962; NAACP resolution, July 1962, NAACP Papers, series III, box A14, "Resolutions" folder; Lester Granger, "Manhattan and Beyond" column, July 7, 1962, LBJ Vice Presidential Papers, Subject file, box 139, "Labor, PCEEO, July–September" folder; Reedy to LBJ, July 20, 1962, ibid.; MacLaury, *To Advance Their Opportunities,* 205–6, 213.

34. PCEEO draft press release, August 20, 1962, LBJ Vice Presidential Papers, Civil Rights file, box 12, "Press Releases" folder; White House press release, August 23, 1962, LBJ Vice Presidential Papers, Subject file, box 139, "Labor, PCEEO, July–September" folder.

35. PCEEO press release, April 7, 1964, AFL-CIO Papers, RG 1–038, box 73, folder 12; Richard Allen Burns, "Taylor, Hobart T., Sr.," *The Handbook of Texas Online,* http://www.tsha.utexas.edu/handbook/online/articles/TT/fta30.html (accessed November 17, 2007).

36. Graham, in *Civil Rights Era* (58–63), does not see the resolution of the Trout-man affair as the watershed moment that I do, noting that the performance of the PCEEO before Troutman's resignation was not as lackluster as civil rights groups con-tended. But Graham cites no non-administration sources for his opinion.

37. PCEEO press releases, January 17 and 23, 1963, and PCEEO newsletter, Janu-ary 1963, Reedy Collection, box 23, "Press Releases 1963" folder; MacLaury, *To Advance Their Opportunities*, 211.

38. Hobart L. Taylor to LBJ, February 27, 1963, LBJ Vice Presidential Papers, Subject file, box 198, "Labor, PCEEO, March–May" folder; Reedy to LBJ, March 2, 1963, ibid.; PCEEO press release, May 29, 1963, LBJ Vice Presidential Papers, Civil Rights file, box 12, "Press Releases" folder.

39. Theodore Spaulding, "Philadelphia's Hate Strike," *The Crisis*, September 1944.

40. Ibid.; Allan M. Winkler, "The Philadelphia Transit Strike of 1944," *Journal of American History* 59, no. 1 (June 1972): 73–89; Countryman, *Up South*.

41. Leon H. Sullivan, *Build, Brother, Build* (Philadelphia: Macrae Smith, 1969), 54. For "defended" neighborhoods, see Sugrue, *Origins of the Urban Crisis*, 209–58.

42. Sullivan, *Build, Brother, Build*, 56–58. For more on internal colonialism, see Peter Bohmer, "African-Americans as an Internal Colony: The Theory of Internal Colonialism," in *Readings in Black Political Economy*, ed. John Whitehead and Cobie Kwasi Harris (Dubuque, IA: Kendall/Hunt, 1999).

43. "Jim Crow's Sweetheart Contract."

44. Inez L. Thompson, "NAACP Prexy Outlines Militant Program," *Philadel-phia Afro-American*, January 19, 1963; Chet Coleman, "Board of Education Sets up $31-Million Program, All for Schools in Negro Areas," *Philadelphia Tribune*, Febru-ary 19, 1963; Countryman, *Up South*, 85–86, 95–98; Early, *This Is Where I Came In*, 89; Aldon D. Morris, *Origins of the Civil Rights Movement* (New York: Free Press, 1984), 285–86; Thomas J. Sugrue, *Sweet Land of Liberty: The Forgotten Struggle for Civil Rights in the North* (New York: Random House, 2008), 292–93.

45. "CORE Pickets Tate's Home and City Hall," *Philadelphia Bulletin*, April 14, 1963; "CORE Says It Will Prod Tate until City Job Bias Ends," *Philadelphia Bulletin*, April 17, 1963; Sugrue, *Sweet Land of Liberty*, 292.

46. August Meier and Elliott Rudwick, *CORE: A Study in the Civil Rights Move-ment, 1942–1968* (Urbana: University of Illinois Press, 1975); Allen J. Matusow, *The Unraveling of America: A History of Liberalism in the 1960s* (New York: Harper and Row, 1984); David Halberstam, *The Children* (New York: Random House, 1998).

47. "Mayor's Office Sit-in Forces Building Trades Study," *Philadelphia Tribune*, April 27, 1963; Philadelphia Commission on Human Relations resolution, April 2, 1963, Records of the Philadelphia Jewish Labor Committee, box 3, folder 13, Urban Archives, Temple University, Philadelphia (hereafter cited as PJLC Records); George Schermer to Alex Wollod, April 23, 1963, ibid.

48. Philadelphia Urban League testimony before the Philadelphia Commission on Human Relations, May 3, 1963, NUL Papers, series II, box D66, "1963" folder; Orrin Evans, "CORE Urges City Take over Project Hiring," *Philadelphia Bulletin*, May 6, 1963.

49. Fred Bonaparte, "Court Orders Go out to Unions from CHR Office," *Phila-*

delphia Tribune, May 11, 1963; Mark Bricklin, "Craft Union Bias Blamed on Wish to Stymie Rivals," *Philadelphia Tribune,* May 14, 1963; Orrin Evans, "Head of Electrical Union Denies It Bars Negroes," *Philadelphia Bulletin,* May 17, 1963; Philadelphia Jewish Labor Committee–Negro Trade Union Leadership Council meeting minutes, February 16, 1966, PJLC Records, box 3, folder 12.

50. "20 from CORE Stage Sit-in in Tate's Office," *Philadelphia Bulletin,* May 14, 1963; James H. J. Tate, "Mayor Asks Support for Effort to End Bias," *Philadelphia Bulletin,* May 15, 1963.

51. Philip Fine, "He Tells CORE Unions Must Admit Negroes," *Philadelphia Bulletin,* May 15, 1963.

52. "NAACP Plaza Sit-in Cancelled with Warning," *Philadelphia Tribune,* May 18, 1963. On the image of the nonviolent southern protester, see Steven F. Lawson, "Freedom Then, Freedom Now: The Historiography of the Civil Rights Movement," *American Historical Review* 96, no. 2 (April 1991): 456–71; and Henry Hampton (director), *Eyes on the Prize* (Blackside Productions, 1987). On the image of the militant northern protester, see Sugrue, *Sweet Land of Liberty,* and Courtney Lyons, "Burning Columbia Avenue: Religious Undertones of the 1964 Philadelphia Race Riot" (paper presented at Civil Rights Conflict in the North: Under-Emphasized Elements of the African-American Civil Rights Movement, 2010 meeting of the American Historical Association, San Diego, CA). The quotation is from Lyons.

53. Douglas H. Bedell, "McShain's Crew Is Pulled off Job," *Philadelphia Bulletin,* May 16, 1963; "3 Firms Warn City It Will Pay for Shutdown" and "City Won't Pay 5 Unions Idled in Shutdown," *Philadelphia Bulletin,* May 17, 1963.

54. Douglas H. Bedell, "Negroes Urged to Seek Cards in Building Trades Unions," *Philadelphia Bulletin,* May 19, 1963.

55. Coleman, "Board of Education Sets up $31-Million Program"; James Jones to Philadelphia AFL-CIO Executive Board, February 27, 1963, AFL-CIO Papers, RG 1–098, box 95, folder 9; "NAACP Urges Schools to Stop All-White Jobs," *Philadelphia Bulletin,* May 20, 1963; Lou Potter, "NAACP Gives City until Friday to Oust Biased Unions on City Projects, Will Face Mass Picketing if No Action Taken," *Philadelphia Tribune,* May 21, 1963.

56. "Negro Labor Quota on Jobs Set by CORE," *Philadelphia Bulletin,* May 22, 1963.

57. "All Night Talks Reach Pact," *Philadelphia Bulletin,* May 31, 1963; Palladino, *Skilled Hands,* 159.

58. Wilkins to JFK, May 28, 1963, NAACP Papers, series III, box A174, "Kennedy Correspondence" folder; NAACP press release, May 30, 1963, ibid., box A190, "Labor, Pennsylvania" folder; John F. Morrison, "Protests Here Only the Start, NAACP Warns," *Philadelphia Bulletin,* May 30, 1963. Clarence Taylor, in *Knocking On Our Own Door: Milton A. Galamison and the Struggle to Integrate New York City Schools* (New York: Columbia University Press, 1997), 128, reports on Wilkins's testy relationship with similar charismatic leaders in New York.

59. Velma Hill, "Harlem Pickets Force City Hall to Halt Project," *New America,* June 10, 1963; Milton Honig, "Discrimination Protests Rising in Newark," *New York Times,* June 16, 1963; Gertrude Samuels, "Even More Crucial Than in the South," *New York Times Magazine,* June 30, 1963.

60. On the racial violence in Birmingham, see, for instance, Matusow, *Unraveling of America*, 86–89, and Judith Stein, *Running Steel, Running America: Race, Economic Policy, and the Decline of Liberalism* (Chapel Hill: University of North Carolina Press, 1998), 37–38. Extended footage of the use of dogs and water cannons to quell protests can be seen in Spike Lee (director), *Four Little Girls* (40 Acres Productions, 1997).

61. PCEEO press release, May 1963, LBJ Vice Presidential Papers, Subject file, box 198, "Labor, PCEEO, March–May" folder.

62. John F. Kennedy, civil rights address, June 11, 1963, http://www.americanrhetoric.com/speeches/jfkcivilrights.htm (accessed November 17, 2007).

63. J. Francis Polhaus to Roy Wilkins, May 1963, NAACP Papers, series III, box A175, "Kennedy Miscellany 2" folder.

64. "Jobs Available for Negroes, Wirtz Testifies," *Philadelphia Bulletin,* June 27, 1963; DOL draft policy, June 27, 1963, AFL-CIO Papers, RG 1–038, box 73, folder 17; Anderson, *Pursuit of Fairness,* 63; Chen, *Fifth Freedom,* 218.

65. John F. Kennedy, Executive Order No. 10925, NUL Papers, series II, box A3, folder B, 1961, §§304–5; W. Willard Wirtz to LBJ, August 19, 1963, Reedy Collection, box 26, "Wirtz, Willard" folder.

66. PCEEO press release, June 25, 1963, AFL-CIO Papers, RG 1–038, box 73, folder 6.

67. PCEEO press release, July 24, 1963, Reedy Collection, box 23, "Press Releases, 1963" folder.

68. DOL draft procedures, September 27, 1963, NUL Papers, series II, box D33, "DC, 1963, 3" folder.

69. Young, TV interview, August 18, 1963, ibid., box E49, "TV Interviews, 1963–4" folder.

70. Remarks of Roy Wilkins, Walter Reuther, and Whitney Young at the March on Washington, August 28, 1963, NAACP Papers, series III, box A227, "March on Washington Speeches and Statements" folder. For more on the march, see Taylor Branch, *Parting the Waters: America in the King Years, 1954–1963* (New York: Simon and Schuster, 1988); Patrik Henry Bass, *Like a Mighty Stream: The March on Washington, August 28, 1963* (Philadelphia: Running Press, 2002); Robin S. Doak, *The March on Washington: Uniting against Racism* (Minneapolis: Compass Point Books, 2008).

71. See, for instance, Dickerson, *Militant Mediator,* and Rudi Williams, "Whitney M. Young, Jr.: Little Known Civil Rights Pioneer," *Defenselink News,* February 1, 2002.

72. Whitney Young, "Domestic Marshall Plan," *New York Times,* October 6, 1963.

73. Quoted in a DOL press release, December 30, 1963, NUL Papers, series II, box A17, "DOL, 1964, 1" folder.

74. DOL press release, December 9, 1963, ibid.

75. Young, TV interview, December 8, 1963, NUL Papers, series II, box E49, "TV Interviews, 1963–4" folder; Dickerson, *Militant Mediator,* 245–46.

76. U.S. Congress, Civil Rights Act of 1964, H.R. 7152, July 2, 1964.

77. "The Nation: Now Philadelphia," *New York Times,* August 30, 1964; DOL press release, July 27, 1964, NUL Papers, series II, box A17, "DOL, 1964, 4" folder. Between June 1962 and June 1964, the unemployment rate for white youths (aged

fourteen to twenty-four) increased from 13.2 to 14.7 percent, while the rate for non-white youths increased from 19.1 to 24.0 percent. Among those aged twenty to twenty-four, white unemployment increased from 8.0 to 8.5 percent, and nonwhite unemployment decreased slightly, from 15.8 to 15.0 percent. Between 1962 and 1964, therefore, the average age of the unemployed black worker fell; unemployed blacks as a group were becoming *younger.*

3. Grasping at Solutions

1. Herbert Hill, testimony on equal opportunity contract compliance, December 5, 1968, in *Construction Labor Report* 690 (December 11, 1968); George D. Zucker-man, "Sheet Metal Workers' Case: A Case History of Bias in the Building Trades," *New York Law Journal,* September 8, 1969.

2. Otis E. Finley, "Statement before the House Committee on Labor and Educa-tion," November 4, 1961, NUL Papers, series II, box E36, "Finley, House Committee on Labor and Education" folder.

3. U.S. Conference of Mayors, "Changing Employment Practices"; Linder, *Wars of Attrition,* 113–14; Palladino, *Skilled Hands,* 143.

4. "Jim Crow's Sweetheart Contract," *Greater Philadelphia Magazine,* February 1963; Leonard J. Biermann, file memo, February 10, 1965, Records of the Department of Labor, Collection of Secretary W. Willard Wirtz, box 236, "PCEEO 3b" folder, National Archives and Records Administration, College Park, MD (hereafter cited as Wirtz Collection); William C. Webb to Meany, February 15, 1965, AFL-CIO Papers, RG 1–038, box 72, folder 12; John F. Henning to David G. Filvaroff, May 3, 1965, Wirtz Collection, box 246, "PCEEO, 5" folder; Hugh C. Murphy to Arthur Chapin, March 2, 1965, ibid.; "Employers, Unions Train Apprentices," *Cleveland Press,* April 16, 1966; MacLaury, *To Advance Their Opportunities,* 160, 226–27.

5. Clifford P. Froehlich, "Career Guidance with Minority Group Youth: A Coop-erative Effort," address to the Youth Training-Incentives Conference, February 4, 1957, NUL Papers, series I, box G7, "PCGC, Reports and Miscellaneous Material" folder; NAACP press release, March 7, 1964, NAACP Papers, series III, box A191, "Labor, S Miscellaneous, 1" folder; U.S. Conference of Mayors, "Changing Employ-ment Practices"; "Employers, Unions Train Apprentices"; Anderson, *Pursuit of Fair-ness,* 56; MacLaury, *To Advance Their Opportunities,* 232; Palladino, *Skilled Hands,* 142–43; Sugrue, *Origins of the Urban Crisis,* 118. Brennan quoted in Palladino (143).

6. Froehlich, "Career Guidance"; U.S. Conference of Mayors, "Changing Employment Practices"; "Employers, Unions Train Apprentices"; NUL brochure, January 18, 1967, NUL Papers, series III, box 134, "Project LEAP, Brochure" folder.

7. U.S. Conference of Mayors, "Changing Employment Practices."

8. NAACP press release, March 7, 1964, NAACP Papers, series III, box A191, "Labor, S Miscellaneous, 1" folder; U.S. Conference of Mayors, "Changing Employ-ment Practices"; "Employers, Unions Train Apprentices."

9. "Hit Unions on Hiring of Negroes," *Cleveland Press,* February 19, 1966; Anderson, *Pursuit of Fairness,* 104.

10. Jack Adler to Wilkins, January 14, 1965, NAACP Papers, series III, box A190, "Labor, Pennsylvania" folder; Joseph B. Meranze, "Negro Employment in the

Construction Industry," in *The Negro and Employment Opportunity: Problems and Practices,* ed. Herbert R. Northrup and Richard L. Rowan (Ann Arbor: University of Michigan Press, 1965), 199–206; "Hit Unions on Hiring"; Sugrue, *Origins of the Urban Crisis,* 116.

11. California FEPC press release, December 31, 1965, NUL Papers, series II, box A34, "Miscellany, A" folder; "Hit Unions on Hiring."

12. "Hit Unions on Hiring"; Marie Hurley to Vincent G. Macaluso, April 17, 1967, OFCC ADC, box 26, "St. Louis Correspondence, 1967" folder.

13. MacLaury, *To Advance Their Opportunities,* 232–44; Palladino, *Skilled Hands,* 161–62.

14. John D. Pomfret, "U.S. Will Attack Job Bias in Construction Industry; Two-Part Program to Seek Cooperation of Contractors—Special 40-Man Force Will Concentrate on 10 Regions," *New York Times,* June 8, 1964.

15. Ibid.

16. PCEEO press release, June 8, 1964, AFL-CIO Papers, RG 1–078, box 73, folder 12; Cernoria D. Johnson to Macaluso, June 12, 1964, NUL Papers, series II, box A42, "1964, 1" folder.

17. Macaluso interview with the author, January 4, 2008.

18. Ibid.

19. Macaluso to Hobart Taylor Jr., December 16, 1964, Wirtz Collection, box 245, folder 1a.

20. Plans for Progress press release, May 1, 1964, ibid., box 154, folder 5a; DOL press release, July 6, 1964, NUL Papers, series II, box A17, "DOL, 1964, 3" folder; PCEEO press release, July 16, 1964, Wirtz Collection, box 154, folder 7b.

21. DOL press releases, July 27 and August 17, 1964, NUL Papers, series II, box A17," DOL, 1964, 4" folder; "The Nation: Now Philadelphia," *New York Times,* August 30, 1964; Arthur A. Chapin, "Remarks to the Job Development and Education Council Session of the 1964 NUL Annual Conference," August 5, 1964, NUL Papers, series II, box F19, "1964, A–K" folder.

22. DOL press release, July 20, 1964, NUL Papers, series II, box A17, "DOL, 1964, 3" folder; DOL press releases, October 5 and 12 and November 9, 1964, ibid., "DOL, 1964, 4" folder; NUL press release, October 9, 1964, ibid., box E34, "October, 9b" folder.

23. PCEEO press release, March 18, 1965, Records of President Lyndon Baines Johnson, Collection of White House aide Lee C. White, box 4, "Committee on Equal Employment Opportunity, 1964" folder (hereafter cited as White Collection).

24. Taylor to agency heads, April 26, 1965, Wirtz Collection, box 246, folder 4b; PCEEO press release, April 30, 1965, ibid., folder 5; remarks of Woody Zenfell to the Associated General Contractors of St. Louis, May 13, 1965, OFCC ADC, box 26, "Newsclips" folder; PCEEO press release, May 21, 1965, AFL-CIO Papers, RG 1–038, box 73, folder 16; Desmond H. Sealy to NUL affiliates, May 26, 1965, NUL Papers, series II, box D34, "1964–5" folder.

25. Macaluso to area coordinators, April 21, 1965, White Collection, box 4, "Committee on Equal Employment Opportunity, 1964" folder.

26. LBJ, "The American Promise: Remarks of the President to a Joint Session of the Congress," March 15, 1965, Records of President Lyndon Baines Johnson, Col-

lection of White House aide Harry C. McPherson, box 21, "Civil Rights, 1965" folder (hereafter cited as McPherson Collection).

27. NUL press release, March 16, 1965, NUL Papers, series II, box E35, "1965" folder.

28. Richard C. Wells to Sterling Tucker, December 20, 1961, ibid., box D31, "PCEEO, 1961–2" folder; PCEEO draft press release, August 20, 1962, LBJ Vice Presidential Papers, Civil Rights file, box 12, "Press Releases" folder; PCEEO press release, November 14, 1962, Reedy Collection, box 22, "Press Releases, 1962" folder; PCEEO press releases, January 17 and 23, 1963, ibid., box 23, "Press Releases, 1963" folder; Young, "Domestic Marshall Plan," *New York Times,* October 6, 1963; "Shuffling the Planks," *Time,* July 17, 1964; Todd Gitlin, *The Sixties: Years of Hope, Days of Rage* (Toronto: Bantam Books, 1987), 168.

29. U.S. Congress, Civil Rights Act of 1964, H.R. 7152, July 2, 1964; "Statement of Civil Rights Organization Leaders," July 29, 1964, NAACP Papers, series III, box A73, "Statements" folder; Clare Booth Luce, "Summit Meeting or Surrender," *New York Herald-Tribune,* August 11, 1964.

30. Civil Rights Act of 1964; Matusow, *Unraveling of America,* 210–11; Chen, *Fifth Freedom,* 29–30, 171, 178–79, 190.

31. PCEEO press release, January 4, 1965, Wirtz Collection, box 245, folder 1a; Hubert H. Humphrey to LBJ, January 4, 1965, White Collection, box 4, "President's Council on Equal Opportunity [V.P.]" folder; LBJ to Humphrey, February 5, 1965, Records of President Lyndon Baines Johnson, White House Central files, box FG403, "President's Committee on Equal Employment Oppportunity, 1/1/65–" folder; White House press release, May 10, 1965, Records of President Lyndon Baines Johnson, Collection of White House aide Will R. Sparks, box 8, "Equal Employment Opportunity" folder.

32. LBJ, "To Fulfill These Rights: Remarks of the President at Howard University, Washington, DC," June 4, 1965, McPherson Collection, box 21, "Civil Rights, 1965" folder. Terry Anderson (*Pursuit of Fairness,* 89) sees the 1965 Howard University speech—rather than Troutman's 1962 dismissal in favor of Hobart Taylor at the PCEEO—as the key moment in Johnson's shift. The Howard speech made the earlier shift clear to the public.

33. NUL press release, June 9, 1965, NUL Papers, series II, box E35, "1965" folder.

34. Leonard H. Carter to Wilkins, September 10, 1965, NAACP Papers, series III, box A333, "Watts Riot" folder. For more on Watts, see Guichard Parris and Lester Brooks, *Blacks in the City: A History of the National Urban League* (Boston: Little, Brown, 1971), 435, and Matusow, *Unraveling of America,* 196, 360–61. For the inner-city riots, including Watts, see, for instance, Sugrue, *Sweet Land of Liberty;* Kevin Mumford, *Newark: A History of Race, Rights, and Riots in America* (New York: New York University Press, 2007); and Frances Piven and Richard Cloward, *The Politics of Turmoil: Essays on Poverty, Race, and the Urban Crisis* (New York: Vintage, 1975).

35. A. Philip Randolph, "How to Prevent Race Riots," *New York Amsterdam News,* September 4, 1965; Daryl Michael Scott, *Contempt and Pity: Social Policy and the Image of the Damaged Black Psyche, 1880–1996* (Chapel Hill: University of North Carolina Press, 1997), 153, 156–57.

36. Alfred Friendly, "Official Watts Riot Report Pulls No Punches," *Washington Post,* December 13, 1965; Matusow, *Unraveling of America,* 361.

37. Lee C. White to LBJ, September 20, 1965, White Collection, box 4, "President's Council on Equal Opportunity [V.P.]" folder; Humphrey to LBJ, September 24, 1965, AFL-CIO Papers, RG 1–038, box 73, folder 14; LBJ, Executive Order No. 11246, September 24, 1965, ibid.; Wirtz, "Secretary's Notice No. 94–65," October 5, 1965, OFCC ADC, box 18, "Wirtz, Correspondence with" folder; Anderson, *Pursuit of Fairness,* 92, 96; Palladino, *Skilled Hands,* 162; Chen, *Fifth Freedom,* 29–30, 171, 178–79, 190.

38. Graham, *Civil Rights Era,* 285. Subsequent scholarship includes Anderson, *Pursuit of Fairness,* 104–5, and Yuill, *Richard Nixon and the Rise of Affirmative Action,* 138.

39. Matt Schudel, "Labor, Hill Official Edward Sylvester Dies," *Washington Post,* February 18, 2005; Wirtz, "Secretary's Notice No. 94–65."

40. Wirtz, "Secretary's Notice No. 94–65;" Donald Slaiman, labor news conference, October 24, 1965, NAACP Papers, series III, box A178, "NAACP, 1965" folder; Robert Dietsch, "Bans Hiring Bias on U.S. Contracts," *Cleveland Press,* February 10, 1966; Macaluso to Edward C. Sylvester, November 4, 1965, OFCC ADC, box 26, "Correspondence, 1965–1966" folder; Anderson, *Pursuit of Fairness,* 96, 103.

41. Macaluso to Sylvester and Ward McCreedy to Sylvester, November 4, 1965, and Biermann to Sylvester, November 22, 1965, OFCC ADC box 26, "Correspondence, 1965–1966" folder; OFCC Suggested Programs, December 22, 1965; F. V. Helmer to Paul McDonald, February 2, 1966; F. Peter LiBassi to Sylvester, Richard M. Schmidt to Sylvester, Clyde C. Cook to Sylvester, and Paul McDonald to Sylvester, February 3, 1966; Richard F. Lally to Sylvester, February 9, 1966; Harry S. Traynor to Sylvester, February 14, 1966; Jack Moskowitz to Sylvester, February 23, 1966; and Alfred S. Hodgson to Sylvester, February 25, 1966, all in OFCC ADC, box 19, "Federal Contract Construction Program" folder; Sylvester to agency heads, June 8, 1966, OFCC ADC, box 18, "Transition" folder.

42. Dietsch, "Bans Hiring Bias."

43. Donald Janson, "Arch in St. Louis Inching Skyward," *New York Times,* August 30, 1964; PCEEO press release, April 30, 1965, Wirtz Collection, box 246, "PCEEO, 5" folder; Leslie McCarthy, "Arch Memories," *Webster-Kirkwood Times,* October 21, 2005. The quotations are from McCarthy.

44. Zenfell to Macaluso, August 27 and 31, 1965, OFCC ADC, box 26, "Correspondence, 1965–1966" folder, and September 24, 1965, ibid., box 25, "Unions Practicing Discrimination" folder.

45. Macaluso to Sylvester and Ward McCreedy to Sylvester, November 4, 1965; Paul Boyajian to Ward McCreedy, November 9, 1965; Biermann to Sylvester, November 22, 1965; Hugh C. Murphy to Joseph W. Beetz, November 30, 1965; and Leroy R. Brown to Zenfell, December 23, 1965, OFCC ADC box 26, "Correspondence, 1965–1966" folder; "AFL-CIO Unions Deny Arch Boycott; Long Legal Battle Opens over Practices on Visitor Center," *St. Louis Globe-Democrat;* "Tells of Effort to Get Firm at Arch to Quit; Witness Says Union Council Made Plea to U.S. on E. Smith," *St. Louis Post-Dispatch,* February 4, 1966.

46. Arthur A. Hunn, policy statement, December 27, 1965, OFCC ADC, box 26,

"Correspondence, 1965–1966" folder; Ted Schafers, "Dispute Stops Riverfront Visitor Center Project Work," *St. Louis Globe-Democrat,* January 12, 1966; "A Principle at Stake," *St. Louis Post-Dispatch* editorial, January 22, 1966; "U.S. Charges Bias to AFL-CIO Unit; Labor Department Requests Action in St. Louis Dispute," *New York Times,* January 23, 1966; Graham, *Civil Rights Era,* 285–86; MacLean, *Freedom Is Not Enough,* 92–93.

47. Sylvester to agency heads, January 5, 1966; Sylvester to Thomas D. Morris, January 7, 1966; Sylvester to Wirtz, January 20, 1966; Sylvester to Nicholas deB. Katzenbach, January 21, 1966; Sylvester to Franklin D. Roosevelt Jr., and Sylvester to Stewart L. Udall, January 24, 1966, OFCC ADC, box 26, "Correspondence, 1965–1966" folder; "St. Louis Union Group Accused of Interfering with Race Hiring Law; Labor Agency Requests Action against the Area's Building Trades Council of AFL-CIO," *Wall Street Journal,* January 1966; "AFL-CIO Unions Deny Arch Boycott," *St. Louis Globe-Democrat,* February 4, 1966; "Unions Charged; Justice Department Files First Job Bias Suit," *Cleveland Plain Dealer;* "U.S. Charges Unions Deny Negroes Jobs," *St. Louis Globe-Democrat,* February 5, 1966; Palladino, *Skilled Hands,* 8, 133.

48. "End Secondary Boycott, Union Told in St. Louis; Racial Charges Pending," *Wall Street Journal,* February 8, 1966; Anderson, *Pursuit of Fairness,* 104; Macaluso interview with the author.

49. Ted Schafers, "Negro Contractor, IBEW Sign Pact," *St. Louis Globe-Democrat,* February 21, 1966; Hurley to Zenfell, March 10, 1966, and Hurley to Macaluso, March 31, 1966, OFCC ADC, box 26, "Correspondence, 1965–1966" folder; Maury E. Rubin, "Pipefitters Local 562 Gives Advanced Job Opportunities to 10 New Negro Members Now Working on the Job in Training Program," *St. Louis Labor Tribune,* February 17, 1966; "Steamfitters' Crash Program Enrolls 10 Negroes; Men Will Be Paid Journeymen's Wages throughout Training Project," *St. Louis Argus,* February 18, 1966.

50. "LBJ to Get Area Report on Rights," *Cleveland Press,* March 24, 1966.

51. Ibid.; Doris O'Donnell, "City Gets Rights Mandate," *Cleveland Plain Dealer,* April 10, 1966.

52. Julian Krawcheck and Don Baker, "Rights Probers Told of Racial Hiring Practices," *Cleveland Press,* April 6, 1966; O'Donnell, "City Gets Rights Mandate."

53. Ibid.; William O. Walker, "Down the Big Road: 'This Has Been a Sorry Story'" column, *Cleveland Call & Post,* April 16, 1966; Biermann, file memo, February 10, 1965, Wirtz Collection, box 246, "PCEEO, 3b" folder.

54. Charles Doneghy, area coordinator's log, January 13, 14, and 25, 1966, OFCC ADC, box 2, "Cleveland, 1966" folder.

55. "Electrical Groups Seek to Train Negro Youths," *Cleveland Press,* June 28, 1966; Harry A. Lenhart Jr., "U.S.-Aided Negroes Pass Union Exam," *Cleveland Plain Dealer,* July 29, 1966.

56. "The Riot's Real Causes," *Cleveland Press* editorial, August 10, 1966; Marc E. Lackritz, *The Hough Riots of 1966* (Cleveland: Regional Church Planning Office, 1968); "Hough Riots," *Encyclopedia of Cleveland History,* http://ech.case.edu/ech-cgi /article.pl?id=HR3 (accessed December 24, 2007); "Hough Heritage," http://www. nhlink.net/ClevelandNeighborhoods/hough/history.htm (accessed December 24, 2007); Report of the United States Civil Rights Commission, March 1, 1967, OFCC

ADC, box 8, "Cleveland Correspondence" folder; Ramsey Clark Oral History Interview IV, April 16, 1969, by Harri Baker, electronic copy, LBJ Library, pp. 1–2, 8.

57. Lenhart, "U.S.-Aided Negroes"; "Negro Apprentices," *Cleveland Plain Dealer* editorial, July 30, 1966; Wilbert Baker to EEOC, September 27, 1966, NUL Papers, series III, box 137, "EEOC, 1965–9" folder; Ernest Jackson to EEOC, September 27, 1966, ibid.

58. Kenneth D. Roberts to EEOC, September 27, 1966, NUL Papers, series III, box 137, "EEOC, 1965–9" folder.

59. *U.S. v. IBEW Local 38*, 59 L.C. 9226 (1969); *Local 53, International Association of Heat and Frost Insulators and Asbestos Workers v. Vogler*, 59 L.C. 9195 (1969). For more on these cases, see Paul D. Moreno, *From Direct Action to Affirmative Action: Fair Employment Law and Policy in America, 1933–1972* (Baton Rouge: Louisiana State University Press, 1997), 257–59.

60. "Federally Financed Construction," November 4, 1966, OFCC ADC, box 13, "San Francisco Related Material, 2" folder.

61. Tom O'Leary, "Rapid Transit Hits Rough Spot," *Christian Science Monitor*, November 11, 1965; "Now under Construction: Rapid Transit for the Bay Area," brochure, winter 1967, OFCC ADC, box 13, "San Francisco Related Material, 1" folder. Although there was a terminus in San Mateo County, just south of the border with San Francisco County, San Mateo did not participate in the management of, or fundraising for, the system.

62. Leonard H. Carter to Wirtz, January 13, 1967, OFCC ADC, box 12, "San Francisco Correspondence, 1967, January–March" folder.

63. O'Leary, "Rapid Transit"; JOBART to BART, March 1966, OFCC ADC, box 3, "San Francisco" folder.

64. Palladino, *Skilled Hands*, 98.

65. "Fair Hire Meeting Set," *Daily Pacific Builder*, March 11, 1967; Robert C. Magnusson to Sylvester, July 1, 1966, and Magnusson to Macaluso, August 22, 1966, OFCC ADC, box 3, "San Francisco" folder. For more on grassroots civil rights organizing in the Bay Area, see Robert O. Self, *American Babylon: Race and the Struggle for Postwar Oakland* (Princeton, NJ: Princeton University Press, 2003).

66. General and Specialty Contractors' Association resolution, October 1, 1966, and Ray Dones to LBJ, October 10, 1966, LBJ White House Central files, box BE16, "Construction" folder; B. R. Stokes to Robert C. Weaver, October 21, 1966, OFCC ADC, box 3, "San Francisco" folder.

67. "Construction Unions Warn of Job Crisis," *San Francisco Chronicle*, February 24, 1967; "S.F. and Oakland Poverty Areas; Survey Finds Bleak Job Picture," *San Francisco Chronicle*, February 16, 1967; Rubin, "Pipefitters Local 562"; Macaluso to Sylvester, February 14, 1967, OFCC ADC, box 8, "Cleveland Correspondence" folder; Magnusson to Macaluso, February 1967, ibid., box 24, "Monthly Reports, 1967, January–June" folder; Sylvester to agency heads, December 22, 1966, ibid., box 3, "San Francisco" folder.

68. Robert A. Sauer to Department of Housing and Urban Development, January 6, 1967, OFCC ADC, box 12, "San Francisco Correspondence, 1967, January–March" folder.

69. Sylvester to agency heads, February 6, 1967, ibid.

70. Sylvester to agency heads, June 29, 1967, ibid., "San Francisco Correspondence, 1967, April–June" folder; Adrian Dove to Sylvester, July 25, 1967, OFCC ADC, box 12, "San Francisco Correspondence, 1967, July–September" folder; Graham, *Civil Rights Era,* 286; Anderson, *Pursuit of Fairness,* 104.

71. Sylvester to agency heads, February 10 and March 15, 1967, OFCC ADC, box 8, "Cleveland Correspondence" folder.

72. Linder, *Wars of Attrition,* 254–55.

73. Doneghy to Macaluso, January 16, 1967, and Macaluso to Sylvester, February 14, 1967, OFCC ADC, box 8, "Cleveland Correspondence" folder.

74. Ted B. Sennett to Ben D. DeJohn, April 13, 1967; Thomas Ruble to Federation Towers, Inc., May 3, 1967; Dove to Sylvester and Clifford E. Minton to Howard L. Graham, June 7, 1967; Nick J. Mileti to Robert D. Sauer, June 19, 1967; and H. D. Conant to DeJohn, August 7, 1967, all in OFCC ADC, box 8, "Cleveland Correspondence" folder; Mileti to Sauer, July 20, 1967, ibid., box 9, "Cleveland Correspondence, 1967, July" folder; Sam Chambers to Doneghy, September 6, 1967, ibid., "Cleveland Correspondence, 1967, September–December" folder.

75. Doneghy to Macaluso, April 1967, OFCC ADC, box 24, "Monthly Reports, 1967, January–June" folder; William F. Miller, "Negroes in Trades Is His Goal," *Cleveland Plain Dealer,* August 24, 1967; Palladino, *Skilled Hands,* 162.

76. Sylvester to agency heads, March 15, 1967, OFCC ADC, box 8, "Cleveland Correspondence" folder; Graham, *Civil Rights Era,* 286.

77. Thomas A. Johnson, "N.A.A.C.P. Opens a Drive for Jobs in Construction," *New York Times,* June 28, 1967; Robert B. Semple Jr., "Ruling May Spur Fight on Job Bias; U.S. Aides Assay Ohio Court Action in Building Case," *New York Times,* July 3, 1967.

78. Antony Mazzolini, "U.S. Stops Funds on Projects Here," *Cleveland Press,* May 18, 1967; "U.S. Stalls $43 Million in Projects Here, Citing Unions' Bias," *Cleveland Plain Dealer,* May 19, 1967; "Union Bias Halts Projects, Cleveland," *San Francisco Chronicle,* May 19, 1967; Wilkins, news conference statement, June 27, 1967, NAACP Papers, series IV, box A21, "Civil Rights, Wilkins" folder.

79. Sylvester to Wirtz, June 27, 1967, and Sylvester to Harry R. Van Cleve Jr., June 28, 1967, OFCC ADC, box 8, "Cleveland Correspondence" folder.

80. Harold S. Stern to HUD, May 24, 1967; Minton to Howard L. Graham, June 7, 1967; Doneghy to Minton, June 14, 1967; Earl B. Raymer to Frank J. Lausche, June 16, 1967; Ray M. White to Raymer and Lausche to Sylvester, June 19, 1967; Sylvester to Lausche, June 30, 1967; and Conant to DeJohn, August 7, 1967, ibid.

81. Doneghy, file memo, June 22, 1967, ibid.; George Hudak to Mechanical Contractors' Association of Cleveland, Inc., May 25, 1967, ibid., box 9, "Cleveland Correspondence, 1967, July" folder.

82. Sylvester to Wirtz, June 27, 1967, OFCC ADC, box 8, "Cleveland Correspondence" folder; Graham, *Civil Rights Era,* 286–87; Anderson, *Pursuit of Fairness,* 104–5; Palladino, *Skilled Hands,* 163.

83. Anderson, *Pursuit of Fairness,* 62; Graham, *Civil Rights Era,* 42 (emphasis in original).

84. Anderson, *Pursuit of Fairness,* 126.

85. Wilkins to state governors and Wilkins to Wirtz, June 27, 1967, NAACP Papers, series IV, box A40, "Labor, Ohio" folder.

86. "A Significant But Little Publicized Report" editorial and "The Press Paid No Attention to This Report," *Construction Craftsman* 6, no. 5 (July–August–September 1967).

87. F. Ray Marshall and Vernon M. Briggs Jr., *Negro Participation in Apprenticeship Programs* (Baltimore: Johns Hopkins Press, 1967), quoted in "A Significant But Little Publicized Report" and "The Press Paid No Attention to This Report."

88. "A Significant But Little Publicized Report"; Howard G. Foster, "Nonapprentice Sources of Training in Construction," *Monthly Labor Review,* February 1970; Graham, *Civil Rights Era,* 280.

89. Sylvester to Wirtz, June 27, 1967, OFCC ADC, box 8, "Cleveland Correspondence" folder; Bennett O. Stalvey Jr. to Macaluso, July 14, 1967, and Stalvey to Philadelphia Federal Executive Board Subcommittee on Contract Compliance in Construction (FCCCS), July 25, 1967, ibid., box 14, "Correspondence, July–October" folder.

90. Chen, *Fifth Freedom,* 46.

91. Zuckerman, "Sheet Metal Workers' Case."

92. For more on the political impact of the riots, see Gitlin, *The Sixties,* 168, 221, 302; Kearns, *Lyndon Johnson,* 259–60; Matusow, *Unraveling of America,* 215–16; and Mumford, *Newark,* 125, 149–50, 173.

4. Pushing the Envelope

1. "U.S. Mint Project Slowed by Dispute," *New York Times,* May 8, 1968; "3 White Electricians Lose Appeal on Discrimination," *New York Times,* May 21, 1968.

2. Graham, *Civil Rights Era,* 287; Anderson, *Pursuit of Fairness,* 105. The quotation is from Graham.

3. Mastbaum Vocational Technical School 1952 Yearbook, p. 32; John Dingle to Alex Wollod, May 29, 1963, PJLC Records, box 3, folder 14; Frank V. Loretti to Macaluso, April 29, 1966, and Stalvey to Macaluso, August 26, 1966, OFCC ADC, box 3, "Philadelphia Correspondence" folder; Richard J. Levin to Philadelphia Commission on Human Rights, August 1966, OFCC ADC, box 14, "Philadelphia Correspondence, 1966, January–June" folder; "U.S. Warns 200 Unions against Bias in Training," *Philadelphia Bulletin,* March 29, 1967; Stalvey, monthly reports, June 1967, OFCC ADC, box 24, "Monthly Reports, 1967, January–June" folder, and August 1967, ibid., "Monthly Reports, 1967, July–December" folder.

4. Harry G. Toland, "Negroes in Trades," *Philadelphia Bulletin,* September 24, 1963; Loretti to Macaluso, April 29, 1966; Stalvey to Macaluso, August 26, 1966; Levin to Philadelphia Commission on Human Rights; "U.S. Warns 200 Unions"; Stalvey, monthly reports, June and August 1967.

5. Stalvey to Macaluso, April 14, 1967, OFCC ADC, box 14, "Philadelphia Correspondence, 1967, January–June" folder; Philadelphia Chamber of Commerce press release, November 23, 1967, ibid., "Philadelphia Correspondence, 1967, November–December" folder; Anderson, *Pursuit of Fairness,* 115–16.

6. Martin J. Herman, "Training Expert Says Manual Trades Have Hard Time Finding Apprentices," *Philadelphia Bulletin,* November 24, 1966.

7. DOL Apprenticeship Outreach Reports, December 1968, AFL-CIO Papers,

RG 9–002, box 28, folder 54, and March 1969, NUL Papers, series III, box 142, "Reports, 4" folder; Philadelphia Jewish Labor Committee–Negro Trade Union Leadership Council meeting minutes, January 22, 1963, PJLC Records, box 3, folder 11, and February 16, 1966, ibid., folder 12; Dingle to Wollod, May 29, 1963, ibid., folder 14; "Need a Job? Want a Promotion?" Philadelphia Jewish Labor Committee–Negro Trade Union Leadership Council training flyer, n.d. [1963], ibid.; Palladino, *Skilled Hands,* 163.

8. "Hot Summer—Philadelphia: Peaceful; Tampa: Shaky Control," *New York Amsterdam News,* June 17, 1967; "Fast Police Action Halts Disturbance in S. Phila. Area," *Philadelphia Tribune,* July 29, 1967; Randolph, Wilkins, Young, and Martin Luther King Jr. joint statement, *AFL-CIO News,* July 29, 1967; Wirtz to LBJ, November 3, 1967, LBJ White House Central files, box FG235, "9/28/67–11/30/67" folder; Gitlin, *The Sixties,* 168, 221, 302; Kearns, *Lyndon Johnson,* 259–60; Matusow, *Unraveling of America,* 215–16; Sugrue, *Origins of the Urban Crisis,* 259.

9. Lawrence H. Geller, "500 Jobs Available for Jobless; Other Demands Being Met," *Philadelphia Tribune,* August 1, 1967. For more on the causes of riots, see Parris and Brooks, *Blacks in the City,* 435; Matusow, *Unraveling of America,* 196, 360–61; Randolph, "How to Prevent Race Riots," September 4, 1965; Scott, *Contempt and Pity,* 153, 156–57; and Friendly, "Official Watts Riot Report Pulls No Punches," December 13, 1965.

10. Kos Semonski, "Tate to Meet Employers to Avert Strife," *Philadelphia Bulletin,* July 31, 1967; "Human Relations Chief Hails Excellence of Jobmobile Recruits," *Philadelphia Inquirer,* August 23, 1964; Stalvey to Macaluso, October 18, 1966, OFCC ADC, box 3, "Philadelphia Correspondence" folder; Stalvey, monthly report, August 1967, ibid., box 24, "Monthly Reports, 1967, July–December" folder; Graham, *Civil Rights Era,* 287.

11. Housing and Home Finance Agency press release, September 27, 1961, Papers of the Urban League of Philadelphia, Clippings box, "Philadelphia Bulletin, Phelan," folder, Temple University Urban Archives, Philadelphia.

12. Macaluso to Stalvey, July 28, 1966, OFCC ADC, box 3, "Philadelphia Correspondence" folder. Additional biographical information is from two published works by Stalvey's wife at the time, Lois Mark Stalvey: *The Education of a WASP* (New York: William Morrow, 1970) and "The Urban Child: Getting Ready for Failure," in *Children, Nature, and the Urban Environment: Proceedings of a Symposium-Fair* (Upper Darby, PA: U.S. Department of Agriculture, Forest Service, Northeastern Forest Experiment Station, 1977), 38–41.

13. Stalvey to Macaluso, October 18, 1966, OFCC ADC, box 3, "Philadelphia Correspondence" folder.

14. Stalvey, monthly reports, December 1966, ibid., box 24, "Monthly Reports, 1966" folder, and January and March 1967, ibid., "Monthly Reports, 1967, January–June" folder; Stalvey to Macaluso, February 10 and 27, March 27, April 27, June 21, 1967, ibid., box 14, "Philadelphia Correspondence, 1967, January–June" folder, and July 10, 1967, ibid., "Philadelphia Correspondence, 1967, July–October" folder; Federal Contract Construction Compliance Subcommittee (FCCCS) of the Critical Urban Problems Committee, Philadelphia Federal Executive Board meeting minutes, February 20 and April 5, 1967, OFCC ADC, box 14, "Philadelphia Correspondence, 1967,

January–June" folder; FCCCS membership list, August 28, 1967, ibid., "Federal Executive Board Meeting" folder; Stalvey to Richard Bourbon, March 7, 1967; Warren P. Phelan, invitation to FCCCS membership, March 22, 1967; Phelan to Stalvey, June 16, 1967; and Phelan to FCCCS, June 22, 1967, ibid., "Philadelphia Correspondence, 1967, January–June" folder.

15. FCCCS meeting minutes, February 20, 1967; Phelan, invitation to FCCCS membership, March 22, 1967; Stalvey to Macaluso, July 14, 1967, OFCC ADC, box 14, "Philadelphia Correspondence, 1967, July–October" folder.

16. Phelan to FCCCS, April 27, 1967, OFCC ADC, box 14, "Philadelphia Correspondence, 1967, January–June" folder; FCCCS meeting minutes, February 20, 1967; OFCC, proposed agenda, August 1, 1967, and summary, August 1967, OFCC ADC, box 14, "FEB Meeting" folder.

17. Stalvey to Macaluso, August 4, September 13 and 22, 1967; Phelan to agency heads, August 7, 1967; DOL draft press release, August 15, 1967; Sylvester to Wirtz, August 28, 1967; Stalvey to FCCCS, September 12, 1967; Paul Boyajian to Phelan, Lorimer Peterson to Phelan, and William J. Kendrick to Phelan, September 15, 1967; Timothy J. May to Phelan, September 18, 1967; Jack Moskowitz to Phelan, September 19, 1967; and Sylvester to Roger W. Wilkins, September 21, 1967, OFCC ADC, box 14, "FEB Meeting" folder; Harold T. Hunton to Phelan, September 26, 1967; Macaluso to Sylvester, September 28, 1967; and John W. Macy Jr. to FEB chairmen, October 30, 1967, ibid., "Philadelphia Correspondence, 1967, July–October" folder; Hurley to Macaluso, August 16, 1967, ibid., "FEB Meeting" folder; FEB press release, October 25, 1967, ibid., "Philadelphia Correspondence, 1967, November–December" folder; Graham, *Civil Rights Era,* 288. For more on Weaver, see Wendell E. Pritchett, *Robert Clifton Weaver and the American City* (Chicago: University of Chicago Press, 2008).

18. Stalvey to Macaluso, September 8 and 11, October 3, 1967, OFCC ADC, box 14, "Philadelphia Correspondence, 1967, July–October" folder, October 24, November 3, 1967, ibid., "Philadelphia Correspondence, 1967, November–December" folder; Donald M. Durkin to Leonard LaRosa, October 2, 1967, ibid., "Philadelphia Correspondence, 1967, July–October" folder; Stalvey, monthly report, October 1967, ibid., box 24, "Monthly Reports, 1968–9" folder; Macaluso to Sylvester, November 7, 1967, and Dove to Macaluso, December 21, 1967, ibid., box 14, "Philadelphia Correspondence, 1967, November–December" folder.

19. George F. Fenton to Robert G. Bartlett, February 21, 1968; Bartlett to Fenton, February 22, 1968; William E. Dunn to James J. Reynolds, March 5, 1968; Reynolds to Dunn, March 25, 1968; and Cushing N. Dolbeare to Wirtz, April 20, 1968, Records of the Department of Labor, Collection of the Office of the Secretary, Chronological file, 1968 (hereafter cited as DOL, Office of the Secretary).

20. "Union-Government Consultation, Not Conflict, on Tough Issues Urged at BTD Convention," *Construction Labor Report* 637, December 6, 1967.

21. Damon Stetson, "Unions Told to Aid Entry of Negroes, But Meany Warns Building Trades to Keep Standards," *New York Times,* December 2, 1967.

22. Sylvester to Philip N. Savage, May 15, 1968, and Sylvester to Andrew G. Freeman, May 21, 1968, DOL, Office of the Secretary, Chronological file, 1968.

23. Stalvey, monthly reports, February, March, and September 1968, OFCC ADC,

box 24, "Monthly Reports, 1968–9" folder; "City Is Asked Not to Patronize 1,447 Firms That Discriminate," *Philadelphia Tribune,* July 27, 1968.

24. Stalvey, monthly reports, June, August, September, October, November, and December 1968 and January 1969, OFCC ADC, box 24, "Monthly Reports, 1968–9" folder; Graham, *Civil Rights Era,* 288–89.

25. Stalvey, monthly report, December 1968, OFCC ADC, box 24, "Monthly Reports, 1968–9" folder.

26. Richard J. Levine, "Construction Unions to Alter Negro Policy, But Shift Won't Fill Rights Groups Goals," *Wall Street Journal,* July 17, 1968; "Group Plans to Block Model Cities Renewal If Labor Bias Found; NAACP Says It'll Go to Court If U.S. Accepts Hiring Policy Set by Building Trades Unions," *Wall Street Journal,* July 18, 1968; Graham, *Civil Rights Era,* 294.

27. Graham, *Civil Rights Era,* 292.

28. Ibid.

29. Ibid., 293.

30. Elmer Staats to Wirtz, May 22, 1968, DOL, Office of the Secretary, Chronological file, 1968; Graham, *Civil Rights Era,* 294.

31. U.S. Congress, Civil Rights Act of 1964, H.R. 7152, July 2, 1964; Wirtz to Lawrence G. Williams, May 24, 1968, DOL, Office of the Secretary, Chronological file, 1968.

32. Staats to William C. Cramer and to Wirtz, November 18, 1968, DOL, Office of the Secretary, Chronological file, 1968.

33. On the "third pillar" of public policy and its relationship with the first two, see H. George Frederickson, *The New Public Administration* (Tuscaloosa: University of Alabama Press, 1980), and "Public Administration and Social Equity," *Public Administration Review* 50, no. 2 (March–April 1990): 228–37.

34. Theories of bureaucracy and representative bureaucracy are copious. See, for instance, Max Weber, *Essays in Sociology,* trans. and ed. H. H. Gerth and C. Wright Mills (New York: Oxford University Press, 1958); J. Donald Kingsley, *Representative Bureaucracy: An Interpretation of the British Civil Service* (Yellow Springs, OH: Antioch Press, 1944); Seymour Martin Lipset, *Bureaucracy and Social Change* (Berkeley: University of California Press, 1950); Frederick C. Mosher, *Democracy and the Public Service* (New York: Oxford University Press, 1968); Samuel Krislov, *Representative Bureaucracy* (Englewood Cliffs, NJ: Prentice-Hall, 1974); Kenneth John Meier and Lloyd G. Nigro, "Representative Bureaucracy and Policy Preferences: A Study in the Attitudes of Federal Executives," *Public Administration Review* (July/August 1976); Julie Dolan and David H. Rosenbloom, eds., *Representative Bureaucracy: Classic Readings and Continuing Controversies* (Armonk, NY: M. E. Sharpe, 2003), 78; David H. Rosenbloom and Jeannette Featherstonhaugh, "Passive and Active Representation in the Federal Civil Service: A Comparison of Blacks and Whites," *Social Science Quarterly* (March 1977); Mary M. Hale and M. Frances Branch, "Policy Preferences on Workplace Reform," in *Women and Men in the States,* ed. Mary E. Guy (Armonk, NY: M. E. Sharpe, 1992); Alfred Blumrosen, "Administrative Creativity: The First Year of the Equal Opportunity Commission," *George Washington Law Review* 38, no. 4 (May 1970): 695–751; Dennis D. Riley, *Controlling the Federal Bureaucracy* (Philadelphia: Temple University Press, 1987); Alan Alt-

shuler, "Rationality and Influence in Public Service," *Public Administration Review* 25, no. 3 (September 1965); and Cornell G. Hooton, *Executive Governance: Presidential Administrations and Policy Change in the Federal Bureaucracy* (Armonk, NY: M. E. Sharpe, 1997).

35. Stalvey, monthly reports, December 1968 and January, February, and March 1969, OFCC ADC, box 24, "Monthly Reports, 1968–9" folder; Graham, *Civil Rights Era*, 296–97; MacLean, *Freedom Is Not Enough*, 96.

36. Tom Wicker, "Johnson Says He Won't Run; Halts North Vietnam Raids; Bids Hanoi Join Peace Moves," *New York Times*, April 1, 1968; John M. Barry, "Labor-Negro Ties Stressed as 40,000 March for King," *AFL-CIO News*, April 13, 1968; John G. Morris, "Kennedy Claims Victory, and Then Shots Ring Out," *New York Times*, June 5, 1968. On voter demographics in 1968, see Kevin P. Phillips, *The Emerging Republican Majority* (New Rochelle, NY: Arlington House, 1969).

37. Graham, *Civil Rights Era*, 302–3; Stein, *Running Steel*, 148–49; Yuill, *Richard Nixon and the Rise of Affirmative Action*, 122–25.

38. Anderson, *Pursuit of Fairness*, 96; Chen, *Fifth Freedom*, 29–30, 171, 178–79, 190.

39. EEOC Annual Report, January 1969, NAACP Papers, series VI, box A23, folder 5; Congress of the United States, S. 2029, April 29, 1969, Papers of President Richard M. Nixon, Collection of White House aide Leonard Garment, box 86, folder 168, National Archives and Records Administration, College Park, MD (hereafter cited as Garment Collection).

40. "Alexander under Fire for 'Doing His Job,'" *Washington Afro-American*, April 1, 1969; Marjorie Hunter, "Dirksen Upbraids U.S. Rights Official," *New York Times*, March 28, 1969; Clifford L. Alexander Jr. to Richard Nixon, April 8, 1969, Garment Collection, box 86, folder 168; "Alexander's Troubles" editorial, "Alexander 'Fired' for 'Doing Job,'" and "Al'xndr Gains Support," *New York Amsterdam News*, April 12, 1969; "Job Discrimination Must Go!!" editorial, and "Top U.S. Bias Fighter Shot Down; Nixon May Launch Local Man," *Philadelphia Tribune*, April 15, 1969; "Cause to Pause" editorial and Gertrude Wilson, "Is Dirksen Setting the Tone?" column, *New York Amsterdam News*, April 19, 1969. On Dirksen's motivations regarding civil rights and free enterprise, see Graham, *Civil Rights Era*, 336–342; Moreno, *From Direct Action to Affirmative Action*, 223; MacLean, *Freedom Is Not Enough*, 97–98; and Chen, *Fifth Freedom*, 29–30, 171, 178–79, 190.

41. Arthur F. Burns to Nixon, August 8, 1969, and U.S. Congress Bill S. 2806, August 8, 1969, Garment Collection, box 84, "EEOC, 1969, 4" folder.

42. "Nixon Names William Brown Head of EEOC," *AFL-CIO News*, May 10, 1969; "Ex-Asst. D.A. Called 'Front Man' for Nixon's Lax Anti-Bias Bill," *Philadelphia Tribune*, August 16, 1969; Warren Hoge, "Nixon's Gentle Job Crusader," *New York Post*, September 13, 1969.

43. Henry T. Aubin, "Brown Called Incompetent; Staffers Quit Rights Agency," *Philadelphia Bulletin*, August 12, 1969; Philip Shandler, "Job Bias Agency Slows to Crawl," *Washington Evening Star*, December 6, 1969; Graham, *Civil Rights Era*, 428–30.

44. "Ex-Asst. D.A."; Anderson, *Pursuit of Fairness*, 113–14.

45. Graham, *Civil Rights Era;* Hoff, *Nixon Reconsidered;* Richard Reeves, *Presi-*

dent Nixon: Alone in the White House (New York: Simon and Schuster, 2001); Stein, *Running Steel;* Yuill, *Richard Nixon and the Rise of Affirmative Action;* Anderson, *Pursuit of Fairness,* 113.

46. Bruce Rabb to Leonard Garment, July 23, 1969, Records of President Richard M. Nixon, Collection of White House aide Bradley Patterson, box 66, "Supreme Court Appointment" folder (hereafter cited as Patterson Collection); Office of Senator Strom Thurmond, press release, August 18, 1969, and Committee for a Fair, Honest, and Impartial Judiciary, draft complaint, September 5, 1969, NAACP Papers, series VI, box A26, "Federal Government, Supreme Court, Haynsworth, 4" folder.

47. "Rumored Consideration," *Wall Street Journal,* August 1, 1969; NAACP press releases, August 9 and 18, 1969, and Wilkins to Leadership Conference for Civil Rights, August 21, 1969, NAACP Papers, series VI, box A26, "Federal Government, Supreme Court, Haynsworth, 2" folder; "A Turn Back," *New York Amsterdam News* editorial, August 23, 1969; "Labor Hits Nixon Choice for Supreme Court Seat; Haynsworth Record Scored as 'Hostile,'" *AFL-CIO News,* August 23, 1969; "Judge Clement Haynsworth," *Time,* August 29, 1969; Lewis Ets-Hokin to Meany, August 31, 1969, AFL-CIO Papers, RG 1–038, box 130, folder 3; Stephen Gill Spottswood to Nixon, September 9, 1969, NAACP Papers, series VI, box A18, "Board Resolutions" folder; AFL-CIO press release, September 13, 1969, AFL-CIO Papers, RG 1–038, box 82, folder 39; "Haynsworth: No," *New York Amsterdam News* editorial, September 27, 1969; "NAACP Continues Haynsworth Fight," *New York Amsterdam News,* October 18, 1969; "Nixon Should Give up on Judge Haynsworth," *Bremerton Sun* editorial, October 21, 1969; "F.Y.I.," *Washington Post* editorial, October 22, 1969; "Rights Leaders Hail Haynsworth Denial," *New York Amsterdam News,* November 29, 1969; Anderson, *Pursuit of Fairness,* 113–14.

48. Stalvey, monthly report, April 1969, OFCC ADC, box 24, "Monthly Reports, 1968–9" folder.

49. Ibid.; John Brantley Wilder, "Detail Methods Unions Use to Bypass Negroes," *Philadelphia Tribune,* March 22, 1969.

50. Macaluso interview with the author.

51. Nixon to U.S. Senate, March 14, 1969, Records of President Richard M. Nixon, Collection of the Department of Labor, box 5, "Executive, 1" folder; "Negro Named to Key Position in Labor Department," *Philadelphia Bulletin,* March 15, 1969; Peter H. Binzen, "U.S. to Revise and Reinstate 'Phila. Plan' on Minority Hiring," *Philadelphia Bulletin,* June 12, 1969; Anderson, *Pursuit of Fairness,* 116.

52. Michael Flynn, "Former Pro Football Star: 'Black Capitalism' Founder Battles for Lieutenant Governorship," *Philadelphia Bulletin,* September 30, 1968; John Whitaker to Bill Casselman, February 25, 1969, Records of President Richard M. Nixon, Collection of the Department of Labor, box 5, "Executive, 1" folder; "A Hard-Driving Black Official: Arthur Allen Fletcher," *New York Times,* December 2, 1971; Graham, *Civil Rights Era,* 326; Arthur Fletcher biography at The History Makers, from an interview conducted May 29, 2003, http://www.thehistorymakers.com/biography/biography.asp?bioindex=526&category=lawMakers (accessed March 14, 2008); "Presidential Adviser Arthur Fletcher, 80, Dies; 'Father of Affirmative Action' Counseled Nixon, Ford, Reagan, G. H. W. Bush," Associated Press, July 13, 2005; Arthur Fletcher interview, April 9, 2003, by Political Science Department, Washburn

University; Paul Fletcher interview with the author, July 30, 2010, by and in possession of the author.

53. Arthur Fletcher interview, April 9, 2003.

54. Graham, *Civil Rights Era*, 327, 330.

55. Philadelphia Jewish Labor Committee—Negro Trade Union Leadership Council meeting minutes, February 16, 1966, PJLC Records, box 3, folder 12; Arthur Fletcher to agency heads, June 27, 1969, AFL-CIO Papers, RG 1–038, box 72, folder 15; Richard J. Levine, "U.S. Takes New Step to End Discrimination in Federally Aided Construction Programs," *Wall Street Journal,* June 30, 1969; Fletcher, address to the Annual NAACP Convention, July 2, 1969, NAACP Papers, series IV, box A9, "1969 Convention, Speeches" folder; Skrentny, *Minority Rights Revolution,* 132.

56. Martin J. Herman, "6 of 7 Unions Boycott Meeting on Phila. Plan," *Philadelphia Bulletin,* July 10, 1969; "U.S. Aide Calls Phila. Plan Just 'a Beginning'; Says Labor Dept. Will Institute Project Despite Problems," *Philadelphia Bulletin,* August 28, 1969; Fletcher to George P. Shultz, August 29, 1969, Records of the Department of Labor, Collection of Undersecretary James D. Hodgson, box 14, "Philadelphia Plan" folder (hereafter cited as Undersecretary Hodgson Collection); John Brantley Wilder, "Biased Unions Are Blasted by Black Workers: Want Philadelphia Plan to Become Law of Land; All-Out Fight Pledged," *Philadelphia Tribune,* August 30, 1969; Henry T. Aubin, "U.S. Guidelines Are Issued for Minority Hiring," *Philadelphia Bulletin,* September 23, 1969; Anderson, *Pursuit of Fairness,* 117.

57. Fletcher to agency heads, June 27, 1969, AFL-CIO Papers, RG 1–038, box 72, folder 15.

58. Jerris Leonard to Laurence H. Silberman, June 26, 1969, Garment Collection, box 143, "Philadelphia Plan, 2" folder; "Shultz Defends New Plan to Get Jobs for Negroes," *New York Times,* July 6, 1969; Fletcher to Wilkins, July 18, 1969, NAACP Papers, series VI, box G9, "Labor, Department of Labor, 1969–71" folder; "Breaking Down the Bars," *New York Times* editorial, August 12, 1969.

59. Clay Dillon, "Construction Work Bidders Required to Hire Blacks for Better-Pay Jobs," *Philadelphia Tribune,* July 8, 1969; "To Push Quota Hiring," *New York Amsterdam News,* August 16, 1969; "Biased Unions Are Blasted," *Philadelphia Tribune,* August 30, 1969; William H. Lindsay Jr. to Horace Menasco, October 17, 1969, Undersecretary Hodgson Collection, box 14, "Philadelphia Plan" folder.

60. Moreno, *From Direct Action to Affirmative Action,* 56–62.

61. Abram L. Sachar, *A Host at Last* (Boston: Little, Brown, 1976), 258. For more on the American Jewish opposition to quotas in particular, see Chen, *Fifth Freedom,* 108–9. In "The Bugaboo of Employment Quotas," *Wisconsin Law Review* 341, no. 21 (1970): 341–403, James E. Jones Jr. argues that the American distaste for employment quotas to help minority groups stems from collective guilt at using quotas *against* minority groups and immigrants from countries deemed "unworthy," such as China.

62. Staats to Shultz, August 5, 1969, Garment Collection, box 143, "Philadelphia Plan, 2" folder; Anderson, *Pursuit of Fairness,* 121.

63. U.S. Congress, Civil Rights Act of 1964, H.R. 7152, July 2, 1964.

64. Staats to Shultz, August 5, 1969.

65. Graham, *Civil Rights Era,* 331–32.

66. "The Question of Quotas," *Philadelphia Bulletin* editorial, July 8, 1969;

Damon Stetson, "Meany Doubtful on Hiring Quota Plan," *New York Times,* August 9, 1969; "'Philadelphia Plan' Impasse," *Philadelphia Bulletin* editorial, August 14, 1969.

67. John N. Mitchell to Shultz, September 22, 1969, Garment Collection, box 142, "Philadelphia Plan, 1" folder.

68. Graham, *Civil Rights Era,* 192; Anderson, *Pursuit of Fairness,* 97–129.

69. *United Steelworkers v. Weber,* 99 S.Ct. 2721 (US S.Ct., 1979), 20 EPD par. 30,026; David E. Robertson and Ronald D. Johnson, "Reverse Discrimination: Did *Weber* Decide the Issue?" *Labor Law Journal* 31 (November 1980): 793–99; Frymer, *Black and Blue,* 88.

70. LBJ transcripts, Burke Marshall Oral History Interview I, October 28, 1968, p. 21, and Clarence Mitchell Oral History Interview I, April 30, 1969, pp. 19–20, by Thomas H. Baker; Stein, *Running Steel,* 84; Graham, *Civil Rights Era,* 151.

71. Skrentny, *Minority Rights Revolution,* 96–100.

72. DOL press release, September 23, 1969, Garment Collection, box 143, "Philadelphia Plan, 2" folder; "'Philadelphia Plan' Contract," *New York Times,* October 23, 1969; Stalvey to Menasco, December 22, 1969, DOL, Office of the Secretary, Chronological file, 1969, folder 2.

73. Clayton Willis to Garment, September 18, 1969, Garment Collection, box 84, "EEOC, 1969, 4" folder; Western Pennsylvania Master Builders' Association statement, August 28, 1969, AFL-CIO Papers, RG 9–002, box 10, folder 1.

74. Michael Stern, "Effort to Train Blacks for Construction Jobs Falters in Pittsburgh; Graduates Get Top Pay Running Heavy Equipment, But Black Control Irks Unions, Firms," *Wall Street Journal,* July 24, 1969; "Five Building Projects Halted in Pittsburgh by Demands of Blacks; Demonstrators at Construction Sites Seek the Placement of Negroes in Area Trade Unions," *Wall Street Journal,* August 26, 1969; "Job Protest Spurs Pittsburgh Clash; Negroes Battle Policemen—180 Arrested, 45 Injured" and Donald Janson, "Construction Job Rights Plan Backed at Philadelphia Hearing, *New York Times,* August 27, 1969; "U.S. Steel Won't Halt Building in Pittsburgh over Negroes' Demands; But Company Says It Has Begun to Intercede on Blacks' Behalf; Further Demonstrations Seen," *Wall Street Journal,* August 28, 1969; "Race Conflict over Jobs" editorial and Donald Janson, "Whites Denounce Pittsburgh Mayor; 4,500 Protest at City Hall over Loss of Pay in 2-Day Construction Shutdown," *New York Times,* August 30, 1969; "Pres. Nixon Should Forget the White Backlash and Help Negroes Get Jobs," *Philadelphia Tribune* editorial, August 30, 1969; "Demonstrations against Bias Halted in Pgh.," *Philadelphia Tribune,* September 6, 1969; "Federal Agencies Move in to Put out Fire of Racial Unrest in Chicago Construction," *Construction Labor Report* 730, September 17, 1969; Macaluso to John L. Wilks, October 16, 1969, Garment Collection, box 1, "Memos, 1969, October" folder; Anderson, *Pursuit of Fairness,* 121; Palladino, *Skilled Hands,* 163.

75. "20 Chicago Building Projects Shut Down by Hiring Protests," *New York Times,* August 10, 1969; "Chi Blacks Renew Job Site Protests," *New York Amsterdam News,* August 30, 1969; "Race Conflict over Jobs," *New York Times* editorial, August 30, 1969; "Federal Agencies Move in to Put Out Fire," *Construction Labor Report* 730, September 17, 1969; "Jesse Jackson Writes from Chicago Jail," *Philadelphia Tribune,* September 20, 1969; "Nationwide Black Walkout Urged to Back Job Demand,"

New York Times, September 22, 1969; Seth S. King, "4,000 Negroes in Chicago Rally in Bid for Skilled Building Jobs," *New York Times,* September 23, 1969; "Showdown on Negro Jobs in the Building Trades," *U.S. News and World Report,* September 29, 1969; Macaluso to Wilks, October 16, 1969, Garment Collection, box 1, "Memos, 1969, October" folder; Palladino, *Skilled Hands,* 163.

76. Damon Stetson, "Negro Groups Step up Militancy in Drive to Join Building Unions; Blacks, Dissatisfied with Slow Pace of Job Integration, Increase Picketing and Work Stoppage at Projects," *New York Times,* August 28, 1969; "Federal Agencies Move in to Put out Fire," *Construction Labor Report* 730, September 17, 1969; A. P. Toner to John Ehrlichman, September 24, 1969, Garment Collection, box 86, "Ehrlichman, 65" folder; James Strong, "Trades Talk Delayed as 500 Jam Room; Workers Shout Down U.S. Aids," *Chicago Tribune,* September 25, 1969; Seth S. King, "Whites in Chicago Disrupt Hearing; 5 Hurt and 9 Arrested in Dispute on Job Bias," *New York Times,* September 26, 1969; Seth S. King, "Whites in Chicago Continue Protest; A Plan to Take More Blacks into Building Union Scored," *New York Times,* September 27, 1969; "2000 Construction Union Members Attack Negroes Outside U.S. Building," *Philadelphia Tribune,* September 30, 1969; Macaluso to Wilks, October 16, 1969, Garment Collection, box 1, "Memos, 1969, October" folder; "Seattle," *New York Amsterdam News,* October 18, 1969; Arthur Fletcher, *The Silent Sell-out: Government Betrayal of Blacks to the Craft Unions* (New York: Third Press, 1974), 70–73.

77. James D. Hodgson to Joseph Loftus, October 20, 1969, and Wilks to agency heads, October 29, 1969, Undersecretary Hodgson Collection, box 8, "OFCC" folder; Wilks to Leonard, October 31, 1969, Records of the Department of Labor, Collection of Secretary Shultz, box 69, "FCC, 8" folder; "Chicago Building Trades Promote Job Opportunities for 4,000 Blacks," *AFL-CIO News,* September 13, 1969; Fletcher, *Silent Sell-out,* 70–73; Anderson, *Pursuit of Fairness,* 121.

78. "Shultz Assigned: Nixon Orders Study of Key Labor Issues," *AFL-CIO News,* March 15, 1969; Palladino, *Skilled Hands,* 170. The notion that White House backing of the RPP was connected to Nixon's policy of weakening unions was first discussed by Linder in *Wars of Attrition* (3–8, 239–40, 253–60, 415, 421); Stein in *Running Steel* (314) and Anderson in *Pursuit of Fairness* (118) concurred.

79. "Wages, Civil Rights Need an Answer," *Engineering News-Record,* December 11, 1969; Linder, *Wars of Attrition,* 3–8, 239–40, 253–60, 415, 421.

80. Stephen Clapp, "Divide and Rule," *Public Information Center News* 1, no. 12 (June 1971): 1–4; Graham, *Civil Rights Era,* 344, 328; J. Larry Hood, "The Nixon Administration and the Revised Philadelphia Plan for Affirmative Action: A Study in Expanding Presidential Power and Divided Government," *Presidential Studies Quarterly* 23 (winter 1993): 145–67; Hoff, *Nixon Reconsidered,* 91–92; Stein, *Running Steel,* 314; MacLean, *Freedom Is Not Enough,* 99–100; Anderson, *Pursuit of Fairness,* 120; Palladino, *Skilled Hands,* 164; Yuill; *Richard Nixon and the Rise of Affirmative Action,* 145–146; Garment, National Association of Manufacturers speech, November 12, 1971, Garment Collection, box 29, "NAM11" folder; Fletcher, "Address at Annual Convention of Associated General Contractors," *Construction Labor Report* 808, March 17, 1971; John Ehrlichman, *Witness to Power: The Nixon Years* (New York: Simon and Schuster, 1982), 228–29.

81. "Administration Fight on Construction Bias Opposed by U.S. Aide; Comptroller General Contends So-Called 'Philadelphia Plan' Violates '64 Civil Rights Act," *Wall Street Journal,* August 6, 1969; *Congressional Record—Senate,* August 13, 1969, S9952–54.

82. On Fannin and McClellan, see Kearns, *Lyndon Johnson,* 184–85, and Stein, *Running Steel,* 22–23.

83. Sam J. Ervin to William H. Brown III, October 15, 1969; Brown to Ervin, October 24, 1969; and Staats, testimony before the Subcommittee on the Separation of Powers, Senate Committee on the Judiciary, October 28, 1969, DOL, Office of the Secretary, Chronological file, 1969, folder 1; Shultz to Ervin, November 28, 1969, Garment Collection, box 143, "Philadelphia Plan, 2" folder; Graham, *Civil Rights Era,* 336; Anderson, *Pursuit of Fairness,* 121.

84. Paul Delaney, "U.S. Aide to Block Hiring Plan Pact; Controller General Will Act against First Participant," *New York Times,* November 9, 1969; Staats to Shultz, November 12, 1969, DOL, Office of the Secretary, Chronological file, 1969, folder 1.

85. Graham, *Civil Rights Era,* 338–39.

86. *Congressional Record—Senate,* December 18, 1969, S17133.

87. "Senate Upholds Ruling against Anti-Bias Plan on Construction Hiring; Setback Is Seen for Nixon in Bid to Establish Minimum Job Quotas on Federal Work," *Wall Street Journal,* December 19, 1969; George Lardner Jr., "Senate Votes against Philadelphia Work Plan; Hands Nixon Setback in Rejecting Move to Put More Negroes in Building Jobs," *Los Angeles Times,* December 19, 1969; Robert B. Semple Jr., "Philadelphia Plan: How White House Engineered Major Victory," *New York Times,* December 26, 1969; Graham, *Civil Rights Era,* 339–40; Anderson, *Pursuit of Fairness,* 122–24.

88. *Congressional Record—Senate,* December 18, 1969, S17131–57; "Quotas and Goals," *Washington Post* editorial, December 22, 1969; "Aid to Jim Crow," *New York Times* editorial, December 22, 1969; Robert B. Semple Jr., "Congress and Nixon: Fight Grows Sharper," *New York Times,* December 22, 1969; Meany to members, House of Representatives, and Staats to Biemiller, December 22, 1969, AFL-CIO Papers, RG 9–002, box 38, folder 42; George Lardner Jr., "Hill Battle Is Escalating over Equal Jobs Plan," *Washington Post,* December 22, 1969; "Nixon Acts to Save Philadelphia Plan Which Aids Black Workers," and "The Philadelphia Plan Killers" editorial, *Philadelphia Tribune,* December 23, 1969; Semple, "Philadelphia Plan."

89. John R. Price to Ehrlichman, December 22, 1969, Garment Collection, box 143, "Philadelphia Plan, 2" folder; Semple, "Philadelphia Plan"; Garment, backgrounder on the Philadelphia Plan vote, December 31, 1969, Garment Collection, box 143, "Philadelphia Plan, 2" folder.

90. Nixon, press statement, December 19, 1969, Garment Collection, box 143, "Philadelphia Plan, 2" folder.

91. Shultz, Fletcher, and Ronald L. Ziegler, White House press conference, December 18, 1969; Nixon, press statement, December 19, 1969; and Ziegler and Garment, White House press conference, December 19, 1969, ibid.; Shultz, press statement, December 20, 1969; and Shultz and Fletcher, White House press conference, December 20, 1969, DOL, Office of the Secretary, Chronological file, 1969, folder 2; David

E. Rosenbaum, "Shultz Appeals to House on Jobs; Urges Defeat of a Move to Halt Philadelphia Plan," *New York Times,* December 21, 1969; Nixon, press statement, December 22, 1969, DOL, Office of the Secretary, Chronological file, 1969, folder 2; "Congress Ends Session; Nixon Gains a Victory; Senate Drops Its Bid to Kill the Philadelphia Plan for Minority Jobs in Building," *Wall Street Journal,* December 24, 1969; Semple, "Philadelphia Plan"; Garment, backgrounder on Philadelphia Plan vote, December 31, 1969; MacLean, *Freedom Is Not Enough.*

92. Shultz, "Why Vote to Recommit," and Ford to House Republicans, December 20, 1969, DOL, Office of the Secretary, Chronological file, 1969, folder 2.

93. *Congressional Record—House,* December 22, 1969, 40903–21; UPI Newswires, December 22, 1969, DOL, Office of the Secretary, Chronological file, 1969, folder 2; Spencer Rich, "Negro Job Ratio Plan Is Upheld by Congress," *Detroit News,* December 23, 1969; Warren Weaver Jr., "Congress Avoids Tie-up on Rights, Prepares to Quit; Heeds Nixon Appeal to Turn Down a Rider Blocking Negro Hiring Plan; Windup Today Is Likely; Tax Bill Approved by Both Houses, But Foreign Aid Measure Is Postponed," and Tom Wicker, "In the Nation: Quotas, Goals and Tricks," *New York Times,* December 23, 1969.

5. Constructing Affirmative Action

1. "Steamfitters Union Object of Fed Suit," *New York Amsterdam News,* March 13, 1971.

2. "Gains Made in Unions in New York, New Jersey," *New York Amsterdam News,* September 23, 1967; "Steamfitters Union Object of Fed Suit"; *George Rios et al., Plaintiffs-Appellees, v. Enterprise Association Steamfitters Local 638 of U.A. et al., Defendants-Appellants, and United States of America, Plaintiff Appellee, v. Enterprise Association Steamfitters Local 638 of U.A. et al., Defendants-Appellants* (hereafter cited as *Rios et al. v. Enterprise*), U.S. Court of Appeals, Second Circuit, 501 F.2d 622 (June 24, 1974).

3. "Steamfitters Now Recruit Apprentices, *New York Amsterdam News,* December 21, 1968; "Steamfitters' Union Offers Apprenticeship," *New York Amsterdam News,* December 27, 1969; "Steamfitters Union Object of Fed Suit"; Sewell, "Contracting Racial Equality," 238.

4. "Gives Qualified OK to Bldg. Construction," *New York Amsterdam News,* November 16, 1968; Marion K. Sanders, "James Haughton Wants 500,000 More Jobs," *New York Times,* September 14, 1969; "NAACP Threatens Court Action," *New York Amsterdam News,* December 26, 1970; Janine Jackson, "James Haughton on Racism in the House of Labor," 1999 interview at History Matters, http://historymatters.gmu.edu/d/7038/ (accessed November 8, 2009). On the protests at Downstate, see Clarence Taylor, *The Black Churches of Brooklyn* (New York: Columbia University Press, 1994). That Fight Back was aligned with a Columbia University entity was ironic, in that only months earlier the organization had picketed a Columbia construction site. For more on Fight Back's protests at Columbia, see Sewell, "Contracting Racial Equality," 223.

5. "Steamfitters Union Object of Fed Suit"; "Court Orders Union to Stop Race Bias," *New York Times,* March 25, 1971; *Rios et al. v. Enterprise* (June 24, 1974).

6. *Rios et al. v. Enterprise* (June 24, 1974); *Rios et al. v. Enterprise,* U.S. Court of Appeals, Second Circuit, 520 F.2d 352 (June 24, 1975), and U.S. Court of Appeals, Second Circuit, 542 F.2d 579 (September 7, 1976); *United Steelworkers v. Weber* (1979); Robertson and Johnson, "Reverse Discrimination"; *Rios et al. v. Enterprise,* as amended, U.S. Court of Appeals, Second Circuit, 860 F.2d 1168 (December 1, 1988).

7. Paul Delaney, "Blacks Still Say 'Show Us' Despite Nixon Effort on Philadelphia Plan," *New York Times,* January 11, 1970; "Courting the South with Judge Carswell," *St. Petersburg Times* editorial, January 21, 1970; "New Nominee," *New York Amsterdam News* editorial, January 24, 1970; Bayard Rustin, "Two Steps Backward" column, *New York Amsterdam News,* February 7, 1970; Bayard Rustin, "Why Carswell Lost" column, *New York Amsterdam News,* April 18, 1970; "Meany Asks Solidarity on Civil Rights," *AFL-CIO News,* July 4, 1970; Dickerson, *Militant Mediator,* 263; Hoff, *Nixon Reconsidered,* 44; Reeves, *President Nixon,* 160–61.

8. John A. Morsell, statement, Marion Palfi to Wilkins, and NAACP press release, January 21, 1970, NAACP Papers, series VI, box A25, "Carswell, 1" folder; "Carswell Disavows '48 Speech Backing White Supremacy," Associated Press, January 21, 1970; Fred P. Graham, "Meany Will Fight Carswell Choice; He Calls Nomination 'a Slap in the Face' to Negroes—Senate Hearings Today," *New York Times,* January 27, 1970; Wilkins to James O. Eastland and Clarence Mitchell to Philip A. Hart, January 27, 1970, NAACP Papers, series VI, box A25, "Carswell, 1" folder; Thomas W. Matthew to Morsell, January 28, 1970, ibid.; Young, "The Carswell Appointment" column, January 28, 1970, NUL Papers, series III, box 441, "To Be Equal" folder; Morsell to Matthew, January 29, 1970, NAACP Papers, series VI, box A25, "Carswell, 1" folder; Wilkins, Dorothy Height, Bayard Rustin, Young, Ralph Abernathy, and Randolph to Nixon, January 30, 1970, ibid.; Rustin, "Two Steps Backward"; "Washington," *New York Amsterdam News,* February 28, 1970; "Against Carswell," *New York Amsterdam News* editorial, March 7, 1970; "More Carswell," *New York Amsterdam News* editorial, March 21, 1970; "Administration Accused of 'Writing off' Negro," *AFL-CIO News,* April 4, 1970; NAACP press release, April 8, 1970, NAACP Papers, series VI, box A25, "Carswell, 3" folder; Morsell to Nixon, April 10, 1970, ibid., "Nixon, 1" folder; "Carswell's Views Beat Him; Racism Called Factor," *New York Amsterdam News,* April 11, 1970; "The Carswell Defeat" editorial and Rustin, "Why Carswell Lost" column, *New York Amsterdam News,* April 18, 1970; "Meany Asks Solidarity on Civil Rights"; Hoff, *Nixon Reconsidered,* 46–48; Reeves, *President Nixon,* 161.

9. James Boyd, "Harry Dent, the President's Political Coordinator, Says: 'I Gave Thurmond 100% Loyalty and Now I Give Mr. Nixon 100%,'" *New York Times,* February 1, 1970; Reeves, *President Nixon,* 160.

10. "Nixon Selects Carswell for Seat on High Court," *AFL-CIO News,* January 24, 1970; Graham, "Meany Will Fight Carswell Choice"; "Contempt of Court," *New York Times* editorial, January 28, 1970; "Nomination of Carswell Called Slap at Negroes," *AFL-CIO News,* January 31, 1970; "AFL-CIO Urges Senate to Reject Carswell," *AFL-CIO News,* February 7, 1970; "An Appalling Appointment," *AFL-CIO News* editorial, February 21, 1970.

11. Meany, address at the 1959 National Urban League Equal Opportunity Day Dinner, November 17, 1959, NUL Papers, series I, box E31, folder M; David L. Perlman, "Nixon Suffers 2nd Defeat on Filling Court Vacancy; GOP Votes Key to Loss

of Carswell," *AFL-CIO News,* April 11, 1970; Rustin, "Why Carswell Lost"; "Meany Asks Solidarity on Civil Rights"; Robinson, *George Meany,* 123–40, 287.

12. "The U.S. Senate's Duty to Our Highest Court," *St. Petersburg Times* editorial, January 24, 1970; Nixon to William B. Saxbe, April 1, 1970, Records of President Richard M. Nixon, Collection of White House aide Charles W. Colson, box 44, "Carswell, 1" folder (hereafter cited as Colson Collection); "Judge Carswell: The President's 'Right of Choice,'" *Wall Street Journal* editorial, April 2, 1970; Robert B. Semple Jr., "Strike Fever Speeds up Wage-Price Spiral," *New York Times,* April 5, 1970; NAACP press release, April 8, 1970, NAACP Papers, series VI, box A25, "Carswell, 3" folder; Nixon, statement, April 9, 1970, Colson Collection, box 44, "Carswell, 1" folder; Morsell to Nixon, April 10, 1970, NAACP Papers, series VI, box A25, "Nixon, 1" folder; William S. White, "Carswell Affair Is a Tragedy at American, Personal Levels" column, *Wall Street Journal,* April 11, 1970; Perlman, "Nixon Suffers 2nd Defeat"; "The Carswell Defeat," *New York Amsterdam News* editorial, April 18, 1970; Reeves, *President Nixon,* 185; Anderson, *Pursuit of Fairness,* 114.

13. Homer Bigart, "War Foes Here Attacked by Construction Workers; City Hall Is Stormed," *New York Times,* May 9, 1970; Gertrude Wilson, "Brown Shirts—Hard Hats" column, *New York Amsterdam News,* June 20, 1970; Reeves, *President Nixon,* 216; Anderson, *Pursuit of Fairness,* 138.

14. Peter B. Levy, *The New Left and Labor in the 1960s* (Urbana: University of Illinois Press, 1994); Nelson Lichtenstein, *Walter Reuther: The Most Dangerous Man in Detroit* (Urbana: University of Illinois Press, 1995), 32–46. On the labor-Democratic split, see Gareth Davies, *From Opportunity to Entitlement: The Transformation and Decline of Great Society Liberalism* (Lawrence: University Press of Kansas, 1996), and Chen, *Fifth Freedom,* 240–45. On the history of civil rights liberalism, see Chen, *Fifth Freedom,* 42–43.

15. Wilson, "Brown Shirts—Hard Hats."

16. Graham, *Civil Rights Era,* 344; Anderson, *Pursuit of Fairness,* 138; Linder, *Wars of Attrition,* 286, MacLean, *Freedom Is Not Enough,* 100–101; Jefferson Cowie, "Nixon's Class Struggle: Romancing the New Right Worker, 1969–1973," *Labor History* 43, no. 3 (August 2002): 257–83.

17. AFL-CIO draft statement, January 12, 1970, AFL-CIO Papers, RG 1–038, box 107, folder 9; Nixon, press statement, March 17, 1970, Garment Collection, box 143, "Philadelphia Plan, 2" folder; Charles W. Colson to Nixon, April 15, 1970, Colson Collection, box 20, "Building Trades Meeting, March 23, 1970" folder; Reeves, *President Nixon,* 165, 215–16; Linder, *Wars of Attrition,* 3–8, 239–40, 253–60, 415, 421; Stein, *Running Steel,* 314.

18. "Brennan Appointment to Secretary of Labor Draws Varied Reactions from Labor, Civil Rights Groups," *Construction Labor Report* 897, December 6, 1972; "An Outspoken Union Man at Head of Labor Department: Peter Joseph Brennan," *New York Times,* November 30, 1972.

19. Colson to Nixon, April 15, 1970; Ziegler, press conference; and Colson to Nixon, May 26, 1970, Colson Collection, box 20, "Building Construction Trades Council" folder; Colson to Hodgson, February 2, 1971, and Colson to Dwight L. Chapin, February 5, 1971, ibid., box 95, "New York City, Workers Building Construction Council" folder.

20. Colson to Peter Brennan, April 1970, and Tom Charles Huston to Ehrlichman, May 12, 1970, Colson Collection, box 95, "New York City, Workers Building Construction Council" folder; Ziegler, press conference, and Colson to Nixon, May 26, 1970; "Being Patriotic," *New York Amsterdam News* editorial, June 6, 1970; Colson to Nixon, September 12, 1970, Colson Collection, box 20, "Building Construction Trades Council" folder; "Nixon and the Bums," *Scanlan's Magazine* editorial, September 1970; Victor Riesel, "Soft on Hard Hats? Nixon Rejects Advisers Urging Him to Declare War on Labor" column, December 7, 1970, Colson Collection, box 73, "Riesel" folder.

21. Ziegler, press conference, May 26, 1970; "Official Sees Racist Ruse in Marches Backing Nixon," *St. Louis Post-Dispatch,* May 27, 1970; John E. Burnett to Hill, June 8, 1970, NAACP Papers, series VI, box G3, "1970, 2" folder; Milton Viorst, "Judging Deeds and Not the Words" column, *Washington Evening Star,* July 30, 1970; Hill, press statement, September 7, 1970, NAACP Papers, series VI, box G10, "Labor, Herbert Hill, Speeches and Testimonies" folder; *Rios et al. v. Enterprise* (June 24, 1974).

22. Building Construction Trades Department, AFL-CIO, Chicago Plan, January 12, 1970, AFL-CIO Papers, RG 1–038, box 107, folder 9; Meany, address to the National Press Club, January 12, 1970, ibid., RG 9–002, box 38, folder 42; Tom Wicker, "In the Nation: Philadelphia, Chicago, and Meany," *New York Times,* January 18, 1970; Meany, "To End Job Bias," letter to the editor, *New York Times,* February 7, 1970; Robinson, *George Meany,* 289–92.

23. John Herling's labor letter, January 24, 1970, AFL-CIO Papers, RG 21–001, box 6, folder 20; John Herbers, "Gains Are Made in Federal Drive for Negro Hiring; Philadelphia Plan, Showing Some Success, Is Being Cautiously Extended; Urban Talks Pressed; Hundreds of Suits under '64 Civil Rights Act Expected to Spur New Progress," *New York Times,* January 25, 1970; DOL press release, January 26, 1970, AFL-CIO Paper, RG 21–001, box 6, folder 20; Garment to Patrick J. Buchanan, and Fletcher, press conference, January 28, 1970, Garment Collection, box 142, "Philadelphia Plan, 1" folder; "Job Bias Fighters Win Big Boosts in Nixon's First Full Budget," *Wall Street Journal,* February 3, 1970; Frank C. Porter, "U.S. to Extend Hiring Plan to 20 Cities," *Washington Post,* February 7, 1970; "Unions Ordered to Hire More Blacks; Philadelphia Plan Opposed by Industry," *Florida Star,* February 14, 1970; "Minority Job Plans Pushed by Labor Dept.," *AFL-CIO News,* February 14, 1970; "Shultz Selects 19 Cities for Philadelphia Plan; Is Opposed Strongly by AFL-CIO," *Indianapolis Labor Tribune,* February 20, 1970; "Job Equality Drive Pushed," *Federal Times,* March 4, 1970; "Labor Dept. Approves Grant to 'Chicago Plan,'" *AFL-CIO News,* May 16, 1970; Byron Calame, "Labor Department Setting up Unit to Spur Local Solutions to Construction Job Bias," *Wall Street Journal,* June 7, 1970; Anderson, *Pursuit of Fairness,* 125–26.

24. Dana Bullen, "Job Bias Guidelines Tightened," *Washington Star,* January 15, 1970; "Ervin Criticizes Orders on Hiring; Says Congress Is Deceived by New Racial Quotas," *New York Times,* January 16, 1970; "U.S. Issues, Recalls New Racial Job Code," *Washington Post,* January 16, 1970; Graham, *Civil Rights Era,* 343; Hood, "Nixon Administration and Revised Philadelphia Plan," 161–62; Skrentny, *Minority Rights Revolution,* 132–33.

25. Graham, *Civil Rights Era,* 344–45.

26. Atlanta Building Trades Council, Atlanta Plan, April 19, 1970; Robert McGlotten to Slaiman, April 13, 1970; Slaiman to Biemiller, April 14, 1970, AFL-CIO Papers, RG 21–001, box 6, folder 20; "Minority Hiring in Construction in 2 Cities," *New York Amsterdam News,* July 11, 1970; Reagan to Nixon, July 14, 1970, in Hugh Davis Graham, ed., *Civil Rights during the Nixon Administration, 1969–1974* (Frederick, MD: University Publications of America, 1989), reel 7, p. 107; "Kansas City Building Trades Sign Minority-Hiring Plan," *Wall Street Journal,* July 21, 1970; "Minority Youths Start Training in Chicago Plan," *AFL-CIO News,* August 15, 1970; "Minority Jobs Plan Approved in Indianapolis," *AFL-CIO News,* August 29, 1970; DOL press releases, July 9, 1971, and January 18, 1972, Garment Collection, box 142, "Philadelphia Plan, 1" folder; James D. Williams to Madelyn Andrews, March 15, 1972, NUL Papers, series III, box 32, "Labor, Labor Affairs Program, 1971–2" folder; DOL press releases, May 28, 1972, Patterson Collection, box 56, "OFCC" folder, July 24, 1972, ibid., box 57, "Philadelphia Plan" folder, and September 21, 1972, Garment Collection, box 142, "Philadelphia Plan, 1" folder; Jon Katz, "Labor Dept. Mulls Plan to Cut Construction Minority Quota," *Washington Post,* September 7, 1972.

27. "New York Plan," *New York Amsterdam News* editorial, March 28, 1970; "New York Plan Keyed to Minority Training," *AFL-CIO News,* March 28, 1970; Thomas P. Ronan, "Construction Men Sign Trainee Pact; Governor and Mayor Praise Plan to Expand Education of Minority Workers," *New York Times,* December 11, 1970; Hill to Fletcher, December 11, 1970, NAACP Papers, series VI, box G9, "Labor, DOL, 1969–71" folder; Simon Anekwe, "NAACP Threatens Court Action," *New York Amsterdam News,* December 26, 1970; Simon Anekwe, "NYC vs. Philly," *New York Amsterdam News,* January 2, 1971.

28. Damon Stetson, "Unions Accepting Negro Members: Referral Panel Here Cites Gains in Building Trades," *New York Times,* December 19, 1963; Sewell, "Contracting Racial Equality," 264.

29. Hill to Fletcher, December 11, 1970, NAACP Papers, series VI, box G9, "Labor, DOL, 1969–71" folder; Simon Anekwe, "Slip NY Plan into Law; Unannounced, Unpublicized," *New York Amsterdam News,* January 30, 1971.

30. "Uncle Sam Looks at NY Plan," *New York Amsterdam News,* March 6, 1971; Emanuel Perlmutter, "Building Unions Defend Hiring Policy," *New York Times,* March 10, 1971; Simon Anekwe, "Blast New York Plan," *New York Amsterdam News,* March 13, 1971; Napoleon B. Johnson II, statement to the United States Commission on Civil Rights, March 23, 1971, NUL Papers, series III, box 32, "Labor, Labor Affairs Program, 1971–2" folder; Simon Anekwe, "Solid Anti-NY Plan," *New York Amsterdam News,* March 27, 1971; Henry C. Cashen II to Colson, April 28, 1971, and Colson to Ehrlichman, May 5, 1971, Colson Collection, box 69, "Hardhats" folder; Colson to Haldeman, May 6, 1971, ibid., box 65, "Arthur Fletcher" folder; Colson to Nixon, July 26, 1971, ibid., box 23, "Brennan" folder.

31. Alexander to Garment, January 23, 1970; Alexander, statement, January 26, 1970; and Garment to Fletcher, February 2, 1970, Patterson Collection, box 2, folder A; Philip Shandler, "Blacks Still Lagging in Construction Pay," *Washington Star,* February 4, 1970; Fletcher to Garment, February 17, 1970, and Garment to Alexander, February 24, 1970, Patterson Collection, box 2, folder A; Austin St. Laurent to United States Congress, March 2, 1970, AFL-CIO Papers, RG 21–001, box 6, folder 20; Dan-

iel Patrick Moynihan to Ellis S. Perlman, April 20, 1970, Records of President Richard M. Nixon, Collection of the Department of Labor, box 5, "General, 2" folder; "Labor Agency Imposes Minority Hiring Rules on Builders in Capital; 'Washington Plan' Quotas for U.S.-Aided Job Contractors Stiffer Than in Philadelphia," *Wall Street Journal,* June 2, 1970; "D.C. Construction Unions Protest New Racial Quota Hiring Directive," *AFL-CIO News,* June 6, 1970; "Labor Secretary Orders 'D.C. Plan,'" *Philadelphia Tribune,* June 9, 1970; AMCO board members to Hodgson, December 18, 1970, and Wilks to Fletcher, December 21, 1970, Records of the Department of Labor, Collection of Secretary James D. Hodgson, box 52, "Fletcher" folder; "Washington, D.C." *New York Amsterdam News,* June 26, 1971; OFCC, St. Louis Plan, July 7, 1971, and Patrick H. Gannon to Garment, July 8, 1971, Garment Collection, box 142, "Philadelphia Plan, 1" folder; Wilks to Washington Plan Review Committee, July 31, 1971, Patterson Collection, box 56, "OFCC" folder; Paul Delaney, "Minority Job Aid by U.S. Questioned; Magnuson Challenges Race Formulas in Nixon Plans," *New York Times,* August 15, 1971; DOL press release, June 1, 1971, Garment Collection, box 143, "Philadelphia Plan, 2" folder; Merelice K. England, "Minority Hiring Pushed in Big Cities; U.S. Aims to Put Black Faces under Hard Hats," *Christian Science Monitor,* June 7, 1971; DOL press release, June 10, 1971, Garment Collection, box 142, "Philadelphia Plan, 1" folder; John Evans to Todd Hullin, October 5, 1972, in Graham, *Civil Rights during the Nixon Administration,* reel 19, p. 253; Richard L. Rowan and Lester Rubin, *Opening the Skilled Construction Trades to Blacks: A Study of the Washington and Indianapolis Plans for Minority Employment,* Labor Relations and Public Policy Series Report No. 7 (Philadelphia: Industrial Research Unit, the Wharton School, University of Pennsylvania, 1972), 110, 193; Anderson, *Pursuit of Fairness,* 129–30.

32. "HUD Advises Action against IBEW Local and 17 Subcontractors; Alleged Hiring Prejudice Is Issue in Complaint against Electrical Concerns, Union in Pittsburgh," *Wall Street Journal,* June 5, 1970; "NAACP Threatens a Lawsuit," *Wall Street Journal,* October 27, 1970; Colson to Arnold R. Weber, April 29, 1971, Colson Collection, box 40, "Building Construction Trades" folder; "White House Plans Offensive on Job Bias in Construction Trades until '72 Election," *Wall Street Journal,* May 6, 1971; Weber to Colson, May 12, 1971, Colson Collection, box 40, "Building Construction Trades" folder; England, "Minority Hiring Pushed in Big Cities"; "Washington, D.C.," *New York Amsterdam News,* June 12, 1971; DOL press release, June 18, 1971, Garment Collection, box 142, "Philadelphia Plan, 1" folder; Bob Smith, editorial, June 18, 1971, Patterson Collection, box 56, "OFCC" folder; Paul Delaney, "Blacks Eye Militancy for Building Jobs," *New York Times,* June 28, 1971; William B. Gould, "Blacks and the General Lockout; In Spite of the Various Plans Put Forward in the Trades, Minorities Are Still Blocked," *New York Times,* July 17, 1971; Gannon to Garment, May 10, 1972, and DOL press release, May 11, 1972, Patterson Collection, box 56, "OFCC" folder; Rowan and Rubin, *Opening the Skilled Construction Trades to Blacks,* 187, 193; Anderson, *Pursuit of Fairness,* 125–26.

33. Paul Delaney, "Nixon Is Seeking to Placate Black Aides Ready to Quit," and Fletcher, "Quote of the Day," *New York Times,* January 4, 1971; "New Look in D.C.?" *New York Amsterdam News* editorial, January 9, 1971; Jack Anderson, "All-out Effort Failed to Nip Black Boycott" column, *Philadelphia Bulletin,* February 6, 1971; Chen, *Fifth Freedom,* 29–30, 190–210.

34. Floyd L. Ruch to Roy L. Ash, September 21, 1970, and Andrew M. Rouse to Ruch, October 5, 1970, Garment Collection, box 84, "EEOC, 1969, 3" folder; Philip E. Hoffman, "Open Letter to the Candidates," August 4, 1972, Patterson Collection, box 30, "EEO" folder; Nixon to Hoffman, August 11, 1972, in Graham, *Civil Rights during the Nixon Administration,* reel 19, p. 271; McGovern to Hoffman, August 14, 1972, Patterson Collection, box 30, "EEO" folder; Paul Delaney, "Nixon Held Likely to Drop Program of Minority Jobs; Is Reported Ready to Scrap the Philadelphia Plan for Construction Industry; Quotas Being Reviewed; Fletcher, Former U.S. Aide Who Administered Policy, Denounces President," *New York Times,* September 4, 1972; John P. Mackenzie, "Quotas and Politics," *Washington Post,* September 24, 1972; Sachar, *Host at Last,* 258; Anderson, *Pursuit of Fairness,* 143.

35. "The Philadelphia Dilemma," *Washington Star* editorial, September 13, 1972; Garment, "On Quotas and Affirmative Action," October 9, 1972, in Graham, *Civil Rights during the Nixon Administration,* reel 19, pp. 257–69; Evans to Bud McFarlane, October 31, 1972, Garment Collection, box 142, "Philadelphia Plan, 1" folder; Jack Anderson, "Viet War Communication 'Mess' Told" column, *Wall Street Journal,* November 11, 1972; Anderson, *Pursuit of Fairness,* 138; Skrentny, *Minority Rights Revolution,* 340.

36. "Chiefs of Nine Building Trades Unions Endorse Candidacy of Nixon for Second Term in Office" and "Statement of General Presidents of Building Trades Unions Endorsing the Reelection of President Nixon," *Construction Labor Report* 887, September 27, 1972; Damon Stetson, "200 Labor Chiefs in City Form Nixon Committee," *New York Times,* September 28, 1972; John H. Lyons, "The President's Page," *Ironworker,* October 1972; Anderson, *Pursuit of Fairness,* 138–39.

37. James M. Naughton, "Construction Union Chief in New York Is Chosen to Succeed Hodgson," "Second-Term Cabinet" editorial, and "An Outspoken Man," *New York Times,* November 30, 1972; "Brennan Appointment to Secretary of Labor Draws Varied Reactions from Labor, Civil Rights Groups," *Construction Labor Report* 897, December 6, 1972; Philip Shabecoff, "U.S. Inaction Seen on Minority Jobs; Officials Say Administration Lets Contractors Evade Hiring Requirements," *New York Times,* December 19, 1972; Anderson, *Pursuit of Fairness,* 140; Cowie, "Nixon's Class Struggle," 281.

38. Gresham C. Smith to Silberman, January 6, 1970, Undersecretary Hodgson Collection, box 14, "Philadelphia Plan" folder; "Contractors File Suit to Roadblock Philadelphia Plan," *Philadelphia Tribune,* January 13, 1970.

39. Martin J. Herman, "U.S. Aide Sees Court Consent to Phila. Plan," *Philadelphia Bulletin,* February 5, 1970; "City Fights Protest to Phila. Plan," *Philadelphia Tribune,* February 7, 1970; "Phila. Plan Likened to 1954 Ruling," *Philadelphia Bulletin,* February 26, 1971.

40. Donald Janson, "U.S. Judge Upholds Controversial Philadelphia Plan to Increase Hiring of Minorities in Building Industry," *New York Times,* March 15, 1970; Donald Janson, "Minority Hiring Upheld by Court; Philadelphia Plan Is Termed 'Valid Executive Action,'" *New York Times,* April 24, 1971; Fred P. Graham, "High Court Lets Hiring Plan Stand; Rejects Pleas by Contractors Who Oppose Program of Quotas in Philadelphia," *New York Times,* October 13, 1971; Anderson, *Pursuit of Fairness,* 126–27.

41. Robert Samuel Smith, *Race, Labor & Civil Rights: Griggs versus Duke Power and the Struggle for Equal Employment Opportunity* (Baton Rouge: Louisiana State University Press, 2008).

42. Moreno, *From Direct Action to Affirmative Action*, 265–66; MacLean, *Freedom Is Not Enough*, 95–96, 109; Frymer, *Black and Blue*, 87–88, 96–97; Chen, *Fifth Freedom*, 225–26. Paul Frymer, in "Acting When Elected Officials Won't: Federal Courts and Civil Rights Enforcement in U.S. Labor Unions," *American Political Science Review* 97, no. 3 (August 2003): 483–99, agrees that *Contractors Association* was more operative here than *Griggs;* Smith, in *Race, Labor & Civil Rights,* notably focuses on the impact of *Griggs* on Title VII alone.

43. "Results Cited in Efforts to Aid Minorities," *AFL-CIO News,* February 28, 1970; "Say Unions Need Do More," *New York Amsterdam News,* May 30, 1970; "Outreach Helps 6,900 Youths Enter Crafts," *AFL-CIO News,* October 10, 1970.

44. "Philadelphia Plan Fails Its Early Tests," *New York Times,* May 3, 1970; Wilks to Hodgson, May 19, 1970, and Wilks to Silberman, July 1970, Undersecretary Hodgson Collection, box 14, "Philadelphia Plan" folder.

45. Madeleine Cushman to Philadelphia NUL Action for Jobs Committee, May 21, 1970, Papers of the Equal Employment Opportunity Commission, Collection of Chairman William H. Brown Jr., 1970, "June" folder; Hill, speech, June 30, 1970, NAACP Papers, series VI, box A3, "Convention Speeches" folder; Wilkins, "The Philadelphia Plan" column, *New York Amsterdam News,* August 1, 1970; "Urban League Head Calls Philadelphia Plan 'Flop,'" *Philadelphia Tribune,* August 18, 1970.

46. Hodgson to Wilks, May 25, 1970, and Wilks to compliance officers, June 26, 1970, Undersecretary Hodgson Collection, box 14, "Philadelphia Plan" folder; "HUD and HEW Move against Contractors over Minority Hiring; Show-Cause Orders Issued to 6 Builders in 'Philadelphia Plan' Charging Lack of Good Faith," *Wall Street Journal,* July 10, 1970; Wilks to Silberman, July 1970.

47. Laurence H. Geller, "Sheet Metal Workers, Firms Hit with Discrimination Suit," *Philadelphia Tribune,* August 11, 1970; Wilks to Silberman, August 12 and September 4, 1970, Undersecretary Hodgson Collection, box 14, "Philadelphia Plan" folder; "U.S. Will Terminate a Contract for Failure to Hire Negroes," *New York Times,* August 20, 1970.

48. "Philadelphia Plan Topping Hiring Goals, Labor Agency Says; Minority Workers in Five Skilled Trades Rose to 22.7% of 180 Employees, Survey Shows," *Wall Street Journal,* August 21, 1970; DOL press release, September 10, 1970, Garment Collection, box 142, "Philadelphia Plan, 1" folder; "Hodgson Asserts Philadelphia Plan Exceeds Its Goals," *New York Times,* September 11, 1970; "Philadelphia Plan Ahead of Schedule," *Philadelphia Tribune,* September 22, 1970; Rex Pollier, "Black among Hard Hats: Drama & Reality" column, *Philadelphia Bulletin,* October 1, 1970.

49. Richard Starnes, "Controversy Frustrates 'Philadelphia Plan,'" *Washington Daily News,* September 9, 1970; Elliot Carlson, "A Slow Start: The Philadelphia Plan to Integrate Unions Called Failure by Some; Hiring Goals Still Not Met; Blacks Shifted among Jobs to Fool U.S. Inspectors; But Backers See Potential," *Wall Street Journal,* December 3, 1970; AFL-CIO press release, December 14, 1970, AFL-CIO Papers, RG 1–038, box 82, folder 82; Orrin Evans, "U.S. Accuses Bucks Firm of Racial Bias in Hiring," *Philadelphia Bulletin,* July 9, 1971; "Contractor Barred from

Federal Jobs," *New York Times,* September 18, 1971; DOL press release, September 28, 1972, Garment Collection, box 142, "Philadelphia Plan, 1" folder.

50. OFCC, ESA compliance check, October 8, 1971, Patterson Collection, box 56, "OFCC" folder; DOL press releases, October 15, 1971, March 31, 1972, and September 13, 1972, Garment Collection, box 142, "Philadelphia Plan, 1" folder; Edwin C. Sexton Jr., report to the Republican National Committee, December 21, 1971, NUL Papers, series III, box 29, "Government Affairs Department" folder; "The Philadelphia Dilemma," *Washington Star* editorial, September 13, 1972; John Evans to Ken Cole, October 24, 1972, in Graham, *Civil Rights during the Nixon Administration,* reel 19, pp. 257–61; "Minority Journeymen and Apprentices Admitted to Unions under the Revised Philadelphia Plan," November 21, 1972, AFL-CIO Papers, RG 9–002, box 38, folder 42. Frymer, in "Acting When Elected Officials Won't," conflates the timing of the hometown plans and incorrectly sees them as a Nixonian response to the "failure" of the RPP; he views activist judicial decisions (including *Contractors' Association*) as responsible for the integration of the unions.

51. "Minority Group Youths Account for 11 Percent of New Apprentices," *AFL-CIO News,* March 21, 1970; Philip Shabecoff, "Blacks Making Few Gains in the Construction Trades," *New York Times,* June 27, 1971; Herbert Hammerman, "Minority Workers in Construction Referral Unions," *Monthly Labor Review* (May 1972): 17–26; Herbert Hammerman, "Minorities in Construction Referral Unions—Revisited," *Monthly Labor Review* (May 1973): 43–46. The quotation is from Shabecoff.

52. Frymer, *Black and Blue,* 38, 93.

53. Fletcher, "Address at Annual Convention of Associated General Contractors," *Construction Labor Report* 808, March 17, 1971; "Union Leader Urges Labor Aide's Ouster," *New York Times,* April 5, 1971; "Union Chief Asks Nixon to Fire Labor Official," *Philadelphia Bulletin,* April 5, 1971; Donald F. Rodgers to Henry C. Cashen, April 5, 1971, Colson Collection, box 69, "Hardhats" folder; "Washington, D.C.," *New York Amsterdam News,* April 10, 1971; Bayard Rustin, "Anti-Union and Anti-Black" column, *New York Amsterdam News,* April 17, 1971; Colson to Ehrlichman, May 14, 1971, Colson Collection, box 40, "Building Construction Trades" folder. Fletcher's subsequent resignation may have been partly the result of his ambivalence toward equal employment opportunity for women; in February 1971 he gave a speech in Kansas where he implied that sex discrimination affected only women who were heads of households, and the resulting complaint was discussed by top White House aides Bradley Patterson, Leonard Garment, and Frederick Webber. Skrentny, *Minority Rights Revolution,* 139–40.

54. Robert C. Maynard, "Jobs Could Win Black Votes," *Wall Street Journal,* July 10, 1971; "High Negro Official Is Cast as Administration Defender," *Philadelphia Bulletin,* August 25, 1971; "U.N. Post Expected for High Nixon Black," *Philadelphia Bulletin,* August 27, 1971; Anderson, *Pursuit of Fairness,* 138.

55. Arthur Fletcher interview, April 9, 2003; "Presidential Adviser Arthur Fletcher, 80, Dies," Associated Press, July 13, 2005; Paul Fletcher interview, July 30, 2010.

56. Louis Uchitelle, "Union Goal of Equality Fails the Test of Time," *New York Times,* July 9, 1995; Palladino, *Skilled Hands,* 147, 166–96; Linder, *Wars of Attrition,* 216–17, 331–96; Cowie, "Nixon's Class Struggle."

57. Hill, speech to the Annual NAACP Convention, July 6, 1972, NAACP Papers,

series VI, box A10, "Speeches" folder; Alfred W. Blumrosen, "The Crossroads for Equal Employment Opportunity: Incisive Administration or Indecisive Bureaucracy?" April 5, 1973, Patterson Collection, box 30, "Equal Employment Opportunity" folder; Stein, *Running Steel*, 306. MacLean, in *Freedom Is Not Enough* (100), correctly labels federal construction cutbacks in the face of the RPP "White House cynicism," but she ultimately draws the wrong conclusion on the relative success of the RPP, using the program as an example of the failure to integrate unions in the North (in contrast to the success in integrating the textile industry in the South). As we have seen, the RPP and other mandatory programs succeeded in integrating the unions, if not the job sites.

58. Brennan to James H. Washington, November 28, 1973, in Graham, *Civil Rights during the Nixon Administration,* reel 20, p. 498; "Labor: The Snags in Trying to Get Minorities Hired," *Business Week,* December 1, 1973; William Chapman, "NAACP to Sue on Hiring Plan," *Washington Post,* December 16, 1973; "News Release from Mayor Lindsay," April 17, 1973," quoted in Frymer, *Black and Blue,* 38.

59. Chapman, "NAACP to Sue on Hiring Plan."

60. "Jobless Rate for Negroes Dips in 1969," *AFL-CIO News,* April 18, 1970; NUL Research Department, "Black Unemployment: A Crisis Situation," July 31, 1972, "Black Unemployment Reaches Record Level during 4th Quarter, 1974," "Unemployed Blacks Soar to 3 Million," May 1975, and "Black Jobless Holds at 26%," July 1975, NUL Papers, series III, box 40, "Research Department, 2" folder.

61. Meany to Gerald Ford, June 11, 1975, AFL-CIO Papers, RG 1–038, box 76, folder 21; "Housing: A Bit Better," *Time Magazine,* June 30, 1975; James M. Naughton, "President Vetoes $1.2-Billion Bill for Aid to Housing; Asserts Economy Would Be Damaged But Frees Funds for Buying Mortgages," *New York Times,* June 25, 1975; James M. Naughton, "President Vetoes School Lunch Bill That Widened Aid; Says $2.7-Billion Measure Would Expand Programs for 'Nonneedy' Pupils; Overriding Predicted; Vote Is Scheduled Tuesday—McGovern Calls Ford's Act 'Mindless Exercise,'" *New York Times,* October 4, 1975; "Ford to City: Drop Dead; Vows He'll Veto Any Bail-out," *New York Daily News,* October 30, 1975; Stein, *Running Steel,* 148–53.

62. "Race, Sex Bias Linked to Teamsters, Trades," *Detroit News,* May 11, 1976; Roger Waldinger and Thomas Bailey, "The Continuing Significance of Race: Racial Conflict and Racial Discrimination in Construction," *Politics and Society* 19 (September 1991): 316–17; Uchitelle, "Union Goal of Equality Fails Test of Time"; Frymer, *Black and Blue,* 1–3.

63. Anderson, *Pursuit of Fairness,* 166–92.

64. Ibid., 176–202, 204–6, 210; Frymer, *Black and Blue,* 3; Skrentny, *Minority Rights Revolution,* 330, 340.

65. John R. Hunting, John C. Haas, and Henry H. Nichols to Nixon, September 20, 1973; A. William Hill and Andrew G. Freeman to Nixon, September 25, 1973; James H. Washington and Elvin P. Pierce to Nixon, October 5, 1973; and Brennan to James H. Washington, November 28, 1973, in Graham, *Civil Rights during the Nixon Administration,* reel 20, pp. 480–503; "Labor: The Snags in Trying to Get Minorities Hired," *Business Week,* December 1, 1973; Chapman, "NAACP to Sue on Hiring Plan"; Martin J. Herman, "Blacks Ask Retention of Hiring Goals," *Philadelphia Bulletin,* October 23, 1980; Uchitelle, "Union Goal of Equality Fails Test of Time."

Conclusion

1. *Merriam-Webster's Online Dictionary,* http://www.m-w.com/dictionary /affirmative%20action (accessed November 17, 2007).

2. NUL press release, September 7, 1961, NUL Papers, series II, box E29, "1961, 1" folder; Sugrue, *Origins of the Urban Crisis;* Moreno, *From Direct Action to Affirmative Action;* Ira Katznelson, *When Affirmative Action Was White* (New York: W. W. Norton, 2005).

3. Whitney Young, "To Be Equal" column, November 25, 1964, NUL Papers, series II, box E47, "To Be Equal" folder.

4. LBJ Howard University commencement address, June 4, 1965, McPherson Collection, box 21, "Civil Rights—1965, 2" folder.

5. Anderson, *Pursuit of Fairness,* 216, 221.

6. Wirtz quotation from DOL press release, June 8, 1964, NUL Papers, series II, box A17, folder 3; MacLean quotation from *Freedom Is Not Enough,* 107, and drawn largely from *Report of the White House Conference on Equal Opportunity,* Panel 7: "Affirmative Action," August 19–20, 1965, LBJ White House Central files, box HU2, folder 1.

7. MacLaury, *To Advance Their Opportunities,* 179–81, 221.

8. Harold Hunton, "Implementing 'Affirmative Action' with Air Force Contractors," *Interracial Review,* February 1963.

9. Nichelle Nichols, production interview for the feature film *Star Trek VI: The Undiscovered Country,* 1991.

10. Sullivan, *Build, Brother, Build,* 70–84; Sewell, "Contracting Racial Equality," 101–9; and Anderson, *Pursuit of Fairness,* 58.

11. Hannah Lees, "The Not-Buying Power of Philadelphia's Negroes," *The Reporter,* May 11, 1961; Sullivan, *Build, Brother, Build,* 70–84.

12. Milton Friedman, *Capitalism and Freedom* (Chicago: University of Chicago Press, 1962), 108–11.

13. Ray Marshall, "The Job Problems of Negroes," in Northrup and Rowan, *Negro and Employment Opportunity,* 18.

14. MacLean, *Freedom Is Not Enough,* 61; Davies, *From Opportunity to Entitlement;* Dan T. Carter, *The Politics of Rage: George Wallace, the Origins of the New Conservatism, and the Transformation of American Politics* (Baton Rouge: Louisiana State University Press, 2000), 466; James T. Patterson, *Grand Expectations: The United States, 1945–1974* (New York: Oxford University Press, 1996).

15. Nathan Glazer, *Affirmative Discrimination: Ethnic Inequality and Public Policy,* 2nd ed. (Cambridge, MA: Harvard University Press, 1987).

Selected Bibliography

AFL-CIO. Records. George Meany Memorial Archives, National Labor College, Silver Spring, MD.

AFL-CIO Web site. http://www.afl-cio.org.

Altshuler, Alan. "Rationality and Influence in Public Service." *Public Administration Review* 25, no. 3 (September 1965): 226–33.

American Rhetoric.com. http://www.americanrhetoric.com.

Anderson, Jervis. *A. Philip Randolph: A Biographical Portrait.* Berkeley: University of California Press, 1972.

Anderson, Terry H. *The Pursuit of Fairness: A History of Affirmative Action.* New York: Oxford University Press, 2004.

Arnesen, Eric. "Assessing the Legacy of Herbert Hill: An Introduction." *Labor: Studies in Working Class History in the Americas* 3, no. 2 (summer 2006): 11–12.

———. *Brotherhoods of Color: Black Railroad Workers and the Struggle for Equality.* Cambridge, MA: Harvard University Press, 2001.

Bass, Patrik Henry. *Like a Mighty Stream: The March on Washington, August 28, 1963.* Philadelphia: Running Press, 2002.

Belton, Robert. "Discrimination and Affirmative Action: An Analysis of Competing Theories of Equality and *Weber.*" *North Carolina Law Review* 59 (March 1981): 531–98.

Berg, Manfred. *The Ticket to Freedom: The NAACP and the Struggle for Black Political Integration.* Gainesville: University Press of Florida, 2005.

Blumrosen, Alfred. "Administrative Creativity: The First Year of the Equal Opportunity Commission." *George Washington Law Review* 38, no. 4 (May 1970): 695–751.

Bohmer, Peter. "African-Americans as an Internal Colony: The Theory of Internal Colonialism." In *Readings in Black Political Economy,* ed. John Whitehead and Cobie Kwasi Harris. Dubuque, IA: Kendall/Hunt, 1999.

Boyle, Kevin. *The UAW and the Heyday of American Labor, 1945–1968.* Ithaca, NY: Cornell University Press, 1995.

Branch, Taylor. *Parting the Waters: America in the King Years, 1954–1963.* New York: Simon and Schuster, 1988.

Bryant, Nick. *The Bystander: John F. Kennedy and the Struggle for Black Equality.* New York: Basic Books, 2006.

Caro, Robert. *The Years of Lyndon Johnson, Master of the Senate.* New York: Knopf, 2002.

Chen, Anthony S. *The Fifth Freedom: Jobs, Politics, and Civil Rights in the United States, 1941–1972.* Princeton, NJ: Princeton University Press, 2009.

Civil Rights Act of 1964. H.R. 7152, July 2, 1964.

Clapp, Stephen. "Divide and Rule." *Public Information Center News* 1, no. 12 (June 1971): 1–4.

Clark, Ramsey. Interview IV, April 16, 1969, by Harri Baker. Electronic copy, Lyndon Baines Johnson Presidential Library and Museum, Austin, TX.

Countryman, Matthew J. *Up South: Civil Rights and Black Power in Philadelphia.* Philadelphia: University of Pennsylvania Press, 2006.

Cowie, Jefferson. "Nixon's Class Struggle: Romancing the New Right Worker, 1969–1973." *Labor History* 43, no. 3 (August 2002): 257–83.

Crenshaw, Kimberlé, Neil Gotanda, Gary Peller, and Kendall Thomas, eds. *Critical Race Theory: The Key Writings that Formed the Movement.* New York: New Press, 1995.

Dallek, Robert. *Lyndon B. Johnson: Portrait of a President.* New York: Oxford University Press, 2004.

Davies, Gareth. *From Opportunity to Entitlement: The Transformation and Decline of Great Society Liberalism.* Lawrence: University Press of Kansas, 1996.

Delton, Jennifer. *Racial Integration in Corporate America, 1940–1990.* New York: Cambridge University Press, 2009.

Department of Labor. Records. National Archives and Records Administration, College Park, MD.

Dickerson, Dennis C. *Militant Mediator: Whitney M. Young, Jr.* Lexington: University Press of Kentucky, 1998.

Doak, Robin S. *The March on Washington: Uniting against Racism.* Minneapolis: Compass Point Books, 2008.

Dolan, Julie, and David H. Rosenbloom, eds. *Representative Bureaucracy: Classic Readings and Continuing Controversies.* Armonk, NY: M. E. Sharpe, 2003.

Dyckman, Zachary Yale. "An Analysis of Negro Employment in the Building Trades." Ph.D. diss., University of Pennsylvania, 1971.

Eagles, Charles, ed. *The Civil Rights Movement in America.* Jackson: University of Mississippi Press, 1986.

Early, Gerald L. *This Is Where I Came In: Black America in the 1960s.* Lincoln: University of Nebraska Press, 2003.

Ehrlichman, John. *Witness to Power: The Nixon Years.* New York: Simon and Schuster, 1982.

Encyclopedia of Cleveland History. http://ech.case.edu.

Equal Employment Opportunity Commission. Records. National Archives and Records Administration, College Park, MD.

Ershkowitz, Miriam, and Joseph Zikmund II, eds. *Black Politics in Philadelphia.* New York: Basic Books, 1973.

Fletcher, Arthur. *The Silent Sell-Out: Government Betrayal of Blacks to the Craft Unions.* New York: Third Press, 1974.

Fraser, Steve, and Gary Gerstle, eds. *The Rise and Fall of the New Deal Order, 1930–1980.* Princeton, NJ: Princeton University Press, 1989.

Frederickson, H. George. *The New Public Administration.* Tuscaloosa: University of Alabama Press, 1980.

———. "Public Administration and Social Equity." *Public Administration Review* 50, no. 2 (March–April 1990): 228–37.

Freeman, Joshua B. "Hardhats: Construction Workers, Manliness, and the 1970 Pro-War Demonstrations." *Journal of Social History* (summer 1993): 725–44.

Friedman, Milton. *Capitalism and Freedom.* Chicago: University of Chicago Press, 1962.

Frymer, Paul. "Acting When Elected Officials Won't: Federal Courts and Civil Rights Enforcement in U.S. Labor Unions." *American Political Science Review* 97, no. 3 (August 2003): 483–99.

———. *Black and Blue: African Americans, the Labor Movement, and the Decline of the Democratic Party.* Princeton, NJ: Princeton University Press, 2008.

Garfinkel, Herbert. *When Negroes March: The March on Washington Movement in the Organizational Politics for FEPC.* New York: Atheneum Press, 1959.

Gitlin, Todd. *The Sixties: Years of Hope, Days of Rage.* Toronto: Bantam Books, 1987.

Glazer, Nathan. *Affirmative Discrimination: Ethnic Inequality and Public Policy,* 2nd ed. Cambridge, MA: Harvard University Press, 1987.

Goluboff, Risa L. *The Lost Promise of Civil Rights.* Cambridge, MA: Harvard University Press, 2007.

Gottlieb, Peter. *Making Their Own Way: Southern Blacks' Migration to Pittsburgh, 1916–1930.* Urbana: University of Illinois Press, 1987.

Graham, Hugh Davis. *The Civil Rights Era: Origins and Development of National Policy, 1960–1972.* New York: Oxford University Press, 1990.

———, ed. *Civil Rights during the Nixon Administration, 1969–1974.* Frederick, MD: University Publications of America, 1989.

Gregory, James N. *The Southern Diaspora: How the Great Migrations of Black and White Southerners Transformed America.* Chapel Hill: University of North Carolina Press, 2005.

Griggs v. Duke Power Supply. 401 U.S. 424 (1971), 91 S.Ct. 849.

Grossman, James R. *Land of Hope: Chicago, Black Southerners, and the Great Migration.* Chicago: University of Chicago Press, 1989.

Halberstam, David. *The Children.* New York: Random House, 1998.

Hale, Mary M., and M. Frances Branch. "Policy Preferences on Workplace Reform." In *Women and Men in the States,* ed. Mary E. Guy. Armonk, NY: M. E. Sharpe, 1992.

Haughton, James. "James Haughton on Racism in the House of Labor." Interview by Janine Jackson, History Matters. http://historymatters.gmu.edu/d/7038/ (accessed November 8, 2009).

Hill, Herbert. "A Critical Analysis of Apprenticeship Outreach Programs and the Hometown Plans." *Howard University Institute for Urban Affairs and Research Occasional Paper* 2, no. 1 (1974): 75.

The History Makers. http://www.thehistorymakers.com/.

Hoff, Joan. *Nixon Reconsidered.* New York: Basic Books, 1994.

Hood, Larry J. "The Nixon Administration and the Revised Philadelphia Plan for Affirmative Action: A Study in Expanding Presidential Power and Divided Government." *Presidential Studies Quarterly* 23 (winter 1993): 145–67.

Hooton, Cornell G. *Executive Governance: Presidential Administrations and Policy Change in the Federal Bureaucracy.* Armonk, NY: M. E. Sharpe, 1997.

"Hough Heritage." http://www.nhlink.net/ClevelandNeighborhoods/hough/history.htm.

In Motion: The African-American Migration Experience. http://www.inmotionaame
.org/migrations/topic.cfm?migration=9&topic=2.
Johnson, Lyndon Baines. Records. Lyndon Baines Johnson Presidential Library and
Museum, Austin, TX.
———. *The Vantage Point.* New York: Holt, Rinehart and Winston, 1971.
Jones, James E. "The Bugaboo of Racial Quotas." *Wisconsin Law Review* 341, no. 2
(1970): 341–403.
———. "The Genesis and Present Status of Affirmative Action in Employment: Eco-
nomic, Legal, and Political Realities." *Iowa Law Review* 70 (1985): 901–44.
Katznelson, Ira. *When Affirmative Action Was White.* New York: W. W. Norton, 2005.
Kearns, Doris. *Lyndon Johnson and the American Dream.* New York: Harper and
Row, 1976.
Kingsley, J. Donald. *Representative Bureaucracy: An Interpretation of the British
Civil Service.* Yellow Springs, OH: Antioch Press, 1944.
Krislov, Samuel. *Representative Bureaucracy.* Englewood Cliffs, NJ: Prentice-Hall,
1974.
Lackritz, Marc E. *The Hough Riots of 1966.* Cleveland, OH: Regional Church Plan-
ning Office, 1968.
Lawson, Steven F. "Freedom Then, Freedom Now: The Historiography of the Civil
Rights Movement." *American Historical Review* 96, no. 2 (April 1991): 456–71.
———, ed. *To Secure These Rights: The Report of President Harry S. Truman's Com-
mittee on Civil Rights.* Boston: Bedford/St. Martin's, 2004.
Levy, Peter B. *The New Left and Labor in the 1960s.* Urbana: University of Illinois
Press, 1994.
Lichtenstein, Alex. "Herbert Hill and the Negro Question." *Labor: Studies in Working
Class History in the Americas* 3, no. 2 (summer 2006): 33–39.
Lichtenstein, Nelson. "Herbert Hill in History and Contention." *Labor: Studies in
Working Class History in the Americas* 3, no. 2 (summer 2006): 25–31.
———. *Walter Reuther: The Most Dangerous Man in Detroit.* Urbana: University of
Illinois Press, 1995.
Linder, Marc. *Wars of Attrition: Vietnam, The Business Roundtable, and the Decline
of Construction Unions.* Iowa City: Fănpìhuà Press, 2000.
Lipset, Seymour Martin. *Bureaucracy and Social Change.* Berkeley: University of
California Press, 1950.
*Local 53, International Association of Heat and Frost Insulators and Asbestos Work-
ers v. Vogler.* 59 L.C. 9195 (1969).
Lyons, Courtney. "Burning Columbia Avenue: Religious Undertones of the 1964 Philadel-
phia Race Riot." Paper presented at Civil Rights Conflict in the North: Under-Emphasized Elements of the African-American Civil Rights Movement, panel discussion at
the 2010 meeting of the American Historical Association, San Diego, CA.
Macaluso, Vincent J. Interview, January 4, 2008, by and in the possession of the author.
MacLaury, Judson. *To Advance Their Opportunities.* Knoxville, TN: Newfound Press,
2008.
MacLean, Nancy. "Achieving the Promise of the Civil Rights Act: Herbert Hill and
the NAACP's Fight for Jobs and Justice." *Labor: Studies in Working Class History in the Americas* 3, no. 2 (summer 2006): 13–19.

———. *Freedom Is Not Enough: The Opening of the American Workplace.* New York: Russell Sage Foundation, 2006.

Marshall, Burke. Interview I, October 28, 1968, by Thomas H. Baker. Electronic copy, Lyndon Baines Johnson Presidential Library and Museum, Austin, TX.

Marshall, F. Ray, and Vernon M. Briggs Jr. *The Negro and Apprenticeship.* Baltimore: Johns Hopkins Press, 1967.

Matusow, Allen J. *The Unraveling of America: A History of Liberalism in the 1960s.* New York: Harper and Row, 1984.

McKee, Guian. "Liberal Ends through Illiberal Means: Race, Urban Renewal, and Community in the Eastwick Section of Philadelphia, 1949–1990." *Journal of Urban History* 27 (July 2001): 547–83.

Meier, August, and Elliott Rudwick. *CORE: A Study of the Civil Rights Movement.* Urbana: University of Illinois Press, 1975.

Meier, Kenneth John, and Lloyd G. Nigro. "Representative Bureaucracy and Policy Preferences: A Study in the Attitudes of Federal Executives." *Public Administration Review* (July/August 1976): 458–69.

Mitchell, Clarence. Interview I, April 30, 1969, by Thomas H. Baker. Electronic copy, Lyndon Baines Johnson Presidential Library and Museum, Austin, TX.

Moreno, Paul D. *From Direct Action to Affirmative Action: Fair Employment Law and Policy in America, 1933–1972.* Baton Rouge: Louisiana State University Press, 1997.

Morris, Aldon D. *Origins of the Civil Rights Movement.* New York: Free Press, 1984.

Mosher, Frederick C. *Democracy and the Public Service.* New York: Oxford University Press, 1968.

Mumford, Kevin. *Newark: A History of Race, Rights, and Riots in America.* New York: New York University Press, 2007.

National Association for the Advancement of Colored People. Records. Library of Congress Manuscripts Division, Washington, DC.

National Urban League Online. http://www.nul.org.

National Urban League. Records. Library of Congress Manuscripts Division, Washington, DC.

Nixon, Richard M. Records. National Archives and Records Administration, College Park, MD.

Northrup, Herbert R., and Richard L. Rowan, eds. *The Negro and Employment Opportunity: Problems and Practices.* Ann Arbor: University of Michigan Press, 1965.

O'Reilly, Kenneth. *Nixon's Piano: Presidents and Racial Politics from Washington to Clinton.* New York: Free Press, 1995.

Palladino, Grace. *Skilled Hands, Strong Spirits: A Century of Building Trades History.* Ithaca, NY: Cornell University Press, 2005.

Parris, Guichard, and Lester Brooks. *Blacks in the City: A History of the National Urban League.* Boston: Little, Brown, 1971.

Pfeffer, Paula F. *A. Philip Randolph, Pioneer of the Civil Rights Movement.* Baton Rouge: Louisiana State University Press, 1990.

Philadelphia Urban League. Records. Temple University Urban Archives, Philadelphia, PA.

Phillips, Kimberley L. *Alabama North: African-American Migrants, Community, and*

Working Class Activism in Cleveland, 1915–1945. Urbana: University of Illinois Press, 1999.

Piven, Frances, and Richard Cloward. *The Politics of Turmoil: Essays on Poverty, Race, and the Urban Crisis.* New York: Vintage, 1975.

Pritchett, Wendell E. *Robert Clifton Weaver and the American City.* Chicago: University of Chicago Press, 2008.

Quadagno, Jill. *The Color of Welfare: How Racism Undermined the War on Poverty.* New York: Oxford University Press, 1994.

Randolph, A. Philip. Interview I, October 29, 1969, by Thomas H. Baker. Electronic copy, Lyndon Baines Johnson Presidential Library and Museum, Austin, TX.

Reed, Merl Elwyn. "Black Workers, Defense Industries, and Federal Agencies in Pennsylvania, 1941–45." *Labor History* 27 (June 1986): 356–84.

———. *Seedtime for the Modern Civil Rights Movement: The President's Committee on Fair Employment Practice, 1941–1946.* Baton Rouge: Louisiana State University Press, 1991.

Reeves, Richard. *President Nixon: Alone in the White House.* New York: Simon and Schuster, 2001.

Riley, Dennis D. *Controlling the Federal Bureaucracy.* Philadelphia: Temple University Press, 1987.

Rios et al. v. Enterprise. U.S. Court of Appeals, Second Circuit, 501 F.2d 622 (June 24, 1974); U.S. Court of Appeals, Second Circuit, 520 F.2d 352 (June 24, 1975); U.S. Court of Appeals, Second Circuit, 542 F.2d 579 (September 7, 1976); and as amended, U.S. Court of Appeals, Second Circuit, 860 F.2d 1168 (December 1, 1988).

Robertson, David E., and Ronald D. Johnson. "Reverse Discrimination: Did *Weber* Decide the Issue?" *Labor Law Journal* 31 (November 1980): 793–99.

Robinson, Archie. *George Meany and His Times.* New York: Simon and Schuster, 1981.

Rosenbloom, David H., and Jeannette Featherstonhaugh. "Passive and Active Representation in the Federal Civil Service: A Comparison of Blacks and Whites." *Social Science Quarterly* (March 1977): 97–103.

Rowan, Richard L., and Lester Rubin. *Opening the Skilled Construction Trades to Blacks: A Study of the Washington and Indianapolis Plans for Minority Employment.* Labor Relations and Public Policy Series Report No. 7. Philadelphia: Industrial Research Unit, Wharton School, University of Pennsylvania, 1972.

Sachar, Abram L. *A Host at Last.* Boston: Little, Brown, 1976.

Schultz, Kevin. "The FEPC and the Legacy of the Labor-Based Civil Rights Movement of the 1940s." *Labor History* 49, no. 1 (February 2008): 71–92.

Scott, Daryl Michael. *Contempt and Pity: Social Policy and the Image of the Damaged Black Psyche, 1880–1996.* Chapel Hill: University of North Carolina Press, 1997.

Self, Robert O. *American Babylon: Race and the Struggle for Postwar Oakland.* Princeton, NJ: Princeton University Press, 2003.

Sewell, Stacy Kinlock. "Contracting Racial Equality: Affirmative Action Policy and Practice in the United States, 1945–1970." Ph.D. diss., Rutgers University, 1999.

Shultz, George P. *Turmoil and Triumph.* New York: Charles Scribner's Sons, 1993.

Shuwerk, Robert F. "The Philadelphia Plan: A Study in the Dynamics of Executive Power." *University of Chicago Law Review* (summer 1972): 723–60.

Skrentny, John David. *The Ironies of Affirmative Action: Politics, Culture, and Justice in America.* Chicago: University of Chicago Press, 1996.

———. *The Minority Rights Revolution.* Cambridge, MA: Belknap Press, 2002.

———, ed. *Color Lines: Affirmative Action, Immigration, and Civil Rights Options for America.* Chicago: University of Chicago Press, 2001.

Smith, Eric Ledell, and Kenneth C. Wolensky. "A Novel Public Policy: Pennsylvania's Fair Employment Practices Act of 1955." *Pennsylvania History* 69 (fall 2002): 489–523.

Smith, Robert Samuel. *Race, Labor & Civil Rights: Griggs versus Duke Power and the Struggle for Equal Employment Opportunity.* Baton Rouge: Louisiana State University Press, 2008.

Stein, Judith. *Running Steel, Running America: Race, Economic Policy, and the Decline of Liberalism.* Chapel Hill: University of North Carolina Press, 1998.

Sugrue, Thomas J. *The Origins of the Urban Crisis: Race and Inequality in Postwar Detroit.* Princeton, NJ: Princeton University Press, 1996.

———. *Sweet Land of Liberty: The Forgotten Struggle for Civil Rights in the North.* New York: Random House, 2008.

Sullivan, Leon H. *Build, Brother, Build.* Philadelphia: Macrae Smith, 1969.

Sullivan, Patricia. *Lift Every Voice: The NAACP and the Making of the Civil Rights Movement.* New York: New Press, 2009.

Taylor, Clarence. *The Black Churches of Brooklyn.* New York: Columbia University Press, 1994.

———. *Knocking on Our Own Door: Milton A. Galamison and the Struggle to Integrate New York City Schools.* New York: Columbia University Press, 1997.

———. "Sticking to the Ship: Manhood, Fraternity, and the Religious World View of A. Philip Randolph." In *Black Religious Intellectuals: The Fight for Equality from Jim Crow to the Twenty-first Century.* New York: Routledge, 2002.

United Steelworkers v. Weber. 99 S.Ct. 2721 (US S.Ct., 1979), 20 EPD par. 30,026.

U.S. Mint. Records. National Archives and Records Administration, Mid-Atlantic Region, Philadelphia, PA.

U.S. v. IBEW Local 38. 59 L.C. 9226 (1969).

Waldinger, Roger, and Thomas Bailey. "The Continuing Significance of Race: Racial Conflict and Racial Discrimination in Construction." *Politics and Society* 19 (September 1991): 295–315.

Walker, Clarence E. "The Legacy of Herbert Hill." *Labor: Studies in Working Class History in the Americas* 3, no. 2 (summer 2006): 21–23.

Weber, Max. *Essays in Sociology.* Trans. and ed. by H. H. Gerth and C. Wright Mills. New York: Oxford University Press, 1958.

Weiss, Nancy J. *Whitney M. Young, Jr., and the Struggle for Civil Rights.* Princeton, NJ: Princeton University Press, 1989.

Williams, Linda F. *The Constraint of Race: Legacies of White Skin Privilege.* University Park: Pennsylvania State University Press, 2003.

Willis, Arthur C. *Cecil's City: A History of Blacks in Philadelphia, 1638–1979.* New York: Carlton Press, 1990.

Winkler, Allan M. "The Philadelphia Transit Strike of 1944." *Journal of American History* 59, no. 1 (June 1972): 73–89.

Wolfinger, James D. "'An Equal Opportunity to Make a Living—and a Life': The FEPC and Postwar Black Politics." *Labor: Studies in Working Class History of the Americas* 4, no. 2 (summer 2007): 65–94.

———. *Philadelphia Divided: Race and Politics in the City of Brotherly Love.* Chapel Hill: University of North Carolina Press, 2007.

Woods, Randall B. *LBJ: Architect of American Ambition.* New York: Free Press, 2006.

X, Malcolm. *The Autobiography of Malcolm X, as Told to Alex Haley.* New York: Grove Press, 1965.

Young, Whitney M., Jr. *To Be Equal.* New York: McGraw-Hill, 1964.

Yuill, Kevin L. *Richard Nixon and the Rise of Affirmative Action.* Lanham, MD: Rowman and Littlefield, 2006.

Zangrando, Robert L. "Manuscript Sources for Twentieth-Century Civil Rights Research." *Journal of American History* 74 (1987): 243–51.

Zieger, Robert H. *For Jobs and Freedom: Race and Labor in America since 1865.* Lexington: University Press of Kentucky, 2007.

Index

Breinigsville, PA USA
25 February 2011
256378BV00002B/1/P